MW00684920

ALBERT EINSTEIN COLLEGE OF MEDICINE/
MONTEFIORE MEDICAL CENTER
DEPARTMENT OF PSYCHIATRY
OFFICE OF EDUCATION
3331 BAINBRIDGE AVENUE
BRONX, NEW YORK 10467

MYTHS OF CHILDHOOD

MYTHS OF CHILDHOOD

Joel Paris, MD
Professor of Psychiatry
McGill University
Montreal, Quebec
Canada

BRUNNER/MAZEL
Taylor & Francis Group

| USA | Publishing Office: | BRUNNER/MAZEL
A member of the Taylor & Francis Group
325 Chestnut Street
Philadelphia, PA 19106
Tel: (215) 625-8900
Fax: (215) 625-2940 |
| | Distribution Center: | BRUNNER/MAZEL
A member of the Taylor & Francis Group
7625 Empire Drive
Florence, KY 41042
Tel: 1 (800) 634-7064
Fax: 1 (800) 248-4724 |
| UK | | BRUNNER/MAZEL
A member of the Taylor & Francis Group
27 Church Road
Hove
E. Sussex, BN3 2FA
Tel: +44 (0) 1273 207411
Fax: +44 (0) 1273 205612 |

MYTHS OF CHILDHOOD

Copyright © 2000 Taylor & Francis. All rights reserved. Printed in the United States of America. Except as permitted under the United States Copyright Act of 1976, no part of this publication may be reproduced or distributed in any form or by any means, or stored in a database or retrieval system, without prior written permission of the publisher.

1 2 3 4 5 6 7 8 9 0

Printed by Edwards Brothers, Ann Arbor, MI, 2000.
Cover design by Rob Williams.

A CIP catalog record for this book is available from the British Library.
∞The paper in this publication meets the requirements of the ANSI Standard Z39.48-1984 (Permanence of Paper).

Library of Congress Cataloging-in-Publication Data

Paris, Joel, 1940–
    Myths of childhood / Joel Paris.
        p. cm.
    Includes bibliographical references and index.
    ISBN 0-87630-966-X (alk. paper)
    1. Developmental psychology. 2. Nature and nurture. 3. Psychology, Pathological—Etiology. I. Title.

BF713.P37 2000
155—dc21   00-021546

ISBN 0-87630-966-X (case)

Dedication

This book is dedicated to my teachers, who I have spent a lifetime trying to prove wrong, and to my students, who challenge me to prove I am right.

Nullus addictus iurare in verbo magistri
(I am not bound to believe in the word of any master)
—Horace (First Century BC)

CONTENTS

INTRODUCTION

☐ Primacy: A Cultural Shibboleth

Do childhood experiences determine the course of adult life? Many have thought so. The principle of *the primacy of childhood* describes the basic assumption: that childhood experiences are the crucial factor in psychological development. A related principle might be termed *the primacy of early experience*: that early experiences in childhood are more important than later experiences.

Psychotherapists have been the most influential advocates of these beliefs, which have become received wisdom in the contemporary world. Most people take primacy for granted and assume that science has long since proven it to be true.

Primacy underlies several psychological theories. Generations of therapists have been trained to seek explanations for patients' present problems in their distant pasts. Many parents believe that how they raise their children determines their future, most particularly whether they will be happy or unhappy. Contemporary society is so saturated with these ideas that the primacy of childhood has become a cultural *shibboleth*—usually taken for granted, and rarely questioned.

This idea is not unique to our own time. Jesuit priests thought that if they could only obtain early access to children, they could shape their religious beliefs for life. John Locke believed the mind of a child was a blank slate on which the environment could imprint almost any message. Jean-Jacques Rousseau viewed children as the innocent victims of improper education and social oppression. Wordsworth famously proclaimed, "The child is the father of the man."

In the 20th century, Sigmund Freud had the most profound influence on cultural beliefs about childhood. Freud believed that character is formed in the first 5 years of life. He also proposed that unearthing long-lost memories of childhood experiences was the key to successful therapy. Freud (1917/1955) wrote that the first and earliest recollection in psychoanalysis often "proves to be the most important, the very one that holds the key to the secret pages of the mind" (p. 149).

The extent to which this belief in the importance of early childhood permeates our culture is shown by a recent and highly publicized example. A former professor of mathematics was arrested for a series of bombings that killed and maimed a number of people. The evidence found by the FBI in his isolated cabin provided overwhelming proof that this man was indeed the "Unabomber." He eventually pleaded guilty and was incarcerated for life.

To the surprise of many, the suspect came from a highly educated middle-class family that had no obvious signs of having been "dysfunctional." His brother, a professional man with a family, had turned him in to the police. Reporters interviewed the suspect's distressed and elderly mother. She remembered that when her son was an infant, he had a lengthy hospitalization, after which he became very withdrawn. Both mother and journalists speculated that this experience had somehow warped the child, accounting for his murderous behavior many years later.

This example could be joined by many others. Speculations about the effects of childhood are particularly common when violence is involved. Thus, in the first of several recent incidents, two young boys in a small town killed several of their schoolmates and a teacher. The media trumpeted the report that one of them might have been sexually abused as a child. In my own city of Montreal, a man rejected by an engineering program murdered a number of women students accepted into the faculty. The press speculated about the impact of his early background, most particularly a violent father who had abandoned the family.

When we do not understand an event, we try to explain it. Usually this means making use of whatever ideas lie readily at hand. Social psychologists call such attempts at explanation *attributions*. In every culture, and at every point in human history, some attributions have been favored over others.

At one time, the concept of demonic possession accounted for strange and inexplicable behavior. In the contemporary world, we prefer to attribute irrational behavior to the effects of an unhappy childhood. Paradoxically, this belief gives us hope. We hope that the warping effects of childhood on adults can be reversible through psychotherapy. We hope that if we raise our children properly, we can prevent them from feeling unhappy and protect them from damage by adverse events later in life.

☐ The Purpose of This Book

The goal of this book is to show that the idea of primacy of childhood is wrong. To support my critique, I will review a large body of empirical research that either contradicts or frankly disconfirms this principle. I will then present data that point to a very different model of psychological development.

I have written this book to challenge the assumption that childhood is the main factor shaping the course of adult life. But I am in no way discounting the profound emotional impact of early life experiences. Childhood leaves a powerful mark on the mind. Everyone has meaningful thoughts and emotions rooted in events occurring during this phase of life.

Yet, the quality of childhood does not predict whether life will be happy or unhappy. Nor are early events the main determinants of personality traits. Finally, childhood experiences do not constitute the main cause of mental disorders. Life events play a role in psychopathology but can only be understood using a model of development that focuses on interactions between temperament and experience.

In recent years, a large body of research has demonstrated that people are much less shaped by their childhood than most had previously thought. A new scientific discipline, *behavior genetics*, demonstrates that about half of individual differences in personality and intelligence are due to genetic variations. These findings have achieved wide attention in the media.

In this "golden age" of genetics, few are surprised to learn that heritable factors are as important for the mind as for the body. But many continue to assume that the most important environmental factors in psychological development derive from experiences in the nuclear family. Behavior genetics has challenged this belief as well. Peers, teachers, role models, and the broader influence of the social environment can be as important, and sometimes even more important, than parents.

This research should not be interpreted as proving that childhood experiences have *no* influence whatsoever on adults. Other things being equal, it is still better to have a happy childhood than an unhappy one. The problem is that other things are *not* equal! The point is that the impact of parenting cannot be understood without considering both temperament and the social environment. Interactions among all these factors will shape personality and determine one's vulnerability to mental disorders. This approach provides a much broader theory of human development.

☐ Three Myths

This book will critique three separate but related myths of childhood.

Myth 1: *Personality is formed by early childhood experiences.*

The term *personality* refers to the psychological characteristics unique to every individual. For many years, social scientists believed that differences in personality between one person and another were rooted in early life experiences. The development of personality traits was seen as the outcome of events in childhood, most particularly attitudes of parents towards children. This belief became a crucial element in both psychoanalysis and family therapy.

Research has now shown that this idea is mistaken. First, personality is strongly influenced by genes. Every child is born with specific temperamental characteristics that are heritable. This discovery has come as a surprise to some people, but nurses working with newborn babies might take it for granted. It has also been said that parents with one child believe in the environment, while parents with two children believe in the genes.

Moreover, the environmental influences on personality do not derive from the family alone. Children are not the passive recipients of good or bad parenting. Their lives are shaped by a multitude of unique experiences. Some of these events come unbidden, but others are determined by children themselves.

Myth 2: *Mental disorders are caused by early childhood experiences.*

The idea that the main source of mental illness is an unhappy childhood has had a wide currency indeed. At one time, even the most severe mental disorders, such as schizophrenia, were explained in this way. In the last few decades, research has convincingly shown that psychoses are largely determined by biological factors. Yet some still assume that more common mental symptoms, such as depression and anxiety, are less influenced by heredity and have their primary roots in early experiences.

Some 30 years ago, as a psychiatrist in training, this is precisely what I was taught. Today, researchers have shown that almost *all* mental disorders are influenced by genetic predispositions. Moreover, the environmental factors in these illnesses are much more complex than originally thought. In defense of my teachers, I should note that we knew little at that time about these other causes. But it is no longer acceptable to explain each and every kind of psychological symptom as the outcome of an unhappy childhood.

Myth 3: *Effective psychotherapy depends on the reconstruction of childhood experiences.*

Psychotherapists who believe that most psychological problems derive from childhood events have applied this model to the treatment of their patients. Following Freud, effective therapy focused on the reconstruction of early experiences. Freud's ideas are also the basis of "interpretations" that attempt to demonstrate to patients that their present problems are a recapitulation of past events.

Empirical evidence sheds a different light on the way that psychotherapies *actually* work. Interpretations linking past and present have not been shown to be uniquely effective. They are overshadowed as curative factors by the quality of the relationship between the patient and the therapist and by the quality of collaborative work on current difficulties.

These conclusions have practical implications. First, therapists need to develop a broader and more complex understanding of the origins of symptoms, developing a model that takes temperament into account. Second, therapists need to change the way they actually work. Belief in the primacy of childhood has led to an excessive focus on reconstructing the past, sometimes at the expense of teaching patients new ways of dealing with old problems.

☐ Myths and Research

In earlier times, mental health professionals spoke with enormous cultural authority. They were consulted on almost every issue related to psychology and were even considered to be expert about social and political issues. Flattered by this attention, many came to believe that their clinical expertise qualified them to be all-purpose consultants on human nature.

Ironically, mental health professionals are in a particularly poor position to make such claims. Many have limited scientific experience, or jettisoned their scientific training once they became clinicians. Therapists tend to believe in the validity of their clinical methods, which are based on the assumption that one can draw reliable conclusions about causality simply by listening to what people say about their lives.

As a result, therapists are all too prone to accept plausible but invalid formulations of psychological issues. A generation of clinicians were trained to believe that their "insights" could be generalized into conclusions with universal application. Psychotherapists were asked to advise parents how to raise healthy and happy children. In reality, this is a subject about which hardly anyone can claim to be an expert.

Fortunately, the mental health professions have emerged from this period of grandiosity. When psychiatrists, psychologists, and social workers are consulted today, they are much more cautious. If committed to the scientific method, they will present conclusions in an appropriately tentative way, often accompanied by calls for further research to elucidate unanswered questions.

In a word, the mental health professions have become *evidence based*. This approach is revolutionizing clinical practice. In the past, psychotherapeutic methods were rarely rooted in sound research data. Traditionally, therapists reached conclusions on the basis of clinical inference, i.e., by listening to the stories that patients presented and by applying a predetermined theoretical model to account for these narratives.

In my own profession of medicine, evidence-based practice is a recent development. For centuries, physicians were trained through apprenticeship to their seniors and taught to respect hierarchy and authority. Given that people's lives can often be at stake, there was probably some justification for imposing this "military" regime.

Only 30 years ago, I was taught both medicine and psychiatry in this way. Since our teachers were clearly older and wiser, we did not often question what we were told. Even after completing formal training, we continued to be influenced by what we heard at meetings and conferences. The more charismatic the presenter, the more likely we were to believe what he or she said. Clinical inference ruled, and few of us stood up to ask, "How do you know whether what you are saying is really true?"

I never fully accepted these ideas, but I acted as if they were true. Many years spent evaluating and treating hundreds of patients, followed by extensive experience in research, led me to greater and greater scepticism. Eventually, I reached conclusions that were incompatible with the primacy of childhood.

Epistemology is not a word that falls trippingly on the lips. Yet it is the philosophical term for answering the question, "How we know what we know?" As clinical sciences mature, their knowledge base comes to depend less and less on experience and more and more on scientific methods. The primacy of early experience is based on inadequate epistemology, in which vast conclusions about human nature emerge from a very limited database.

Clinical experiences can only create hypotheses. Any conclusions drawn from these encounters must be tentative. Moreover, it is not possible to understand normal psychological development from experience with patients. To determine the relationship between childhood experiences and adult psychopathology, we must rely on research findings using both clinical and community populations.

In this book, therefore, I will be suspicious of clinical impressions and will lean strongly on empirical evidence. I will approach all questions concerning causality with profound scepticism. I will only consider answers that can, at least in principle, be supported by data. I will therefore avoid using descriptions of patients to support my arguments. (I will, on occasion, make use of illustrative vignettes.)

Readers who are familiar with the literature on child development will already understand the complexity of the pathways from childhood to adulthood. They may not see a need for my critique and may even wonder if I have created a "straw man." If only that were so—then there would be no need to write this book! The thrust of this volume concerns the large gap between *what researchers have found* and *what clinicians believe*.

☐ **What This Book Is and Is *Not* Saying**

There can be no doubt that life experiences affect development. Empirical evidence consistently demonstrates the influence of such events on both personality and psychopathology. However, the role of the environment is much more complex than previously believed.

One consistent conclusion can be drawn from research about the influence of childhood experiences on adult functioning. It is that where relationships between adversities and outcomes *do* exist, they are statistically *weak*. In other words, *some* people are badly affected by early experiences, but many, if not most, people with an unhappy childhood do reasonably well as adults. A predisposed and vulnerable minority is most affected by adversity.

These are the facts. Although those who have managed to survive an unhappy childhood may suffer as a result of their experiences, they do not describe themselves as more distressed than a random sample of the population. At the same time, some people, in spite of having had a fairly happy childhood, become deeply troubled in adult life.

In summary, while the risks of adversity are real, they do not affect a majority of those exposed to them. On the one hand, no parent would want their child to experience events that might lead to sequelae, even if such outcomes only occur 10% or 20% of the time. On the other hand, we can reassure parents that most children are highly resilient to a wide range of adversities.

The clinical point here concerns the error of applying a reverse logic in interpreting research on risks and sequelae. *The presence of psychopathology does not prove the existence of childhood adversities.* It is simply wrong in principle to assume that childhood experiences generally account for symptoms. No matter how severe the psychopathology we see, we need not assume that a patient's childhood must have been traumatic. Even when one finds a history of adversity, such events need not be the primary or only cause of current symptoms.

When challenging common beliefs, one runs the danger of being assumed to take a radically opposite point of view. There is a real danger of having one's ideas dismissed if they are seen as claiming that "parents don't matter" or that neglecting or mistreating children is acceptable.

At the risk of repetition, let me clarify my position. This book is not proposing that childhood experiences can be discounted or that psychopathology is nothing but the result of genes and "chemical imbalances." I am *not* saying that it does not matter what kind of parenting children have or what kind of experiences they have in the home.

Instead, my position is that childhood experiences only have a central influence on personality development and psychopathology in a temperamentally vulnerable minority. It is *these* children who are most likely to be damaged by toxic influences in their environment. Negative experiences are particularly likely to warp such children and lead to serious pathology. This is especially so when stressors are multiple, when they are repeated, and when they fail to be counteracted by positive experiences. Even the strongest constitution can be brought down by a continued onslaught.

For these reasons, we need to maintain our vigilance about child abuse and neglect. A significant minority will be deeply affected by such experiences, and the majority may still bear some emotional scars. Therefore, children need to be protected—by their parents and by society.

Nevertheless, the central issue about the impact of adversity is not whether childhood experiences create unhappy memories, but whether such experiences lead to measurable psychological symptoms. In other words, we need to acknowledge the crucial difference between *distress* and *disorder*.

Clinicians need to keep in mind that there is no *single* cause for psychological problems. Symptoms reflect interactions among temperament, childhood experience, and the social environment. While many psychotherapists are aware of the importance of all these factors, the problem lies in the *weighting* one gives to multiple influences on development. Too often, lip service is given to biological and social influences, while childhood environment is given precedence. This leads to a "knee-jerk" reaction, in which clinicians find a source in childhood for almost every problem in adult life.

Moreover, I am not suggesting that childhood is not worth talking about in psychotherapy. On the contrary, these memories almost always need to be addressed. The story of one's life is a crucial part of personal identity. For these reasons alone, therapists will always need to understand their patients' childhoods. Moreover, symptoms are often more understandable in a historical context, helping therapists to identify consistent patterns.

With all these caveats in mind, I am forcefully challenging many commonly held beliefs about development. Therefore, this book will be explicitly controversial. By calling primacy a "myth," I am consciously playing the role of a gadfly. But I do not intend to confine myself to criticism. I will also offer a model that can replace primacy.

Finally, the issue of the role of childhood in development has important ethical implications. Blaming one's childhood for problems in adult life can be an "abuse excuse." Seeing ourselves as influencing our own fate can be empowering.

☐ How This Book Is Organized

The book will be divided into five sections, focusing on the three myths of childhood described above—Parts I and II on the impact of childhood experience on adult life, Part III on the relationship between childhood experience and psychological problems, and Part IV on childhood experiences in the practice of psychotherapy. Finally, Part V will address the implications of studies of childhood for parenting, and suggest directions for further research.

☐ Acknowledgments

All writers need critics. Otherwise, they run the risk of being overly attached to their own ideas (not to speak of their favorite sentences).

This book benefited from the comments of two people who critically read the entire manuscript. My wife, Rosalind Paris, helped me to make the text more accessible and coherent. My long-time research colleague, Hallie Zweig-Frank, provided detailed feedback that assisted me in shaping the presentation of my ideas into a logical and systematic argument. Phyllis Zelkowitz read the first part of the manuscript, providing many helpful suggestions for revision. In the course of the manuscript review process, Judith Rich Harris carefully read the text, suggesting many useful changes and clarifications.

I am grateful to Judy Grossman, a librarian with great skills in locating obscure references. The "protected time" required to write this book was provided by the McGill University Faculty of Medicine and its Dean, Abraham Fuks; as well as by the Sir Mortimer B. Davis-Jewish General Hospital, and its former Psychiatrist-in-Chief, Phillip Beck.

I would like to thank Lansing Hays, my first editor at Brunner/Mazel, who took an interest in this book, agreeing to publish it entirely on the basis of a proposal. I am also grateful for encouragement and support from his successor, Toby Wahl.

Some of the ideas developed in this volume derive from earlier books and journal articles. I have written three previous volumes on personality disorders: one on borderline personality (Paris, 1994), a second on these disorders as a whole (Paris, 1996c), and a third on psychotherapy (Paris, 1998b). Another previous book (Paris, 1999) presents a detailed description of the predisposition-stress model of mental disorders.

I

CHILDHOOD
AND ADULTHOOD:
THE EVIDENCE

Part I consists of four chapters examining the empirical evidence concerning the impact of childhood experience on adult functioning.

Chapter 1 discusses the problems in establishing cause and effect relationships between life experiences and psychological symptoms. Relying on simple associations between risks and outcomes can lead to surprisingly incorrect conclusions about the causes of psychological problems. The social psychology of attributions helps to explain some of these common errors in logic.

Chapter 2 reviews the theoretical assumptions behind primacy, and shows how the scientific evidence contradicts them. The disconfirming data include discontinuities between childhood and adulthood, the reversibility of effects of early experiences through later experiences, and the fact that an unhappy childhood has very different effects on different people.

Chapter 3 reviews research on the long-term sequelae of various adversities during childhood: poor quality of parenting, marital conflict, separation or divorce, traumatic experiences, and socioeconomic deprivation. In each case, single adversities have weak relationships with outcome, while impacts are greater when adverse event are mulitple and cumulative.

Chapter 4 reviews research on resilience. Only a minority of children exposed to traumatic experiences suffer long-term sequelae. The mechanisms by which people survive a traumatic childhood include intelligence, favorable personality traits, the availability of alternate attachments, and the buffering effects of extended family and social community.

Establishing Cause and Effect

Behavior does not follow simple laws. This is why psychology does not resemble classical physics. The simplest outcome can emerge from a complex matrix of factors. The same outcome can result from many different causes. The same causes can lead to entirely different outcomes.

All these complexities make it difficult to determine whether a risk factor, such as an adverse event during childhood, is the true cause of an outcome, such as problems during adulthood. This chapter will describe a series of problems in scientific methodology bearing on this difficulty:

1. the base rate problem,
2. the difference between risk factors and causes,
3. the difference between correlation and causation,
4. the difference between clinical and community populations,
5. distinguishing the roles of shared environment and shared genes,
6. the problem of retrospective methods,
7. the difference between statistical and clinical significance,
8. the contrast between clinical inference and research data.

When these pitfalls go unrecognized, researchers and clinicians can reach incorrect conclusions. The chapter concludes with a discussion of attribution theory, which sheds light on the reasons *why* we make false inferences.

☐ The Base Rate Problem

Most people experience their share of adversity. This is true at any stage of life. A trauma-free childhood is probably exceptional. Therefore, to the extent that negative childhood experiences are frequent in the general population, many patients are bound to report them. It is important to remember that large groups of nonpatients have had parallel experiences, yet do not develop the same sequelae.

This is a classic example of a *base rate problem*. If a risk factor is sufficiently ubiquitous, then even when it is commonly associated with an outcome, the relationship cannot be considered as truly causal. Thus, reported childhood adversities, even when reported frequently, do not necessarily, by themselves, account for symptoms in adult patients.

To establish whether an adverse life event is a valid cause of clinically significant symptoms, we also need to decide what cut-off point to use. In other words, *What is a case?* This well-known problem in clinical epidemiology arises from the fact that most forms of disorder lie on a continuum with normality, with pathology emerging only on the extremes (Goldberg & Huxley, 1992).

To know what a case is, we must address the difference between *distress* and *disorder*. Everyone is affected by adverse life experiences, but few become clinically ill as a result. For example, although most of us have times when we are unusually sad, the prevalence of clinical depression in the population is only about 5% at any given time, and no more than 20% over the course of a lifetime (Kessler et al., 1994; Robins & Regier, 1991). Thus, while distress is almost universal, disorder is less common.

This problem with determining "caseness" has important implications for measuring resilience. When we are conservative about defining pathology, most people appear highly resilient. But when we are liberal about defining pathology (as the psychodynamic model tends to be), resilience can appear exceptional.

Some might argue that we miss important effects of adversity by counting only those who have clinical levels of psychopathology. In this view, we should give equal weight to those affected in any perceptible way, even if they have no diagnosable disorder. The main reason for rejecting this line of argument derives from the base rate problem.

Epidemiological surveys (Kessler et al., 1994; Robins & Regier, 1991) show that one third of the population have a measurable psychological disorder at any given time. But if we limit consideration to those mental disorders with a severe effect on functioning (i.e., schizophrenia, major mood disorders, severe substance abuse, and severe personality disorders), only about 10% to 15% of the population are affected.

These figures do not take distress into account. *Some* symptoms, that is, complaints that do not meet criteria for a diagnosable disorder, can be found in about another third of the population (Srole, 1980). At some point, being mildly troubled becomes perfectly normal! This issue is particularly relevant to issues raised in the next few chapters of this book.

Unfortunately, many of the studies of the impact of adversity use distress rather than disorder as an outcome (e.g., studying the effects of early experience on self-esteem).

In summary, we need to define caseness in such a way as to avoid making the distinction between normality and pathology meaningless. Life involves many travails, and no one can expect to be happy most of the time. Models that pathologize all human suffering run the risk of applying a standard of mental health that makes almost everyone into a patient. Using distress as a criterion also trivializes the question of whether unhappiness in childhood causes unhappiness in adulthood.

This is not to deny that people can be deeply affected by their childhood. Intuitively, most people are aware of carrying *some* scars from our early lives. But when one measures outcomes too broadly, one ends up concluding that there is no such thing as resilience.

In summary, psychopathology is not just a matter of distress. Clinicians should not diagnose illness without a clearcut impairment in functioning. In that context, when we ask whether childhood experiences cause mental disorders, the answer is: *usually not.*

☐ Risk Factors and Causes

We can open the newspaper almost any day and read about the results of the latest research on risk factors for disease. Over morning coffee, we learn that researchers are arguing about whether too much caffeine increases the risk for cancer. Reading on, we discover that it is a bad idea to drink too much alcohol, that it is dangerous to be too fat or too thin, and that although we need to exercise, we should be careful not to overdo it. One can only conclude that life is a fatal disease!

But we need not become unnecessarily concerned. All of these purported dangers are *risks*, but none of them are *causes*. Risk factors consist of anything that makes disease more likely. But we need to know how likely that outcome is. If the base rate in the population is 1%, and a risk factor doubles it to 2%, such information provides very little reason to change one's lifestyle.

When are risk factors truly etiological? Only when: (a) they precede the development of pathology; (b) they are consistently, strongly, and specifically associated with the disorder; and (c) there is a plausible mechanism linking them with outcome (Regier & Burke, 1989).

Let us consider each one of these criteria in turn. First, a risk factor must precede the development of pathology. If not, both risk and outcome may well be due to a third factor, termed a latent variable. Moreover, it is difficult to determine whether risk or outcome takes precedence when adversities are assessed retrospectively.

Second, the relationship must be consistent, strong, and specific—if not, a risk is unlikely to play a major role in outcome. Actually, the consistency and strength of risks in childhood are not as great as one might expect. As Chapter 3 will show, few adversities during childhood lead to predictable long-term effects. Even in the short term, most risks, by themselves, will affect only a minority of those exposed. Even the most severe traumas are associated with adult pathology in about 25% of cases.

In many ways, 25% looks like a high rate. If, for example, a couple were receiving genetic counseling, that level of risk would be high enough to raise serious questions about conceiving. But we are not comparing 25% to 0%. These numbers have to be seen in the context of relatively high base rates of mental disorder in the population.

Moreover, the risk of sequelae for any adversity is rarely as high as 25%. The vast majority of exposed children do not develop any serious pathology. This is why clinicians can conclude very little, simply from observing symptoms, about the probability of finding any specific risk factor. Moreover, most risks in child development are not very specific. Chapter 3 will provide examples of how similar outcomes can arise from many different causes, while causes do not lead to predictable outcomes. This is another reason why the presence of childhood adversity cannot, by itself, explain the development of adult symptoms. Some other factor is required; Chapters 9 and 10 will suggest what that is likely to be. Finally, we cannot accurately describe the mechanisms by which childhood adversities cause adult pathology. We have many theories, but few certainties.

There are several good examples in medicine of risk factors that meet most criteria for being true risk factors. A good example is the relationship of cigarette smoking to lung cancer and cardiovascular disease. We know that smoking frequently and consistently leads to serious disease, and we also have a very good idea of the mechanism by which tobacco causes pathology. Therefore, there can be little doubt that this relationship is etiological.

In contrast, the association between childhood trauma and mental illness is neither consistent, strong, nor specific. Moreover, it lacks a plausible pathogenic mechanism. Even if the criteria defining a valid risk factor listed above are met (and they rarely are), most people exposed to risk factors never become ill, and if they do, they rarely become ill in the specific way suggested by reported associations with disorders. As will be discussed later in this chapter, when relationships are purely statistical, they need not, and usually do not, apply to any particular individual.

Thus, from the retrospective point of view embodied in the clinical encounter, we cannot readily understand why anyone develops pathology.

Simply knowing that someone has been exposed to specific risk factors is not enough. Even from the prospective point of view of the researcher, we cannot predict which individuals exposed to any risk factor will develop mental disorders.

In summary, risk factors often *contribute* to a pathological outcome but should not generally be thought of as either necessary or sufficient conditions for their development. The causes of psychological symptoms are almost never single but depend on complex interactions between many risk factors.

☐ Correlation and Causation

Correlation does not prove causation. This saying is so well known that it has become a cliché. Yet the principle is often ignored. The difference between correlation and causation is crucial to understanding the relationships between childhood experiences and adult disorders. When researchers find such associations, they need not be etiological in any way. As discussed in the previous section, we need to know whether risk factors are consistently, strongly, and specifically associated with outcome and to establish a plausible mechanism before we can feel confident that any such relationship is truly causal.

Moreover, associations between risk and outcome may result from *latent variables* not measured in the study. For example, people who drink too much are more likely to develop lung cancer. But alcohol does not cause lung cancer. The explanation is that people who drink more also smoke more, so that tobacco is the latent variable leading to disease.

To consider an example closer to the experience of psychotherapists, children who are sexually abused are more likely to develop a wide range of psychological problems as adults (Browne & Finkelhor, 1986). Yet abuse, by itself, need not be the primary or only cause of these outcomes. Children who are traumatized by abuse also tend to come from dysfunctional families. This latent variable is a much more powerful cause of later difficulties than child abuse itself (Beitchman et al., 1992; Nash et al., 1993; Rind & Tromofitch, 1997; Rind, Tromofitch, & Bauserman, 1998).

In summary, childhood adversities are multiple and intercorrelated. As a result, researchers are likely to draw faulty conclusions unless they carry out *multivariate* studies, in which they measure more than one risk. These methods provide a way of assessing a wide range of potential factors, rather than being confined to one or two. Yet, no matter how many additional variables are added, important ones can still be missed. This is why scientific papers so often end with a call for further research!

☐ Clinical and Community Populations

Therapists do not see a random sample of the population. Therefore, observations on patients cannot be generalized to nonclinical groups. Clinical impressions often lead to incorrect conclusions about cause and effect.
Practitioners may find associations between adversities and disorders in
the people they see, but these relationships may not apply to community
populations, since patients are, almost by definition, more vulnerable to
adversity.

A project conducted at my own university department provides a good
example of this principle. Since the end of the Second World War, a number of clinicians had been interested in understanding the effects of the
Holocaust, both on the survivors themselves and on their children. Clinical observations had given the impression that most survivors had post-
traumatic symptoms, and that the second generation suffered difficulties
associated with a guilty attachment to their damaged parents. However,
when a research group examined a community sample of survivors (Eaton,
Sigal, & Weinfelds, 1982), they found that although nearly half had at
least some form of distress, most did not have any diagnosable mental
disorder, and many remained asymptomatic. Similarly, community samples
of children of the Holocaust (Sigal & Weinfeld, 1989) have found no psychopathology in a majority of subjects.

These results should not be interpreted as implying that there are *no*
psychological consequences to experiencing the Holocaust, either in survivors or in their children. Life events cause distress, even if they do not
necessarily lead to disorder. The point is that clinical populations, in which
disorders are more frequently observed, are unrepresentative of community populations. Holocaust survivors who develop disabling disorders may
have had other vulnerability factors; survivors do not necessarily fall ill,
however horrific their experiences were.

☐ Shared Environment and Shared Genes

Studies of the effects of early family life on development do not readily
separate environmental from hereditary influences. Yet apparent associations between adversities and symptoms can often be explained by genetic similarities between parents and children. Thus, the presence of a
history of family dysfunction or parental psychopathology in symptomatic patients does not necessarily prove environmental mechanisms of
causation.

The relation between attachment and anxiety (see Chapter 8) is one good example. Anxiously attached parents tend to have anxiously attached children. This observation has been interpreted as demonstrating the existence of an *intergenerational transmission* of attachment style (Fonagy et al., 1996). Yet this need not be so. Attachment styles are as much measures of temperament as of experience (Kagan, 1989; Rutter, 1995a; Thompson, 1988). It is possible that anxious traits are shaped and modeled by parents who transmit their sense of fear about the world to the next generation. It is also likely that children resemble their parents due to common temperament (Rutter, 1998).

Similar principles apply to the pathways leading to serious mental disorders. In alcoholism (Pihl & Peterson, 1992) and in antisocial personality disorder (Robins, 1966), fathers and sons often have the same symptoms. But this observation does not tell us whether the mechanism of transmission is genetic, environmental, or both.

The best way to sort this matter out is to measure the heritable factors in mental disorders, using twins as a *natural experiment* (see Chapters 9 and 10). Such studies show that genetic factors account for a large portion of the variance in temperament, as well as in disorders such as substance abuse and antisocial personality (Rowe, 1994).

Environmental factors play a large role in the development of psychopathology. But the mechanisms are more complex than simple imitation or modeling of parents' behavior. First, most of the environmental factors leading to mental disorders are *unshared,* that is, unique to the individual rather than a simple result of growing up in a particular family. (See Chapters 9 and 10 for an explanation of this terminology.) Second, genes determine sensitivity to the environment, so that while some individuals become disordered with only a small dose of stress, others require a much larger dose.

☐ Retrospective Methods and Recall Bias

Almost 50 years ago, Akira Kurosawa directed the classic Japanese film *Rashomon*. The plot concerns a crime and how several different observers (the victims, the perpetrator, and witnesses) all had contradictory perceptions of what happened. Even memories of recent events depend on one's point of view. For example, a classic study of psychotherapy (Mintz, Auerbach, Luborsky, & Johnson, 1973) found no relationship among ratings of patients, therapists, and outside observers as to whether a session had been productive or not. The researchers termed this a *Rashomon effect*.

The problem is even more severe for long-term memories. Studies of childhood experience in adult patients typically ask them to recall events many years in the past. Yet, as has been often shown (Maughan & Rutter,

1997), the way we remember childhood is strongly influenced by our present state of mind. In a classic study (Yarrow, Campbell, & Burton, 1970), mothers' and children's memories of the quality of early childhood experiences were compared to direct observations. No relationship existed between the way parents and their offspring recalled the past. Yet, in both cases, memories were strongly associated with quality of current relationships between mothers and children.

The concept of *recall bias* means that the way we remember the past is determined by the present. Those who are happy in the present are more likely to forget bad events and to remember good ones, while those who are unhappy in the present are more likely to focus on bad memories and to discount good ones.

Problems with the validity of past information are even more complex in patients who externalize difficulties, preferring to hold others responsible for their problems. Clinicians should be careful not to agree with patients who blame family members for most of their difficulties. These attributions are common in patients with impulsive disorders. For example, although a large literature (reviewed in Paris, 1996c) shows that patients with borderline personality tend to report unusually traumatic childhood experiences, it is impossible to tell whether these reports represent objective reality or perceptions. Only prospective studies, examining children known to be at risk due to major adversities, and then following them into adulthood, can answer such questions.

Another problem with retrospective methods is that they are often conducted on populations of patients in treatment with therapists who believe that their problems are due to an unhappy childhood and who shape perceptions of the past to conform to these beliefs. It is not just false memories, but *selective* memories that produce difficulties in knowing the truth about the past. Again, only prospective research can determine the true relationship between childhood and adult functioning.

☐ Statistical Significance and Clinical Significance

When perusing scientific journals, most readers, to assess results rapidly, scan the abstract first. When a hypothesis is confirmed, the words *significant* or even *highly significant* may appear. The "take-home message" becomes the demonstration of a cause and effect relationship. Yet a deeper understanding of statistics shows that this need not be the case. To illustrate the problem, let us examine a recent and important prospective study of the impact of marital conflict and divorce on children (Amato & Booth, 1997). The results (discussed further in Chapter 3) show that marital discord and divorce predicted a number of psychological problems among children when they grow up. These research sociologists used sophisticated statistical analyses, making use of regression equations that can sort out which variables, above and beyond any of the others, predicted outcome. In this case, the standardized regression coefficients were *highly* significant, accounting for about 20% to 25% of the outcome variance. In the context of psychosocial research, in which there is always a high "signal-to-noise ratio," this constitutes a remarkable finding.

Nevertheless, one cannot conclude from such results that children of divorce are necessarily likely to be damaged by the experience. The risk is probably high enough to suggest that couples with children should think twice about ending a marriage. But none of the analyses accounted for the *other* 75% of the variance. In other words, while having parents who are unhappily married makes it more likely that children will have problems with intimacy as adults, more often than not, there will be no such association. Thus, most people who come from unhappy families can achieve normal levels of self-esteem and intimacy. Conversely, while coming from a happy family makes it more likely that children will grow up to be happy and successful, there is no assurance that this will be the case.

This example shows why clinicians who follow the research literature need to understand the difference between *statistical significance* and *clinical significance*. As everyone who has taken an introductory statistics course knows, a finding is significant when one can say, at least 95 times out of a 100, that the results in this particular sample represent what would be found if one had conducted the same study on an entire population.

But differences that are statistically significant may not be large enough to be "significant" in the real world. Statistical significance only proves that there is *some* association between the variables under study. It does not mean that the relationship applies to everyone in the sample. Moreover, few studies do as well as that of Amato and Booth (1997) in accounting for a large percentage of the variance. Group differences may mask enormous heterogeneity, with some subjects affected positively, others negatively, and some not at all.

Let us consider some examples. It is quite possible for a finding to be highly significant even if it applies very strongly *only* to a subgroup. This is an important issue in the clinical trials of drugs: A result can be significant if a few patients do extraordinarily well, even when most obtain no benefit at all. Alternatively, a finding that is statistically significant, and that applies to most subjects in the sample, may still be too weak to attain clinical significance. In antidepressant trials, for example, it is possible for a drug to reduce some symptoms but not others, leaving most patients clinically depressed.

Finally, the statistical "power" of any study depends on sample size.

But sometimes a research study can have too much power for its own good! More findings become reportable if the sample is so large that even small differences attain statistical significance. Although this is not often an issue in clinical research (where the problem usually consists of finding enough subjects), it arises frequently in large-scale community surveys.

For all these reasons, Cohen (1990) has argued that statistical significance is not a sufficient criterion, by itself, to determine the strength of a research finding. Instead of a simple "yes/no" question, researchers need to ask "how much." One way this can be accomplished is by determining *effect size*. This statistic describes the quantitative, not just the qualitative, difference between groups.

Let us consider an example of some relevance to clinical practice: the effects of psychotherapy (see Chapter 11). Twenty years ago, Smith, Glass, and Miller (1980) conducted meta-analyses showing that the psychotherapies as a whole lead to improvement in patients. When this effect is quantified as an effect size, it reaches the level of half a standard deviation. (If applied to IQ scores, this would correspond to an increase of about 10 points, a reasonably large effect.)

Another way to determine the quantitative effects of a finding is through multivariate statistical techniques, which can measure how much of the variance in outcome is accounted for by each of several independent variables. Finding factors that explain a quarter of the variance is impressive and relatively rare. In the real world, there are just too many factors, measured or unmeasured, that can influence outcomes.

When an adverse experience is statistically associated with symptoms, and when that relationship is clinically significant, we can conclude that it constitutes a risk factor, that is, that it is at least one among many factors that can lead to this pathological outcome. Yet we will still be a long way from being able to say that the adversity *causes* this outcome or that when we see a specific outcome in a clinical setting, we should expect to find a history of a particular adversity.

These methodological and statistical problems are by no means abstruse and theoretical. On the contrary, these issues are crucial for a precise understanding of the nature of the relationship between childhood experience and adult pathology. *Some* people are very badly affected by their childhoods. It is this vulnerable subgroup that accounts for most of the statistically significant relationships reported in the literature, even when the majority of those exposed are doing reasonably well. For this reason, conclusions about relationships between childhood experience and adult functioning are, in any individual case, more likely to be wrong than right. Clinicians who expect to find adversities that account for symptoms are also likely to be mistaken.

☐ Clinical Experience and Research Data

We can now summarize the implications of all the problems in determining cause and effect discussed in this chapter. No matter how much experience we have, the formulations we use to account for the causes of psychopathology are often wrong. This is because clinical methods are incapable of determining cause and effect relationships. At the same time, research methods can also produce misleading results. Long-term prospective research in community samples (preferably using twins to control for common genes) is the *only* unquestionable way to determine the effects of childhood experience.

Therapists should never forget that no one can make general conclusions about the human condition from clinical experience. Instead of relying on the opinions of prestigious "experts," we would do well to familiarize ourselves with the research literature on child development. In the past, the first thing budding clinicians learned in abnormal psychology was a series of clinical theories, often referred to as the "schools" of psychology. All of these models are quite speculative, and most are, at best, misleading (see Chapter 6). Research in developmental psychopathology, not armchair theories, should be the basic science taught to clinicians.

Therapists can use their training and their tools to find problematic psychodynamics in almost anyone. Since everyone has had unhappy experiences during childhood, the base rates of almost any risk factor are considerable. It is not difficult to give patients direct and indirect cues to offer more information confirming the therapist's theoretical position. Langs (1973) describes *clinical validation* as occurring when patients provide more material after receiving an interpretation. Unfortunately, this sequence is not valid at all—it may prove nothing except for patients' wishes to please therapists and to be comforted by a coherent story that makes sense of their difficulties.

Explanations and Attributions

False beliefs in psychology do not readily die out. Many survive and continue to influence each new generation. Why do new facts not lead to the correction of old errors? Why does illogic so often defeat logic?

Social psychologists have long been interested in understanding why people come to idiosyncratic conclusions about the world. This area of research is termed *attribution theory* (Sutherland, 1994; Weiner, 1999) and consists of formal studies about how people explain sequences of events in their lives.

First and foremost, people prefer any explanation to no explanation. We are all more likely to prove something true than untrue. When confronted with a complex sequence of events, most of us are uncomfortable with not having at least some adequate theory. For this reason, we have trouble withholding judgment about cause and effect. This leads to an *availability bias*, the tendency to explain events on the basis of what lies closest at hand (Dawes, 1994). These explanations provide an illusion that we can control our environment. What is most readily available often derives from beliefs that are commonly held in one's culture. The primacy of childhood experience is a good example.

Attributions based on an availability bias also color clinical observations, leading to misleading associations between risk factors and outcomes. In an instructive example quoted by J. Holmes (1998), physicians once believed that Down's syndrome was caused by birth trauma, largely because mothers of these children, no doubt searching for some explanation of their tragedy, frequently reported such events. When the real cause (an extra chromosome) was discovered, it became clear that the "available" mechanism was entirely wrong.

Second, people overvalue previous harm when experiencing present adversity. This tendency to rewrite one's personal history in the light of present suffering is an example of recall bias (Weiner, 1999). Moreover, people may not prefer to explain present failure in terms of *personal* inadequacy. Blaming one's childhood experience and one's parents provides a readily available explanation that maintains some degree of self-esteem (Deutsch, 1960).

Third, the way patients think affects the way therapists hear their stories. The *fundamental attribution error* describes the fact that individuals typically characterize their *own* behavior as a reaction to a situation, but attribute the behavior of *other* people to internal dispositions such as personality. In other words, when patients tell their stories, they tend to present themselves as victims of circumstance, rather than as the authors of their own distress. Of course, it is the task of therapy to correct these perceptions. But too often, out of a need to be empathic and "on the patient's side," clinicians are inclined to accept and validate these attributions.

The tendency to blame adverse circumstances for one's troubles can also be understood in light of another construct: *locus of control* (Rotter, 1966). One can divide people into those who typically attribute problems to external factors, and those who typically attribute life problems to their own failings. Either an external or an internal locus can be adaptive, depending on the context (Bowman, 1997). However, psychotherapists often do better with patients who have an internal locus (and who can therefore be helped to feel better by blaming themselves less) than with patients who have an external locus (who are all too ready to put the blame on others and reluctant to blame themselves).

Clinicians sometimes say they don't realize the extent of a patient's problems until they work with them for a while. But psychotherapy, by its very nature, tends to pathologize human problems. Seeking causes in the past encourages patients to see themselves as victims of circumstance. Such conclusions are neither fair to the facts nor necessarily therapeutic.

Finally, research findings describe groups, not individuals. Even when relationships are statistically significant, they do not necessarily apply to most people in a sample. For all these reasons, we must be very cautious about interpreting research on adverse childhood experience in patients as demonstrating causality. Moreover, formulations in the clinical situation may be nothing more than attributions. What is most readily available often derives from beliefs commonly held in a culture. The primacy of childhood is a very good example.

☐ Conclusions

Even when adult problems and childhood experience run parallel, it is difficult to prove that causality governs their relationship. There are other possible explanations, most particularly latent variables such as abnormal temperament, that can account for the co-occurrence of problems in early and later life. For all these reasons, we need to be cautious about interpreting adverse childhood experience as the main cause of psychological symptoms.

☐ Are Earlier Experiences More Important than Later Experiences?

Primacy tends to be taken as an axiom. But why *should* early events be more important than later events? Several possible answers have been proposed.

1. Early learning occurs when the brain is more plastic. Thus infants, who have not previously been exposed to a social environment, should be more profoundly affected by the quality of parenting (Millon, 1985).
2. Early learning occurs during sensitive periods of development, when the organism is primed to learn certain patterns more easily. An analogy can be made with those species in which behaviors are imprinted early in life (Lorenz, 1966; Tinbergen, 1951).
3. Early learning occurs when the child is more dependent, making younger children most susceptible to the shaping influence of parents (Millon, 1985).
4. Earlier stages of development must be mastered in order to proceed to later stages (Erikson, 1950).

All these arguments have a prima facie appeal. The apparent logic of primacy makes it intuitively attractive. But ideas, however appealing, can still be wrong. Theory must always be submitted to empirical verification.

The first argument, concerning plasticity, fails to take into account that even if infants are born without prior experience, each child begins life with unique temperamental characteristics. Research on infancy (Stern, 1985) and on the consequences of temperament (Chess & Thomas, 1984) has consistently shown that children are born with innate capacities. These individual differences in temperament are a major determinant of parental responses (Harris, 1995).

There is also no evidence that emotional responses in children are more plastic in infancy than later on in development. Events in the early years might even be *less* important, since, as will be discussed in Chapter 7, most memories are lost, and few people can remember anything from before age 3. It has been thought that very early events might still affect children on a nonverbal level. However, infants lack the cognitive maturity to evaluate their experience. As Kagan (1998b) and Bruer (1999) have pointed out, the brain is still growing in the first 2 years of life, and the frontal lobes, where experience is evaluated, are particularly immature.

The second argument, concerning sensitive periods of development, is also open to serious question. Kagan (1998b), reviewing the literature on imprinting in the wild and on early separation from maternal care in laboratory animals, concludes that sensitive periods exist in mice or monkeys, but not necessarily in humans, who are born with a more flexible program for learning. Critical periods exist for language acquisition, but there is no evidence that they apply to emotional learning. Kagan is also critical of recently popular ideas, such as that infancy is a time when mothers must provide increased stimulation to help lay down neural networks, or that bonding must begin through physical contact in the first few hours of life (Klaus & Kennell, 1976), or that children benefit from prenatal exposure to music.

Finally, little evidence supports the idea that the sensitivity of newborns means that stressful events in infancy must have more long-term consequences. As will be documented in Chapter 4, children are born with resilience, displaying a striking capacity to compensate for early deficits through later learning. Even Harlow's (1958) monkeys, separated at birth from their mothers, recovered when raised with peers.

Kagan (1998b) describes how emotional reactions in humans developed during infancy can become dulled over time:

> Most adults experience the gradual loss, over time, of strong emotional reactions, perhaps fear of an animal, sadness over the death of a parent, anger at a rival, or intense sexual arousal at the sight or thought of another. It strains credulity to argue that infants are exceptions to this universal aspect of human nature and do not lose emotional reactions acquired during the first two years of life. (pp. 126–127)

The third argument, concerning the dependency of young children, is an extension of the concept of critical periods. Again, research shows that later environment can modify the early influence of rearing practices. There are no consistent permanent effects from leaving infants alone and untended for long periods, from being separated from a mother, from being in day care, or even from experiencing multiple fostering or life in an orphanage (Kagan, 1998b).

Moreover, if rearing practices during infancy and early childhood were as important as is often claimed, we should see dramatic differences in the frequency of psychological problems that accord with cultural variations. Yet the prevalence of serious mental disorders is about the same around the world.

The fourth argument, concerning the mastery of sequential stages of development, assumes the reality of fixed developmental stages. Chapter 6 will present a detailed critique of this *epigenetic* approach.

In summary, there is no clear evidence that adversity has a greater effect earlier in life than it does later. As Rutter and Rutter (1993) point out, adversities that begin early tend to continue over time, creating the *illusion* that timing is a crucial factor. It is possible that early adversity can create feedback loops that make it more difficult for improvements in the

treme temperaments that affect children early in life also increase the risk for developing mental disorders in adulthood.

In summary, while most children grow out of early behavioral problems, continuity between child and adult symptoms is most frequent in children with severe temperamental difficulties. The best explanation is based on a general principle: The more severe the psychopathology, the more likely it is to be driven by biological factors (Paris, 1999).

To put these conclusions another way, most children have temperaments that are relatively easy, or at least fall within a normal range. Thus, when problems are caused mainly by an adverse environment, they are likely to remit once that environment changes. This helps to explain why most children seen in clinical settings never develop adult mental disorders (Zeitlin, 1986). In contrast, children with the most vulnerable temperaments are more affected by environmental adversity. This interaction leads to positive feedback loops that maintain pathology over time.

The course of life is never fully determined. By and large, discontinuities are the rule in development. There can always be changes, some for the better, others for the worse. These facts led one developmental psychologist (Lewis, 1997) to publish a book-length critique of the primacy of early experience. Suspicious of determinism, Lewis offered the optimistic view that it is always possible to alter one's fate and that one does not necessarily need therapy to accomplish this goal. Moreover, Lewis, drawing on a wide literature in social psychology, argued that behavior is highly contextual and emphasized that people behave very differently in different environments.

These principles have been confirmed, at least to a large degree, by evidence that children raised in unusually adverse circumstances retain the capacity to develop normally when placed in a better environment. Older studies have consistently supported recovery for damaged children (Clarke & Clarke, 1979), and I will examine recent research on Romanian orphans in Chapter 4.

Rutter (1987a) has made a series of observations supporting the concept of turning points in development. In other words, meeting new people, moving to a new neighbourhood, or attending a new school can break cycles of disadvantage. Continuities are accounted for by children whose temperamental vulnerability prevents them from taking advantage of new opportunities. Given a change in their luck, most adults with an unhappy childhood can have productive lives.

☐ Primacy and Adversity

To what extent is psychopathology in adults the result of adverse events during childhood? A large body of research has found that adults with serious psychological symptoms tend to report a wide range of early adversities. Thus, patients with depression report histories of early loss of parents (Parker, 1992) or of neglectful parental attitudes (Parker, 1983). Patients with impulse disorders, such as substance abuse (Vaillant, 1994) or eating disorders (Steiger, Liquornik, Chapman, & Hussain, 1991), often describe dysfunctional families of origin. Patients with personality disorders, most particularly those with borderline personality, report serious pathology in their parents, as well as histories of trauma, neglect, and early loss (Paris, 1994, 1996c).

At first sight, these findings might seem to support conventional clinical wisdom. Yet, as discussed in Chapter 1, all they demonstrate are *associations*. Moreover, almost all this research is retrospective, and few of the findings have ever been confirmed by prospective studies. Thus, we do not know how many of these observations may only reflect recall biases in patients whose present suffering leads them to remember the past in a negative way. In any case, such reports cannot, by themselves, prove that childhood experiences *cause* mental disorders.

Another problem with retrospective research concerns the base rate of adversity (see Chapter 1). Forty years ago, Renaud and Estes (1961) interviewed 100 highly functioning men to determine what it was about their childhood that made them successful. To their surprise, these nonsymptomatic individuals reported about as many childhood traumas as did patients in therapy. As Freud (1920/1955) himself once acknowledged, therapists make formulations in retrospect, but no one can predict how anyone will function in life from how difficult or easy their childhood has been.

Vaillant (1977), in a long-term study of men who had attended Harvard University before World War II, measured whether their childhoods had been happy or unhappy (based on interviews during adolescence). But the quality of childhood experiences failed to predict in any way how these men functioned in later life. Vaillant (1993) later obtained similar findings from studies of men growing up in inner-city Boston, as well as from a sample of women (part of a famous long-term follow-up of children with high intelligence conducted at Stanford University) and from a large sample of men suffering from alcoholism. Each of these cohorts were marked by great discontinuities between childhood and adulthood.

The most likely explanation is that whether or not childhood is difficult, the way people cope with life depends more on internal than external factors. These intrinsic capacities depend on individual differences affecting negative emotionality (Bowman, 1997), attitudes of optimism (Seligman, 1975), an internal locus of control (Sapolsky, 1998), and the capacity to make use of social supports (Sarason, Sarason, & Pierce, 1990).

Resilience is the rule in human life. For every patient describing adver-

that children need to be cared for, yet must also be allowed to separate from their parents.

Clinical observations suggest that patients tend to report problems during childhood on both dimensions. Many describe feeling unloved, profoundly misunderstood, or not responded to by one or both of their parents. This corresponds to a dimension of *neglect*. Other patients, sometimes the same ones, provide data supporting clinical observations (Bowlby, 1973; Levy, 1943) on the parental practices that interfere with the development of autonomy. This corresponds to a dimension of *overprotection*.

Empirical studies measuring these parenting dimensions have made use of self-report instruments that ask people to remember childhood experiences. The results show that a wide variety of patients describe a failure by their parents to carry out basic tasks. The most striking findings have been reported in clinically depressed individuals (Parker, 1983, 1992), who commonly report emotional neglect and/or overprotection from their parents. Similar observations have emerged from studies of patients with personality disorders (Paris, 1996c).

If we were to take these reports at face value, they would suggest that when parents fail to provide enough love and fail to encourage enough autonomy, they put their children at serious risk. Yet all these results must be approached with great caution.

First, how do we know that adult descriptions of childhood experiences are accurate? Parker (1983), who developed the Parental Bonding Index, one of the best-known instruments used to measure parenting, was aware of the problem and went to some trouble to determine the validity of his scale. His supporting data depended on significant correlations between siblings growing up in the same family and between the perceptions of parents and children. However, the reported correlations were not very large. As shown in many other studies (Robins, Schoenberg, & Holmes, 1985; Rowe, 1981), major differences exist in the perceptions of parenting and family atmosphere between children growing up in the same family. Although parents can, and do, treat different children differently, it is not clear to what extent that is a response to variations in temperament. Thus, it remains unclear whether reports of emotional neglect represent historical reality or are simply a matter of perception.

Second, we cannot rule out the possibility that retrospective measures of parenting reflect a recall bias, in which people in distress tend to remember the past in a negative way. To address this problem, we need prospective studies, in which parenting is directly measured during childhood and in which cohorts of affected children are followed into adulthood.

Moreover, there is evidence suggesting that measures of parental bonding are more perception than fact. The same parental behavior is experienced quite differently by different children. When subjected to behavioral genetic analyses in twin studies (see Chapter 9), parental bonding scales turn out to have a large heritable component (Plomin, DeFries, McClearn, & Rutter, 1997). The most likely explanation is that the personality traits shaping differences in the perception of parenting are heritable.

A third problem, discussed in Chapter 1, is that most associations between risk factors and outcomes show statistical, but not predictable, relationships between parental behavior and psychological symptoms. It is worth reiterating that there is a potential artifact hidden in most statistical analyses. Significant findings are often not quantitatively large, and results can be accounted for by a minority of those in the sample. Thus, it is possible to have reportable findings even when most individuals with the symptoms under study have experienced normal or close-to-normal parenting, while many in nondisordered control groups have been subjected to pathological parenting.

Most children have an innate capacity to overcome defects in their parenting. (Readers who have raised children should find this fact reassuring!) As Winnicott (1958) famously stated, parenting does not have to be good, only *good enough*. Or, as Kagan (1997) argues, children can grow up in their own way unless parents put serious obstacles in their way. Moreover, even when parenting is not "good enough," other factors in a child's experience can compensate for these deficiencies.

In other words, parents have to be *highly* toxic to their children to produce consistent negative effects. One example of this toxicity occurs when parents themselves suffer from mental disorders. A good deal of evidence shows that children raised by seriously disturbed parents are at higher risk. This conclusion has been supported by studies of parents with depression (Downey & Coyne, 1990), with criminal histories (Robins, 1966), and with histories of substance abuse (West & Prinz, 1987). To some extent, these associations reflect common heredity. But one can also imagine how parental mental illness might seriously interfere with parenting, leading to either preoccupation (as in the case of depression) or to neglect and abuse (as in the case of criminality and substance abuse).

Short of overt mental illness, many factors in family life affect children adversely. In particular, children tend to respond badly to severe marital conflict (Cummings, 1996) or to family violence (Rutter, 1987a). At least in the short term, they may even feel relieved if a break-up of the family terminates exposure to these stressors.

Nonetheless, we should still view all these findings cautiously. Although toxic parenting has worse effects than mediocre parenting, most children survive such experiences. They may feel inner scars, but the majority do not become seriously dysfunctional. The ultimate outcome of children's experiences with parenting often depends on other, largely innate characteristics, as well as on factors outside the family environment.

Lambert, 1993; Rind & Tromofitch, 1997; Rind, Tromofitch, & Bauserman, 1998) largely account for observed sequelae. In fact, seriously dysfunctional families are all too common among abused children.

Moreover, a great deal of confusion has resulted from considering sexual abuse as one thing, rather than many things. The ultimate effects of childhood sexual abuse also depend on its *parameters*. The most important of these are severity and the identity of the perpetrator (Browne & Finkelhor, 1986; Russell, 1986). Yet the abuse to which children are most likely to be exposed is a single incident of molestation, not involving penetration, and perpetrated by a nonrelative. These experiences rarely lead to long-term sequelae. In contrast, multiple incidents, abuse involving penetration, or abuse by a family member, especially a father, are much more likely to cause sequelae. Yet even when *all* the parameters of severity are present, most of those exposed grow up to function normally as adults.

Similar findings emerge from studies of the long-term effects of childhood physical abuse (Malinovsky-Rummell & Hansen, 1993). Again, the base rate of these experiences in the community is high (MacMillan, MacMillan, Offord, & Griffith, 1994a, 1994b). About a quarter of children who suffered physical abuse from their parents develop psychological symptoms as adults. There is a significant relationship between severity and outcome, with those who have been injured or consistently beaten showing the most sequelae. Physical abuse is also highly intercorrelated with other adversities: family dysfunction or breakdown and mental illness in parents.

The principle that children who have been beaten are more likely to become violent adults has become a shibboleth, both for therapists and for the media. Yet there is slim empirical support for this relationship. It *is* true that those who suffer violence as children are statistically more likely to be violent as adults (Widom, 1989). It is *not* true, however, that most violent adults have been abused during childhood. It is also *not* true that most children who are physically abused will become violent adults.

Again, the problem has to do with the difference between statistically significant effects, which may be derived from a minority of cases, and true predictability. For example, in one large-scale study of children exposed to family violence, although there was a higher rate of violent behavior by adulthood, the vast majority were never violent at any time (Widom et al., 1989). A subgroup, which could have had higher levels of impulsive and aggressive traits, accounted for the reported association. Thus, common temperament might explain these relationships.

Research on child abuse demonstrates that impressions drawn from clinical cases are not necessarily borne out by community studies. There are enormous discontinuities between adversities and outcomes.

Other Traumatic Events

Researchers have also examined the effects of a wide variety of traumatic events on children. Typically, posttraumatic symptoms are frequent in the short term and much less common in the long term. For example, Terr's (1988) 2-year follow-up of children surviving a kidnapping on a school bus in Chowchilla, California, showed that most of the cohort had vivid recollections of the incident, but few remained clinically symptomatic. Similarly, a long-term follow-up of children involved in a major flood (Green et al., 1994) found that posttraumatic symptoms decreased steadily and strikingly over time.

Few events in this century were as traumatic as the Holocaust. The child survivors of this event lived through the war years, a few emerging from camps, while most remained in hiding under assumed identities. Adult Holocaust survivors tend to report some degree of psychological distress (Sigal & Weinfeld, 1989) but do not necessarily have major psychopathology. A recent study from Israel (Robinson, Rapaport-Bar, Sever, & Rapaport, 1994) found the majority of child survivors to be functioning well. One cannot help but be impressed by these dramatic examples of resilience.

☐ Parental Death, Separation, and Divorce

It is usually tragic to lose a parent during childhood. But do such losses have long-term consequences, leading to outcomes involving serious psychopathology? A large body of research has addressed this issue.

One of the most frequently investigated questions concerns whether early bereavement is a risk factor for later depression. Essentially, this association has been found to be either weak or absent (see review in Parker, 1992). The best research suggests that loss, by itself, does *not* cause depression, unless it is accompanied by *other* adversities. Those most at risk are exposed to other psychosocial risk factors, such as depression in the surviving parent or isolation of the nuclear family from social supports. Moreover, those most affected by such events tend to carry a genetic diathesis for depression (see review in Paris, 1999).

We should keep in mind that parental death must have been a common experience throughout the history of our species, even more so in the past than in the present. From the point of view of natural selection, it should not be surprising that children are not marked permanently by such events.

The results of research concerning separation and divorce present a

expected from a primacy model, the younger parents divorce, the better the outcome is for the children (Wallerstein, 1989). The most likely explanation is that young children have not yet formed a strong attachment to the departing parent and do not suffer as palpable a loss.

Those who divorce early are more likely to remarry, yet the outcome of remarriage is not always beneficial. Remarriage seems to be more helpful for boys, who may have a particular need for a father-substitute, than for girls, who can easily feel excluded by their mother's new relationship (Hetherington, Cox, & Cox, 1985).

Finally, the outcome of divorce depends on the availability of extended family ties and on the social context of the larger community. Structured and positive school environments have a protective effect on children growing up in broken families, as they are known to do in a variety of childhood adversities (Hetherington et al., 1992).

The conclusion of this story is a relatively happy one: Most children of divorce grow up normally and function without developing significant psychopathology. As with other adversities, sequelae are concentrated in a vulnerable minority, and resilience remains the rule.

☐ Poverty

The idea that poverty is a major cause of psychological problems is another cultural shibboleth. Many people sympathize with the poor or consider them to be unfairly oppressed. For this reason, a belief in the pathogenicity of poverty has a strong political significance.

There is no doubt that it is better to be rich than poor. (It is also better to be good-looking, smart, and talented.) Higher socioeconomic status is associated with better physical and mental health, even when other factors are controlled for (Sapolsky, 1998). Social class is a strong predictor of psychological symptoms, with many mental disorders being more common in lower socioeconomic groups (Robins & Regier, 1991).

There will always be social classes. Yet most people who live in developed countries are becoming richer, not poorer. The paradox is that even as Western civilization becomes wealthier, many mental disorders have become *more* common. The list includes some of the most common and important of psychological problems: depression, substance abuse, and criminality. Some might think that it is depressing to be poor, that despair about deprivation leads to substance abuse, and that a lack of resources leads people to turn to crime. None of these assumptions turn out to be true.

Prospective studies show that most people born into poverty do not end up on welfare lists. Instead, many work hard to improve themselves.

In the Boston inner-city study (Vaillant, 1993), most of the cohort achieved some form of upward mobility. This research also identified the most important protective factors against the effects of poverty: well-functioning families and strong community networks.

Here we have still another example of the problem of statistical versus clinical significance. Whereas most children born into poverty become well-functioning adults, there are specific subgroups at risk for psychopathology. Thus, even though slums are plagued with drugs and crime, most people do not participate in these activities (and are more likely to be victims than perpetrators).

Poverty acts in the same way as other adversities. By itself, it is only a statistical risk factor for psychological sequelae, with most people being resilient to its effects. As with other adversities, cumulative risks are more pathogenic, with the *combination* of poverty with severe family dysfunction being a potent toxin for children.

☐ Cumulative Adversities

Our immune system allows us to remain healthy even when exposed to pathogens. But when this protection breaks down, we can readily fall victim to disease. In the same way, many individuals never develop any form of mental disorder, even when exposed to the most severe stressors. On the other hand, even in relatively normal individuals, defenses can be broken down by cumulative levels of adversity.

When enough bad things happen over time, psychological symptoms tend to develop. In children, the total number of adversities during childhood has a stronger relationship to a pathological outcome than the presence of any one risk factor (Deater-Deckard et al., 1998; Rutter, 1989). Similar findings apply to adults, as shown by the fact that measures of cumulative life stress predict illness outcomes (Rahe, 1995).

In a series of classic studies, Rutter (1987a, 1989) demonstrated the cumulative effects of adversity in a number of studies on samples of children at high risk, due to psychosocial or socioeconomic adversities. The six variables associated with the greatest long-term risk for psychiatric disorder were: (a) severe discord between parents; (b) low social status; (c) large family size; (d) paternal criminality; (e) maternal psychiatric disorder; (f) child placement. A child with only one of these factors would do as well as those with none. But as additional factors were added on, the risk of disorder increased—in those with four or more, the rate reached 20% (although one must note an 80% rate of resilience).

One possible mechanism for the effects of cumulative life stressors involves Seligman's (1975) concept of "learned helplessness." We can usu-

Yet, if anything, they show higher levels of resilience. The environment in which our species evolved was, in the famous phrase of the English philosopher Thomas Hobbes, "nasty, brutish, and short." In hunter-gatherer societies, starvation was always a possibility, and predation was far from unheard of, particularly for children. Disease was endemic, and there was no medical treatment to speak of. Parents often died young, and children did not always survive for long. Strangers were often physically dangerous. In short, traumatic events in prehistory would have been much more common than they are now.

Yet our species did not become extinct. Evolution must therefore have developed mechanisms to deal with exposure to trauma. Humans are characterized by an unusually long childhood, providing an opportunity to learn the complex tasks required of an adult. Therefore, children have to be born with a certain toughness and an ability to rise above adversity.

☐ Individual Differences in Resilience

Resilience, like any other capacity, varies greatly between individuals. Thus, the impact of the same life events is very different for different people.

How experiences effect us depends on how the mind assimilates them. Personality traits, rooted in temperament, are mechanisms designed to deal with a variety of challenges from the environment (Beck & Freeman, 1990). They play a crucial role in determining how any life event, whether negative or positive, is processed in our minds. These *person-environment interactions* (Kendler & Eaves, 1986) are much stronger predictors of outcome than exposure to adversity alone.

Children who carry predispositions to mental disorders or who have personality profiles that make them unusually sensitive to stress are more likely to experience adverse life events as negative and to react badly to them. In contrast, children with positive personality traits tend to find ways to cope with adversity, making them relatively immune to stressful experiences. Although most children lie on a continuum between these extremes, an average child will have sufficient resourcefulness to weather an average level of adversity.

A large body of research on the effects of trauma (see reviews in Paris, 1999; Yehuda, & McFarlane, 1995) shows how these principles apply to adults. Although the traditional belief is that children are much more vulnerable to stress, empirical evidence has not supported this conjecture. By and large, children tend to emerge from even the most severely stressful circumstances relatively intact.

Studies using prospective methods have consistently demonstrated that children are not easily damaged by life experiences. In fact, researchers who have conducted these long-term follow-up studies have sometimes been amazed to see how problems in childhood, such as serious family conflicts (which they had thought to be seriously pathogenic) prove to have very few long-term effects (Kagan & Zentner, 1996). Although there are exceptions to the rule, children are generally much tougher and more flexible than many people think.

The concept of resilience does not, of course, imply that we should dismiss or discount the negative effects of exposure to adversity. As discussed in the previous chapter, stressful events during childhood do increase the statistical risk for psychopathology later in life (see reviews by Cohler, Stott, & Musick, 1995; Masten & Coatsworth, 1995). Again, it is better to have a happy childhood than an unhappy one. But statistical associations are not strong enough for useful prediction, and there is no *necessary* link between adverse events and long-term sequelae.

As discussed in Chapter 1, associations between variables can be significant even if they are *not* found in most of the subjects in the study, masking the fact that, in most cases, there may be no relationship—or even a negative one (Meehl, 1990). These statistical artifacts commonly occur in research on the long-term effects of adversities. If the most vulnerable children respond *very* badly to life events, there can be statistically significant effects for the group as a whole, even though most children rise above adversity.

Since statistical relationships between risk factors and outcomes can be misleading, we should be very cautious about interpreting them as proof for statements claiming that "A causes B." Even among vulnerable individuals simple associations do not establish causality. We need to remember that single negative events during childhood, however traumatic, do not usually lead to sequelae, while even cumulative adversities do not necessarily break down natural coping mechanisms.

This principle also helps to explain why histories of trauma early in childhood cannot be interpreted as proving that "earlier is worse." When development begins badly, the same risks are likely to continue over time. Early adversities are often a marker for continuous adversities occurring at many other stages of development (Rutter & Rutter, 1993). Moreover, most of the important adverse events during childhood, such as family discord, parental psychopathology, and poor socioeconomic status, are intercorrelated, leading to cumulative effects (Rutter et al., 1997). Chapter 3 noted that Rutter (1987a) found that a combination of cumulative adversities leads to a rate of mental disorder in children of about 20%. This is a very high rate, yet 80% of those with multiple risk factors did not develop *any* mental disorder. We do not know how many of these children with multiple adversities eventually developed psychological symp-

long-term follow-up of a cohort of children who grew up in inner-city Boston. In contrast to the conventional wisdom that slums must breed crime and disorder, most of the subjects eventually led productive adult lives.

The Cambridge-Somerville study was also conducted in the Boston area and had been initiated during the Great Depression (McCord, 1990). It was designed to follow children at risk for delinquency. The original purpose had been to determine whether or not counseling can prevent offending. (It did not!) When the cohort was followed into adulthood, with subjects retraced at ages 45 to 53, criminality in adulthood was most significantly related to measures of deficient child rearing and parental alcoholism and criminality. However, resilience was again the rule, since most of the adults followed were *not* criminals, having "grown out" of their earlier behavioral problems. These findings are supported by long-term outcome studies of conduct disorder (Robins, 1966; Zoccolillo et al., 1992), which show that only the most severely symptomatic children go on to become criminals in adulthood.

Similar findings have emerged from British research, derived from cohorts in Newcastle slums (Kolvin, Miller, Fleeting, & Kolvin, 1988) as well as a cohort in the city of Cambridge (Farrington, 1988). In both studies, the strongest factors favoring resilience to delinquency were a more agreeable temperament, higher IQ associated with good school performance, and better family and peer relationships.

Studies of Institutionalized Children

Children raised in institutions can suffer from severe emotional neglect, an adversity that might be expected to increase the risk for psychopathology. But the results of a major study of women who had been reared in institutions early in their childhood (Rutter, Quinton, & Hill, 1990) only demonstrates the ubiquity of resilience. The data showed that while severe adversity led to a poorer overall outcome, there was enormous variability within the cohort, and only a minority developed severe pathology.

Rutter et al. (1990) also looked at what mechanisms might explain this variability. One of the most important determinants of outcome concerned the way individuals reacted to life events later on in life. Whether or not they left home in a reasonable and planned way, as opposed to getting pregnant and marrying impulsively, was a major factor in protecting them against the impact of prior adversities. It is notable that those women whose marriages broke down proved more sensitive to renewed stress, and it was this subgroup that accounted for most of the differences. In contrast, those who married successfully were eventually indistinguishable from those raised in normal families. Although it is not clear exactly what determined these successful choices, it seems likely that those whose marriages worked made use of favorable temperamental characteristics, such as higher persistence and lower impulsivity.

Another line of evidence supporting this interpretation is that the women with symptoms during adulthood were much more likely to have had temperamental difficulties during childhood. In contrast, those who did well had a more positive temperament, did better in school and in social relationships throughout development, and showed a good capacity to plan their lives. As in the Hawaii study, those who were most intelligent were most resilient. These findings nicely demonstrate the mechanisms by which later events can compensate for earlier events.

Yet when environments are consistently and severely adverse, natural mechanisms of resilience can sometimes be overwhelmed. Clarke and Clarke (1979) reviewed a series of classical studies on multifostered children, a group who clinicians know to be susceptible to long-term damage. When children were placed in a secure and positive environment before age 6, the results of early deprivation were *entirely* reversible. Placement at a later age did not have the same salutary effects, since by that point, many children were too deficient in social skills to take advantage of their new environment. These conclusions, published 25 years ago, have been consistently replicated ever since.

Studies of orphans adopted during World War II (Rathbun et al., 1958) and the Korean War (Winick, Meyer, & Harris, 1975) consistently support the principle that placement in a good home can reverse the effects of early deprivation. Researchers found that these children, in spite of having been exposed to severe malnutrition and other life-threatening adversities, are indistinguishable from their contemporaries only a few years later.

The generalizability of these findings might be limited by the circumstances of adoption, in that parents who die in war need not be pathological and are therefore less likely to pass on problematical temperamental characteristics to their offspring. On the other hand, there is hardly any difference in psychopathology between adopted and nonadopted children as a whole (Singer et al., 1998). Moreover, even among children who were adopted late in childhood, after living in institutions, psychopathology is far from the rule (Hodges & Tizard, 1989).

Adoption of children who have had unusually poor care in the first few months and years of life provides a particularly good test of the principle of primacy. When early adversities are followed by later adversities, one sees a cumulative impact. But adoptions of children who have been traumatized or neglected, and are then placed in good homes, test the theory of primacy more precisely. If early experience is more important, most

To some extent, therefore, resilience may depend on individual differences in temperament. As I will show later in this book, temperamental variations, and the personality trait profiles associated with them, constitute predispositions to psychopathology. Those who are constitutionally vulnerable will suffer the most from negative experiences. At the same time, those who have positive and adaptive traits are most protected against adversity.

Yet, as clinicians know, some constitutional vulnerabilities are strong enough to override entirely the effects of a positive psychosocial environment. This is the case for genetic vulnerabilities for schizophrenia, which can also be amplified by exposure to brain injury (Weinberger, 1987). At the same time, differences in temperament, by themselves, need not lead to symptoms, particularly when environmental conditions are favorable (Beck & Freeman, 1990; Paris, 1996c). Ultimately, the pathway to psychopathology depends on *interactions* between temperament and experience.

Let us consider an example. Some temperamental qualities are better than others for making the best use of environmental opportunities. Returning to the study by Werner and Smith (1992), the most prominent traits promoting resilience were an attractive personality, intelligence, persistence, a variety of interests, the capacity to be alone, and an optimistic approach to life. Thus, these children had a number of capacities that helped them to respond flexibly to environmental challenges. Competent children are not passive recipients of external input but actively shape their environment to meet their needs (Scarr, 1992).

A well-known prospective study conducted by Vaillant (1977) confirms this principle. Somewhat to the surprise of the researcher (a trained psychoanalyst), the quality of childhood experience had little or no predictive value about the extent to which Harvard men eventually achieved psychological maturity. Instead, school performance and defense styles, both of which tend to reflect favorable or unfavorable personality traits, were the best predictors of functioning in later life.

Chapters 9 and 10 will show how genetic factors cause children to differ in exposure to, as well as in sensitivity to, adversity. Thus, the most resilient children have positive and effective traits that lead them to do well at school, gain the positive attention of their teachers, find a supportive peer group, and develop attachments to people in their extended family and community.

In contrast, a vulnerable child is more likely to experience negative events and to respond more strongly to them. These temperamental qualities, reflected in personality trait profiles, prevent them from making good use of their environment, leading to negative feedback loops.

For example, impulsive and irritable children respond to adversity by becoming even more difficult, making it more likely that they will be badly treated (Rutter et al., 1990). A long-term follow-up study of children in New Zealand (Caspi, Moffitt, Newman, & Silva, 1996; Newman et al., 1997) found that observations of impulsivity and anxiety as early as age 3 allow one to predict a statistical risk for adult disorders, with children who show early impulsivity being at long-term risk for externalizing disorders.

Children with an anxious temperament can also respond to adversity in a maladaptive way. Becoming more withdrawn interferes with the ability to make use of crucial alternate attachments outside the nuclear family involving peers, extended family, and community organizations. Caspi et al. (1996) also found that anxious children were at long-term risk for internalizing disorders. (We need to keep in mind, again, that most children in the sample did *not* develop adult psychopathology.)

Differences in resilience can also be driven by environmental factors. Clearly, positive experiences are protective against adversity. The relative availability or unavailability of these opportunities to develop buffers the negative impact of adversity (Kaufman, Gruneman, Cohler, & Gamer, 1979; Rutter, 1987a). To this extent, therefore, resilience reflects not only personal qualities but also good fortune. (Yet, since not every child takes advantage of favorable circumstances, we must never lose sight of temperament.)

The presence of readily accessible social support networks is another important factor in resilience. Social cohesion helps to explain why communities vary in overall levels of psychopathology (Leighton et al., 1963). Social structures are particularly important for children with an abnormal temperament, who may otherwise have difficulty finding a social niche. Traditional societies, which provide guaranteed social roles for almost everyone, protect vulnerable children from developing several forms of psychopathology, most particularly addictions and personality disorders (Paris, 1996c).

In summary, research on resilience shows that even the most troubled children need not develop serious psychopathology later in life. The influence of Freud had created the impression that development is relatively fixed at the end of childhood or adolescence. But many adolescents "straighten out," with two-thirds of children with conduct disorder growing out of delinquency (Robins, 1966). Throughout adult life, people continue to change, sometimes in surprising ways (Vaillant, 1993).

The ubiquity of resilience carries a hopeful message. The past does not determine the present. No matter how unhappy childhood has been, people have the opportunity to achieve something better.

☐ Surviving an Unhappy Childhood

Research on resilience points to specific strategies that children can use to overcome adversity. On the one hand, constitutional advantages such as intelligence and an attractive personality are largely a matter of luck. Yet even for those not well endowed with positive temperamental qualities, some behaviors are more useful than others.

First, children growing up in a dysfunctional family need to get out of the house and spend time with other people. Studies of children with parents who are psychotic, chronically depressed, or alcoholic (Anthony, 1987; Kaufman et al., 1979) all show that the more time is spent at home, the worse the outcome. Conversely, positive interactions with uncles, aunts, or grandparents all lead to a better outcome. Similarly, having friends and spending time at *their* houses with *their* families protects children from parental pathology.

Second, connecting with a social community buffers the effects of family dysfunction. Children are attached not only to family and friends but also to schools, religious groups, and community organizations. A child whose teacher, clergyman, or youth worker takes a special interest in him or her is likely to fare better. Rutter (1989) described how these positive experiences become turning points that can change the course of development.

To find alternative sources of attachment, resilient children must also have the capacity to recognize the nature of their adversities. In particular, seeing how other families work gives them perspective on their own. Children who regard their pathological family as normal or who feel obligated to look after troubled parents can become enmeshed in the lives of others, and will be less likely to develop autonomy later in their own lives.

☐ Conclusion

Research findings on resilience offer a powerful challenge to the primacy of early experience. Most children emerge intact from even the worst experiences, and psychopathology is concentrated among those who are intrinsically vulnerable to stress. The main mechanisms of resilience involve a capacity to maximize opportunities that lead to positive experiences that buffer negative ones.

But resilient children are not invulnerable, an older term that is no longer used by researchers. Moreover, as Rutter (1987a) once pointed out, resilience does not apply to everything. Adults who have survived bad experiences may show better coping in some aspects of their lives than in others. Negative experiences in childhood may sometimes be an Achilles heel, increasing the difficulty of overcoming some adversities later in life.

The most important implication of the resilience literature is that development is not deterministic. Chance plays a major role in shaping the course of development (Kagan, 1997; Lewis, 1997). An unhappy childhood need not determine the rest of one's life. As Harris (1998) states, "There is no law of nature that says misery has to have sequelae" (p. 153).

Clinicians need to understand and absorb the research data on resilience. The findings summarized in this chapter contradict any simple and direct connection between childhood experience and adult difficulties. As will be shown in Part III, psychopathology requires a more complex and comprehensive model.

CHILDHOOD AND ADULTHOOD: MYTHS

Part II consists of four chapters examining the sources of false beliefs about the relationship between childhood and adulthood.

Chapter 5 places the idea that childhood shapes adult life in a historical perspective. This belief can be traced back to the post-Enlightenment belief in unlimited progress through modification of the environment. The chapter will also document the wide currency of primacy in contemporary culture.

Chapter 6 provides an assessment of psychoanalytic theory, the model that has always been, and remains, the most important theoretical basis of primacy. Freud's original ideas have been modified by later theorists, but one can assess the scientific validity of psychoanalysis in the context of modern knowledge about child development.

Chapter 7 presents a critical review of repression and dissociation, ideas derived from psychoanalysis. Research has undermined both of these concepts. The fallacies of the recovered memory movement shed light on the problems inherent in the primacy of childhood.

Chapter 8 will present a detailed critique of attachment

theory, a model derived from both psychoanalysis and developmental psychology. The chapter will briefly evaluate concepts of childhood in cognitive-behavioral theory.

Childhood, History, and Society

☐ Nature and Nurture

Why are people so different from each other? This is one of the greatest puzzles in psychology. We only need to look around us to see how much people vary—not just in physical characteristics, but also in thoughts, feelings, and behavior. Some people are happy, others unhappy. Some are vulnerable to stress and develop mental disorders, while others sail through life unscathed. Does the explanation lie in *nature* or in *nurture*?

The commonsensical answer to this question is, of course, *both*. For example, both genetic and environmental factors are involved in height. Children are more likely to grow tall if their parents are tall, but they also require an adequate diet. In the same way, individual differences in personality and behavior are the result of interactions between genes and environment. Although each child begins life with unique and heritable temperamental characteristics, complex personality traits do not emerge *de novo*, but are shaped by a multitude of life experiences.

The world is made up of interactions, but people have difficulty thinking interactively. It is more comfortable to believe that complex outcomes result from single causes. As a result, history has seen radical swings in intellectual fashion, in which either genes or environment have been favored as *the* explanation for differences in human behavior.

☐ The Nature/Nurture Problem: A History

The polarities between nature and nurture have always been a focus of sharp dispute. We can trace this controversy back at least 400 years. The English philosopher John Locke (1693/1892) believed that the mind was a blank slate at birth and that differences between individuals in thought or behavior are entirely based on social conditioning. In his view, parents and educators would have an almost unlimited capacity to shape children.

The corollary is that human nature itself might be almost infinitely malleable. In the libertarian political program of the Enlightenment, everyone is born with the same potential (or, in a famous phrase, created equal). Therefore, differences in opportunity and achievement are external to the individual and should be redressed through social reforms. These concepts added a powerful political dimension to the debate. Conservatives have often embraced the idea that individual differences are innate, while the political left tends to oppose any and all genetic explanations of human behavior (Paris, 1999).

The romantic movement of the late 18th and early 19th centuries introduced the idea that upbringing deprives a child of natural innocence. In the same way, philosophers came to believe that modernity robs primitive societies of an innate harmony with nature. Jean-Jacques Rousseau promoted the concept of the noble savage, spoiled by contact with civilization. As he famously stated (Rousseau, 1762/1978): "Man is born free, and everywhere he is in chains."

This way of thinking reached a climax in the 20th century. The idea that environment determines a lifelong pattern of behavior came to dominate the ideological climate of psychology and shaped the theory behind clinical practice. Psychotherapists have usually been strong believers in the power of the environment. They have consistently favored explanations of behavior that derive from the uniqueness of life experience. Typically, therapists regard biological explanations with some degree of suspicion. To the extent that genetics is considered at all, it tends to be relegated to a black box labelled "constitution."

The cultural influence of environmentalist ideas has been equally profound. Educated people have been taught that personality is formed in early childhood and that the presence of psychopathology reflects problems in the quality of parenting. Up to recently, there were few credible alternatives to these ideas. The idea that character might be preformed or inherited seemed to be a relic of the past, lacking any firm scientific foundation. Thus, the concept of children being a blank slate on which the environment writes its text has ruled. Let us therefore examine specific ways in which these ideas about the primacy of childhood have dominated our culture.

☐ Childhood, Psychotherapy, and Contemporary Culture

Psychotherapists are influential members of society. Their theories and methods are widely disseminated through the media. Therapeutic beliefs about the causes of mental disorders affect the way people think about a wide range of issues. The principle that psychological problems are rooted in childhood experiences has become central to the culture of our times.

A belief in the centrality of childhood also resonates with deep and universal human feelings. Every generation feels some nostalgia for the past, and the idealization of childhood is hardly a new theme in human history. Adults prefer to think of children as basically good. When children are bad, they are often seen as corrupted innocents. Thus, belief in the primacy of childhood gives hope that even the most severe psychological difficulties can be resolved by changing the environment.

One of the powerful forces behind the belief in the primacy of childhood is psychoanalysis, with its wide impact on contemporary culture. Intellectual leaders are often familiar with the principles of this discipline. They may have read about psychoanalysis or may have undergone the treatment themselves. (Those who have been analyzed will have spent many years committed to the method and are particularly likely to become true believers.) Intellectuals sympathetic to analysis have also applied its concepts to a range of other disciplines.

The primacy of childhood has permeated contemporary thought in the social sciences, the humanities, the arts, and the media. To document these trends in any detail would require another, and different, book. Therefore, I will only offer a brief sketch, illustrating my thesis with examples, while referring the interested reader to scholarly sources.

Let us begin with the *social sciences*. These disciplines have consistently taken the side of nurture as the determining force for human nature (Degler, 1991; Paris, 1999). Until recently, radical environmentalism dominated psychology, with models emphasizing the central roles of early experience and behavioral conditioning. In particular, developmental psychology has been permeated by the assumption of a blank slate, with parental behavior determining almost everything in a child's experience (Harris, 1998).

Cultural anthropology has been equally environmentalist in its assumptions. Both psychologists and anthropologists have generally been resistant to the possibility that individual differences are rooted in temperament. Strong links between psychology and anthropology developed on the principle that personality is determined by culture, most particularly by parental practices shaping the development of young children. Mead (1926/1971) suggested that different cultures, by raising their children differently, can produce individuals with radically different personalities—an idea later popularized by Erikson (1950).

Myths about childhood have had an equally strong influence on the *humanities*. Theories about the childhood origins of psychological problems seemed to explain problems that would otherwise have remained mysterious. The last few decades have been marked by the development of new hybrid disciplines joining psychology to history and biography.

Psychohistory attempts to explain historical events and historical figures by analyzing the unconscious motivation of historical figures (DeMause, 1982; Mazlish, 1963). Erik Erikson was a pioneer in this area, writing about such diverse figures as Hitler (Erikson, 1950), Luther (Erikson, 1959), and Gandhi (Erikson, 1969). Since then, many have followed down the same path. Yet psychohistory has had a checkered course. Its speculative methods do not correspond to standard historical practices, leading the field to fall into a certain decline (Stannard, 1980). Can psychological insight account for the political content and style of Richard Nixon? (See Volkan, Itkovitz, & Dod (1997) for an attempt.) Even more poignantly, can one account for the Holocaust by analyzing the psyche of Adolf Hitler? (See Rosenbaum, 1998.)

Psychobiography has been a more successful enterprise. In fact, psychology has now become a standard tool for most literary biographers. In the past, childhood was only used to place life stories in historical context. Today, many biographies begin by describing their protagonists' unhappy childhoods, the details of which are later invoked to explain both their creativity and their psychological problems. Thus, the novels of Virginia Woolf have been seen as the outgrowth of possible childhood sexual abuse (DeSalvo, 1989). Philip Larkin's bitter poetry and preoccupation with death have been interpreted in the light of the artist's painful relationship with his mother (Motion, 1993).

This approach reverses earlier biographical methods, in which artists and historical figures were often idealized and presented as heroic. Modern biographers are much more likely to debunk their subjects, demonstrating how unhappy childhood experiences led them to be dysfunctional adults. This has led many modern books on the lives of famous people to be termed, with some accuracy, "pathographies."

Even more than academics, artists tend to reflect the spirit of their times. It is therefore not surprising how much myths of childhood have influenced the content of *poetry* and *fiction*. Confessional poetry, as well as autobiographical fiction describing dysfunctional families have become prominent literary phenomena. Famously, Sylvia Plath turned her personal agony, particularly the death of her father, into powerful verse and described her psychotherapy in a widely read novel (Plath, 1963).

In a frequently quoted poem, Philip Larkin (1988) wryly described all parenting as toxic:

Man hands out misery to man.
It deepens like a coastal shelf.
Get out as early as you can,
And don't have any kids yourself. (p. 180)

Modern novels have often dramatized themes involving children victimized by uncomprehending adults. In itself, this is hardly new—consider David Copperfield and Oliver Twist. But, unlike the modern writer, for whom childhood is the beginning of unavoidable tragedy, 19th century novels, such as those of Charles Dickens, ended with their protagonists rising above initial adversity. No one then assumed that childhood had the power to determine the rest of a person's life. *That* concept is relatively unique to contemporary culture.

Not surprisingly, the idea of childhood as a destructive force has appeared in many theatrical productions. The plays of Shakespeare are built on the clash of character and circumstance in the lives of great men and women. But in the dramas of Arthur Miller or Eugene O'Neill, tragedy arises in ordinary lives because no one can resist the impact of family dysfunction.

Cinema is the most widely influential medium of the 20th century. Psychoanalysis and its ideas about childhood have had a particularly powerful influence on Hollywood films (Farber & Green, 1993; Gabbard & Gabbard, 1999). Part of the explanation lies in the way films reflect wider cultural beliefs. Another part may be derived from the popularity of psychoanalysis among writers and producers. But the simpler explanation is that effective cinema requires dramatic situations. For this reason, the discovery of hidden past events has had an irresistible appeal to screenwriters.

Popular films about psychoanalysis, such as John Huston's *Freud*, portrayed therapists as detectives, persistently ferreting out secrets from their patients. Many films seized on the idea that isolated traumatic episodes during childhood, particularly when repressed or forgotten, can lead to widespread consequences in later life. The discovery of repressed childhood trauma is one of the most effective of all dramatic devices, powerfully melding shock and surprise. By now, this device has been used so often in cinema that it might be termed the Hollywood theory of mental illness.

The idea that childhood shapes adult life reached a peak of influence on cinema around the time of the Second World War. In many famous films of this period, the influence of childhood trauma on adult life was used as a central plot device. Citizen Kane suffered for the rest of his life for the loss of a sled! In *Lady in the Dark,* Ginger Rogers played a career woman haunted by a traumatic past, whose therapy allows her to marry (and to give up some of her ambitions). In *Spellbound,* Alfred Hitchcock even engaged Salvador Dali to choreograph a dream sequence delineating the hero's unconscious. The plot concerns a patient (Gregory Peck) who suffers from traumatic amnesia due to a repressed incident from his childhood in which his brother died in an accident. The truth emerges only in therapy with a devoted psychiatrist, Ingrid Bergman (who also finds time to marry Peck at the end of the film).

Radical changes from therapy, usually the result of remembering trauma, continued to appear in later cinematic scripts. In the highly popular film, *Ordinary People,* the trauma is neither distant in time nor repressed (again, there is an accident in which a brother died). The hero (Timothy Hutchins) suffers from communicatively challenged parents but is helped by his psychiatrist (Judd Hirsch) to overcome traumatic memories. After exploring events in therapy, a dramatic and complete cure occurs—almost immediately!

Childhood trauma continues to be a great gift to novelists and scriptwriters. In one popular fiction, *The Color Purple* (Walker, 1982), later filmed by Steven Spielberg, the plucky heroine is shown rising above many travails, among which incest is only one of her many adversities. The resolution of the plot of the popular novel *A Thousand Acres* (Smiley, 1990), later adapted for the cinema, depends on the revelation of a long-lost memory of parental sexual abuse.

Plot twists involving the discovery of repressed memories of childhood threaten to become a cliché. But an accurate description of the slow and gradual ways through which most people overcome their difficulties in life would probably not sell many tickets. By comparison, facts are relatively dull.

Finally, one cannot help noting how strongly the *media* have supported the primacy of childhood. One only has to open the daily newspaper, read popular magazines, or watch television to find examples of this influence. In the Introduction, I provided an illustration that is far from uncommon, in which an unhappy childhood was used to explain a dramatic series of crimes. Political pundits now conduct amateur analyses of almost any public figure, explaining their misbehavior on the basis of childhood neglect or spoiling, as the case may be. At the same time, entertainment personalities trumpet the results of their psychotherapy, announcing their triumph over childhood trauma.

The ubiquity of these ideas, as reported in the media, simply reflects what most people believe. At the same time, what appears in print or on the screen is usually what sells. The more dramatic the story is, the better.

For this reason alone, the primacy of childhood will probably remain alive and well for some time to come.

☐ Conclusion

The principle that childhood has the power to shape adult life has had a long history. Ultimately, this idea derives from the political philosophy of the Enlightenment and the struggle of individuals to break free from social and family bondage. Individualism is a powerful ideology. One of its potential end-points has been hostility against families, with parents seen as oppressors and children seen as victims.

These ideas about childhood belong to the very intellectual air we breathe. Moreover, primacy is a seductive and appealing concept. Its romantic appeal can only be countered by sober and careful consideration of data obtained through scientific methods.

Childhood and Psychoanalysis

Although it is important not to throw out the baby with the bathwater, there is an
awful lot of psychoanalysis that needs to go down the plughole and we also need to
appreciate that psychoanalysis is only one of the parents of the baby and that the
growing infant differs in very important ways from its progenitors.
—Michael Rutter (1995a, p. 565)

The primacy of childhood has always been a cornerstone of psychoanalysis, and it still is. In the 20th century, Sigmund Freud was the most powerful and influential proponent of the concept that adult personality and
adult symptoms are rooted in childhood experiences. As we will see,
modern revisions of Freud, however much they change his original model,
always retain this belief. Therefore, challenging the myths of childhood
requires a confrontation with the myths of psychoanalysis.

In the last two decades, the psychoanalytic movement has been rocked
by criticism—of its theoretical structure, its methodology, and its therapeutic results (see Crews, 1995; Gellner, 1993; Grunbaum, 1984; Hale,
1995; Webster, 1995). Yet in spite of a recent decline in its prestige, the
theory retains an immense influence.

Psychoanalysis is actually not one idea, but many ideas. Therefore, this
chapter must address a large number of separate issues. First, I will review the history of Freud's ideas about childhood and their influence.
Second, I will critique a central tenet of psychoanalysis, the principle of
epigenesis. Third, I will critically review the modern revisions of psychoanalysis. (Attachment theory will be discussed separately and in greater
detail in Chapter 8.) Fourth, I will show how the primacy of childhood

has influenced clinical theory and practice in closely related fields: child therapy and family therapy. Finally, I will assess the scientific status of psychoanalysis, and comment on its probable future.

☐ Childhood and Psychoanalysis

Freud (1916/1963) was of two minds about the role of childhood in human life. On the one hand, he saw the psyche as driven by intrinsic, universal instinctual forces. On the other hand, he believed that the shaping events for any human life occur at its beginning. Freud only gave lip service to the possibility that psychological development depends on differences in temperament.

Freud's ideas mirrored beliefs going back to Plato, whose concept of a perfect republic involved training to shape the character of children. Religious movements have also held the view that a child's personality and ideas can be shaped by early education. However, unlike previous theorists, Freud suggested that the most important events of childhood can occur even *before* they can be remembered. In his view, many of the most important experiences of childhood are subject to repression. Freud's methods of treatment were therefore archaeological, designed to recover past events that would otherwise have remained lost. Chapter 7 will critically review the related assumption that *all* life events are recorded in memory.

Psychoanalysis explains both psychological symptoms and individual differences in personality through the impact of experiences during the earliest years of life. Freud's (1916/1963) model of development described a series of predictable developmental stages, so that fixation at any of these points would explain a wide range of adult pathology. These stages were derived from clinical observation and extrapolation, rather than from systematic observation of children. As we will see later in the chapter, this part of the model is of doubtful validity.

The concept of primacy also influenced the course of psychoanalytic treatment. One of the primary purposes of analysis was to discover the roots of present problems by identifying childhood experiences that interfered with the normal course of development. Thus, Freud (1919/1955, p. 183) stated that his method deserved to be recognized as genuine psychoanalysis only when it had succeeded in recovering from the adult knowledge of childhood from the earliest points of development.

In accordance with his theory of the Oedipus complex, Freud identified ages 4 to 5 as a crucial turning point in childhood. He also aimed to recover key memories from as early as the second year of life. Some of Freud's followers adopted an even more extreme view of the importance of early experiences, pushing the crucial time when development went awry even further back.

Few followed Otto Rank's (1926/1984) proposal that the process of birth itself could cause long-term psychological problems. But others, most particularly Melanie Klein (1946), thought that problems during infancy could be a major source of pathology later in life. Although Klein buttressed her model with the claim that her ideas were based on infant observation, this statement could only have impressed those without scientific training. The fact was that no one could determine what Klein's observations consisted of, on whom they were made, or how any observer could really know what was going on in the mind of an infant.

As the critical events of childhood were located earlier, the focus of psychoanalytic theory shifted from Freud's triangular conflicts between a child and its two parents to the vicissitudes of relationships between mothers and infants. Several British analysts modified Klein's ideas to create an "object relations school," in which the focus moved to the quality of parenting. In this view, the overall quality of rearing in early childhood is more important than mastering psychosexual stages.

Donald Winnicott, a former pediatrician, was a prominent member of this group who promoted the idea that the first year of life is crucial for all future development. Winnicott (1958) thought that failure by the mother to establish an empathic "holding environment" for the young infant could cause a wide range of later disturbances.

Parallel developments occurred on the other side of the Atlantic. The most influential theorist in America was Erik Erikson. Like Klein and Winnicott, Erikson (1950) gave infancy, and the quality of the relationship between mother and child, a primary role in development. He hypothesized that the first stage of life requires the achievement of basic trust. Failure to manage this task could interfere with mastery of all further stages of development. Later, an American version of object relations theory appeared (J. R. Greenberg & Mitchell, 1983). In this view, the primary cause of psychological symptoms is troubled relationships between children and parents, which are the main cause of pathological interpersonal relations in adulthood. (As Chapter 8 will show, this is also the crucial assumption of attachment theory.)

Self-psychology (Kohut, 1970, 1977) also emerged within psychoanalysis in America. This model has had a great influence on clinical practice. Kohut's theory is based on assumptions very similar to those of Winnicott, in which mothers need to provide empathy to children and in which consistent empathic failures lead to narcissistic traits in adulthood.

Common to all these theories is the attribution of enormous power to the quality of mothering during the early years of life. A belief in the primacy of maternal care became a received wisdom for psychoanalysis.

The stage was now set for a generation of therapies in which mothers would be blamed for every form of psychological problem.

These theories, placing the sources of psychopathology in early childhood, led to the development of a general principle for psychoanalytic theory: *The more severe the psychopathology, the earlier in life must be its source.* Thus, neurotic symptoms would be rooted in problems occurring at ages 4 to 5, borderline personality in problems occurring at ages 1 to 2, and psychoses in problems occurring during infancy. These ideas were attractive to many clinicians, even if they had earned little or no support from empirical data.

☐ A Critique of Epigenesis

Epigenesis is the principle that what happens at any point in psychological development depends on what happened before. This concept is associated with the broader principle that development normally proceeds in predictable stages. These sequences, which are an essential element in several psychological theories, assume that success in mastering any milestone is dependent on how well one has dealt with challenges at earlier points.

Epigenetic theories have been associated with several of the most famous names in psychology: Freud, Erikson, and Piaget. It may surprise some readers to learn how questionable the validity of *any* of these models is. Clinicians may assume that, given the prestige of their authors, these ideas must be scientifically well grounded. But researchers in developmental psychopathology give Freud and Erikson (and even Piaget) much less credence. Empiricists must be suspicious, on principle, of all these grand theoretical models.

Let us begin with Freud. His developmental sequence (Freud, 1905/1953) described oral, anal, and phallic stages, based on a hypothesized cathexis of libido to different erogenous zones during the first few years of life. Although these ideas used to be at the very core of psychodynamic theory, they are rarely heard of today, having been quietly dropped as an embarrassment—even to psychoanalysts.

Freud's attempt to reduce complex psychological phenomena to fixations at various stages failed the test of empirical verification. S. Fisher and Greenberg (1996) carefully reviewed the research literature bearing on this schema. Their main conclusion was that while there are identifiable oral (i.e., unusually needy) and anal (i.e., compulsive) personality traits, there is no evidence that these characteristics are associated with any particular stage of development. As Chapter 10 will show, characterological differences are more strongly influenced by temperament than by early childhood experiences.

We can draw similar conclusions about the idea of a universal "Oedipus complex." Although Freud considered this to be a central construct in his system, it has withstood neither the test of time nor the scrutiny of empirical data. For example, Freud (1918/1955), to buttress his proposal, had suggested that the primal scene, i.e., seeing one's parents have sexual intercourse, is a profound trauma for a child. This idea flies in the face of the simple fact that *most* children throughout history have slept in the same room as their parents, and there is no serious evidence that witnessing a primal scene is in any way pathogenic.

Children may express a fantasy of growing up and marrying the parent of the opposite sex. But what is the evidence that these feelings have the profound significance for adult development claimed by Freud? S. Fisher and Greenberg (1996) carefully reviewed the literature and found no evidence for a relationship between events at this stage, or between feelings about Oedipal issues, and any measure of later functioning. Freud's concept is also contradicted by cross-cultural evidence (Durham, 1992) suggesting that incest avoidance is not due to sexual desire for a parent but to an innate mechanism triggered by proximity during childhood. (This is why unrelated children brought up as siblings, as on a Kibbutz, will not marry each other as adults.)

For all these reasons, the Oedipus complex no longer functions as a central tenet of psychodynamic theory. Among psychoanalysts, it is either given lip service, reinterpreted, or quietly shelved (Paris, 1976). Unfortunately, the demise of the Oedipus complex has gone unannounced!

In modern psychoanalysis, Freud's epigenetic stages have been replaced by newer models: object relations theory, attachment theory, and self-psychology. Instead of focusing on sexual or aggressive drives, contemporary analysts are much more interested in how early relationships with caretakers can affect the quality of intimate relationships later in life. Probably the main reason for this shift is that the older models never corresponded well to the issues patients bring to therapists, which usually involve problems with intimacy. It makes more intuitive sense to believe that patients who are unsuccessful in love were never properly loved by their parents.

Thus, to the extent that they use epigenetic models, contemporary therapists are more comfortable with the stages of Erikson than with those of Freud. Redefining development in terms of psychosocial tasks is more acceptable than stages based on drives that may or may not exist. Moreover, Erikson's (1950) epigenetic theory, to which he gave the catchy label, "the eight stages of life" has many virtues. The phases he describes are commonsensical, intuitively appealing, and correspond fairly well to the way patients talk about their life experiences.

Yet, there is hardly any evidence that childhood follows the sequence that Erikson described. The developmental tasks for children and adolescents (basic trust, autonomy, initiative, industry, identity) are real enough, but there is no proof that any of these issues are more important at one stage than another. It seems reasonable that children who are securely bonded should benefit from a good start on life. Yet, early adversities need not necessarily have long-term consequences, while later difficulties can sometimes be equally problematic. For example, basic trust need not have any specific relationship with early childhood. A trusting relationship with a mother during infancy is not necessarily a protection against later adversity and disillusionment. As noted in Chapter 4, problems in trusting others may be just as crucial for a 7-year-old whose family unexpectedly breaks up.

Erikson's epigenetic theory has sometimes been tested by researchers conducting empirical studies using longitudinal designs. Yet one of the prominent investigators in this area (Vaillant, 1993) had to acknowledge that the evidence for the existence of a specific sequence of phases determining development is slim. In the end, Erikson may well be remembered more for his use of colorful clinical terminology (e.g., "identity crisis") than for developing a valid theoretical model.

Erikson's model was at least rooted in observable behaviors. Other epigenetic theories are based on metapsychological entities that are essentially mythical. Unfortunately, students of psychotherapy are still sometimes asked to learn hypothetical stages of early childhood such as Klein's (1946) paranoid and depressive positions or Mahler, Pine and Bergeman's (1975) phases of symbiosis and separation-individuation. Such constructs must count among the more dubious theories added to psychoanalysis since the death of Freud.

The problem with all these theories of epigenesis is that they reflect epistemological problems common to every version of psychoanalysis. If the founder could invent stages of development out of his own head, what is there to prevent others from doing the same thing? Thus, the existence of sequences in development has depended entirely on clinical inference. In other words, ideas or behaviors in patients are assumed to resemble, and therefore to repeat, experiences and patterns presumed to exist in early childhood. The assumption is that when adult behavior is infantile, it must represent a regression, i.e., derive from problems in infancy. Such ideas may be plausible, but they fail to account for behaviors, such as those seen in adults with personality disorders, that would be abnormal even in a child.

Modern psychoanalysis has placed less emphasis on epigenesis, giving more weight to consistent effects over time. For example, object relations models have focused on family atmosphere rather than on traumatic events occurring at any particular stage. Self-psychology is also notable for emphasizing patterns of interactions over time. Kohut (1977) describes a gradual process, like water dripping into a barrel, that can either lead to internalization of "mirroring" responses, or to an empty self. Attachment theory (see Chapter 8) also focuses on the cumulative effects of childhood experience, explicitly stating that later childhood can be as important as infancy.

What will historians conclude about the grand epigenetic theories of the past century? Very likely, their judgment will be that such models were grandiose but premature attempts at reducing complex processes to a few simple stages. It is easy to learn these stages, and their simplicity is appealing. But the world is much more complex than that.

Finally, epigenetic principles do not represent universal truths that apply to everyone. From the earliest years, every child is an individual. Some are more trusting, some more autonomous, some have more initiative, some have more industry, and some have an easier time achieving identity and intimacy. As we will see in Chapter 10, these characteristics need not reflect events related to developmental stages, but can be better understood as traits.

☐ Childhood, Child Psychotherapy, and Family Therapy

Psychoanalysis has had a powerful impact on other forms of psychotherapy. Many approaches to individual therapy are variations on the analytic theme, and group analytic treatment is derived from the same model. This section will address the relationship of the primacy model to child psychotherapy and to family therapy.

A developmental model based on the primacy of early experience should be applicable to the understanding of psychological problems in children. Pioneered by analysts such as Anna Freud (1937), the child psychotherapy movement held that symptoms in children derived from problems earlier in development. Moreover, to the extent that problems in children are due to problems in mothers, therapists would treat them both. The resulting model was the child guidance approach, in which children and parents were offered separate therapies.

This approach had its limitations, in that therapists concluded that children were more influenced by their families than by an hour or two of psychotherapy. As a result, the child guidance method was gradually replaced by an emphasis on family intervention. As Ackerman (1966) argued, therapists could not address the problems of troubled children unless they could also alter the environmental factors believed to create and maintain pathology.

The terminology of the family therapy movement was telling: The child was no longer a patient, but an *identified* patient (Minuchin, Rosman, & Baker, 1978). Thus, psychopathology came to be seen as located within the family *system*, and symptoms in children were understood as the result of unexpressed conflicts in their parents. Differences between siblings were rarely ascribed to temperament, but to differential treatment associated with a process of projective identification. In this view, the child was a blank slate on which the family could imprint an identity, solving structural problems by scapegoating a child.

Like so many other movements in the mental health field, family therapy has suffered from its own excesses. The most striking example was the theory that schizophrenia is the result of family pathology (Bateson & Jackson, 1956; Lidz & Fleck, 1985). In the present era of biological psychiatry, these ideas have become little more than historical curiosities. But family theories of psychosis were part of a larger zeitgeist in which parents were held accountable for any and all problems in their children. In the same way, children with conduct disorder were assumed to be acting out superego lacunae in their parents (Johnson, 1949). In other words, children only misbehave when their parents secretly want them to! Almost every form of symptom in children could be explained in this manner.

Perhaps the most egregious excess of environmentalism in child therapy concerned early infantile autism. This condition, first described by Kanner (1943), is associated with severe and early problems in bonding between mother and child. Some observers (Bettelheim, 1967) assumed that the mother's lack of interest *caused* the child's pathology. Although genetic and biological findings have now convincingly refuted these ideas, a great deal of damage was done to innocent parties—both parents and autistic children themselves (Dolnick, 1998).

The lesson from this story demonstrates the consequences of strict adherence to a theory that psychopathology is due to defective upbringing. Forty years ago, blaming parents was a normative practice in child and family therapy. Parents were told that they could not hope to see improvements in their children's problems unless they dealt with their own problems first.

Today, few child and family therapists adopt such extreme models. Clinicians recognize that children have their own symptoms that may be exacerbated by parenting styles but are not necessarily caused by them. Although earlier models of causation have by no means died out, therapists are much more likely to focus on how a family is coping with the stressor of having an ill child.

☐ Psychoanalysis: A Scientific Assessment

A multitude of interacting factors determine what kind of adult a child eventually becomes. Therefore, psychological models of development have to account for enormous complexity. I quoted Rutter (1995a) at the beginning of this chapter to make the point that while the psychoanalytic model has contributed to developmental theory, it can only be thought of as one of the parents. I will now critically review the basic postulates of psychodynamic theory, so as to assess how many remain viable in the light of current empirical research.

Recently, modern psychoanalytic theorists have been trying to reconcile their model with empirical science. The British analyst, Peter Fonagy, a prominent figure in attachment research, has been a strong advocate of a scientific psychoanalysis. On this side of the Atlantic, Glen Gabbard (1995), long associated with the Menninger Clinic, is a much-quoted exponent for a revised and modernized psychodynamic theory.

As a benchmark for discussion, I have chosen a scholarly and witty defense of psychoanalysis published in a leading psychological journal by Drew Westen (1998; see also Westen & Gabbard, 1999). Westen, a researcher, theoretician, and teacher, defends the thesis that psychodynamic theory remains a valuable model for a scientific psychology. Yet, like other modern analysts, he acknowledges that *most* of the ideas in the works of Sigmund Freud are outdated and can safely be discarded. To quote Westen (1998):

> Psychodynamic theory and therapy have evolved considerably since 1939 when Freud's bearded countenance was last sighted in earnest. Contemporary psychoanalysts and psychodynamic therapists no longer write much about ids and egos, nor do they conceive of treatment for psychological disorders as an archaeological expedition in search of lost memories. . . . [M]ost psychodynamic theorists and therapists spend much of their time helping people with problematic interpersonal patterns, such as getting emotionally intimate or repeatedly getting intimate with the wrong kind of person. (p. 333)

Westen (1998) goes on to list five postulates that define contemporary psychodynamic theory, all of which he believes have earned significant empirical support. It is worth critically reviewing each of the items on Westen's list.

The Existence of Unconscious Processes

Of all the tenets of psychoanalysis, this is still the most central. When presenting doubts to clinicians about issues discussed in this book, I have sometimes been asked, "Don't you *believe* in the unconscious?"

The answer to this question does not depend on belief. Of course, much mental activity is unconscious. Given the cost of thinking through every issue consciously, how could it be otherwise? As Westen (1998) documents, the postulate of an unconscious mind is now widely accepted in psychology and has also become part of cognitive theory (Beck, 1986; Kihlstrom, 1999). As Westen correctly points out, there is good experimental evidence for unconscious processes. Thus, thoughts, memories, emotions, and motivations, even when consciously unavailable, have been shown to influence overt behavior. Finally, research on defense mechanisms also supports the existence of cognitive systems that function to keep painful feelings out of awareness.

However, accepting all these principles does not require us to see the unconscious as Freud did: as the base of a mental iceberg, structured by primary process mechanisms, characterized by powerful sexual and aggressive drives that create constant pressure for conscious expression, and containing memories for each and every event in the course of a lifetime.

It is perfectly possible to describe an unconscious mind whose structure does not correspond to any of these assumptions. Let us consider, for example, the meaning of dreams, one of the main sources for the classical theory of the unconscious. Freud should get credit for recognizing that dreams are metaphors that reflect concerns that may or not be conscious during the day. It does not follow, however, that the language of dreams is intended as a disguise to pass an internal censor. More likely, as Hobson (1988) argues, the distortions characteristic of dreams simply reflect the brain structures activated during REM sleep.

Conflict and Ambivalence

Psychoanalytic theory states that most symptoms (as well as many behaviors) represent compromises between wishes and fears. As Westen (1998) points out, this idea is at least consistent with a well-established principle of cognitive science: that mental symptoms are "modular," that is, they work in parallel and can come into conflict.

Again, we can accept this general principle without supporting the mental modules described by psychoanalytic theory. The id, the ego, and the superego have all become outdated. Although these terms have been replaced by new constructs, the concept of intrapsychic conflict remains central to psychoanalysis.

The problem (see Chapter 12) is that psychodynamic formulations implying conflict between mental mechanisms tend to be ad hoc, invoking processes that are difficult or impossible to measure or prove. Such formulations do not take into account why different people react and behave differently when dealing with the same conflict.

Westen (1998) acknowledges that there has only been a small amount of research testing the postulate of intrapsychic conflict. Yet he is reluctant to discard this idea, falling back on clinical inference and common-sense arguments to back it up. But it is not sufficient to show that a psychological postulate is plausible. The history of science is full of examples in which common sense and folk psychology have been overthrown by new and unexpected ideas.

The Childhood Origins of Psychological Problems

Westen (1998) addresses this issue by underlining the continuities of personality and behavior over time. He acknowledges the role of genes and temperament, but he explains continuities as the result of childhood experiences, particularly in the family.

To support his argument, Westen relies on empirical studies (several of which were reviewed in Chapter 3). On first inspection, much research seems to document consistent associations between parenting styles and the adjustment of children. However, Westen fails to note the limitations of this literature. For example, he ignores the fact that most associations between childhood variables and adult outcomes are quantitatively weak. He also fails to consider that many correlations between the behavior of parents and that of children can be accounted for either by common temperament or by common social background (Harris, 1998).

Westen (1998) does explicitly acknowledge the importance of resilience and that later experiences can be just as important as early experiences in shaping personality:

> None of this is to suggest that childhood experiences inevitably leave indelible marks that later experiences cannot correct or obviate. Many longitudinal studies have shown only modest associations between early childhood experiences and temperament on the one hand and adult personality and psychopathology on the other. . . .[T]he study of resilient children certainly makes clear that the determinism assumed by many psychoanalysts through the 1940s was too extreme. (p. 351)

Yet, in spite of these admittedly modest associations, Westen's belief in the crucial importance of early childhood remains firm:

> [M]ost important human experiences—namely those involving feelings of intimacy and adequacy—have precursors in childhood that leave their precipitates not only in working models of the self, others, and the world but also in motives, emotions, and ways of regulating emotions in later situations that activate these prototypes. To the extent that these processes reflect repeated experiences or experiences that are painful and conflictual and hence have engendered automatized affect-regulatory procedures to

cope with them, they are more likely to be resistant to change to require extraordinary experiences to alter them. (p. 352)

Ultimately, arguments in favor of primacy depend on this last assumption: that childhood experiences create automatized reactions in the mind. Yet it is precisely *this* idea that is lacking in proof. The past creates *tendencies*, not predictable results. New experiences, which need not necessarily be extraordinary ones, can modify these effects (Kagan, 1998b; Rutter, 1995b). It strains credulity to believe that events occurring in childhood, whether in infancy or later, cause reactions so "automatized" that they can last for a lifetime and that are resistant to reversal by a change of environment or by newer, more benign experiences. Clinicians can always find childhood events that *seem* to parallel adult problems. Concluding that these relationships prove cause and effect is another matter.

Mental Representations of Self, Others, and Relationships

This postulate states that behavior and symptoms are influenced by internal models in the mind and that these mental models are generalizations of childhood experience. Westen (1998) quotes attachment research, as well as some of his own investigations, in support of this hypothesis.

The concept of mental representations has been strongly supported by cognitive research. Most of the findings described by Westen are consistent with a cognitive model (Beck, 1986). The question is whether the source of mental representations lies primarily in early experience, or whether they also reflect temperamental variations.

Developmental Trajectories

The principle that development follows epigenetic stages is central to psychoanalysis. Westen (1998), surprisingly for a modern analyst, defends the usefulness of Freud's oral, anal, and Oedipal stages, falling back on anecdotes for support. But, as discussed above, epigenesis is one of the most problematical aspects of developmental theory. Certainly some things come before others in childhood. But evidence for clearcut *stages*, leading to the principle that early experiences must be mastered to deal with later experiences, has not been forthcoming.

Summary

After considering the evidence for the five basic postulates Westen (1998) proposes, which ones deserve empirical support? We can certainly support the construct of an unconscious mind, as well as that of mental representations. The other three postulates (intrapsychic conflict, primacy of childhood, and epigenesis) remain doubtful. Notably, the concepts most worth saving are least unique to psychoanalysis and are fully compatible with cognitive science. In a recent review, Kandel (1999) pointed out that by insulating itself from developments in neurobiology and cognitive science, psychoanalysis has left itself isolated and vulnerable.

☐ Why Psychoanalytic Ideas Remain Attractive to Clinicians

In spite of the uncertain database for psychoanalytic ideas, the model has had a long life and continues to influence the practice of many, if not most, therapists. This striking fact demands an explanation.

Therapists who work with problematical patients want *answers*. They are interested in results and do not readily share the doubts of researchers. It should therefore not be surprising that so many clinicians have a fatal attraction to psychoanalytic theory.

As a former "fellow traveler" of the movement, I have little personal difficulty understanding its appeal. Who, after all, can resist a universally applicable theory of development that explains, in a relatively understandable way, phenomena that would otherwise be inexplicable? Who can resist a method of therapy that claims to be effective for the most intractable problems seen in clinical work, requiring only that the practitioner be unusually skilled and that treatment be continued for a long time?

For all these reasons, psychoanalysis retains many strong defenders. Its theoreticians have argued that revisions can address most of the problems in the model. Moreover, clinicians continue to be attracted by the coherence of its methods. Because of the prestige of psychoanalysis, patients, albeit fewer than in years past, still actively seek out this form of treatment.

Even among highly educated people, emotion is always more powerful than reason. Intelligent people can use their talents and their abilities to justify what they *want* to believe. As history shows, intellectuals have consistently committed themselves to false ideologies. We need look no further than the history of ideas in the 20th century, in the course of which many philosophers, scientists, and artists have unapologetically supported all kinds of ideas, ranging from totalitarian politics to religious orthodoxies.

Over the years, I have had the opportunity to meet brilliant psychoanalytic theoreticians who present deft and creative arguments in favor of their model. Several of these experts have informed me that they actually agree with many critics of analysis and no longer feel obliged to use classical theory. They favor newer models and only quote Freud when he sounds sufficiently modern. Like liberal theologians, analysts can reinterpret scripture to support a contemporary point of view.

☐ Psychoanalysis and Epistemology

Most psychodynamic psychotherapists are humane clinicians who are helpful to many patients. They do not actually reject empiricism. Rather, they believe that the psychoanalytic method is sensitive to aspects of the human experience that empirical methods cannot measure or tap. They resist critiques based on research since, in their view, psychological science is not advanced enough to shed light on the intrapsychic world.

I assume that any reader who has followed me this far will agree that scientific methods, however far they fall from perfection, remain the best way of discovering truths about human nature. I will therefore not even attempt to counter those who want clinical intuition to be granted an epistemological status equal to that of empirical investigation. Nor will I give any credence to the argument, currently fashionable in the humanities, that science itself is a world-view contingent on social or political assumptions. Instead, I will proceed on the assumption that empiricism remains the best standard for knowing how the world works.

One of the primary reasons for the decline of prestige for psychoanalysis is a developing climate of opinion in psychology that demands empirical verification of theoretical models. Freud's method involved drawing universal conclusions about development from speculative interpretations of clinical data. Convinced of his conclusions, he demonstrated a weak commitment to a requirement for measurable data.

Experimental and developmental psychology have long since emerged from a reliance on armchair theories. Yet clinical science remains at a much more immature stage. The problem with many models is that they reflect as much about the mind of the theorist as objective reality. Freud's failure to build a system on an empirical base isolated psychoanalysis, so that the movement he founded never joined the mainstream of science.

Some psychoanalysts have resisted these standards, rationalizing their retreat from playing by scientific rules. These hermeneutic methods of inquiry (Spence, 1992) resemble those of humanists rather than scientists, proposing that the *interpretation* of ideas is as important as facts. This point of view is nothing but an attempt to escape from epistemological problems. Until and unless it submits its theories to empiricism, psychoanalysis will fail to achieve the minimum requirements to call itself a scientific discipline.

Some analysts accept this conclusion, and enlightened practitioners are aware of and respect the latest developments in psychology. But many continue to think in the same way as their predecessors. When one reads the psychoanalytic literature, one finds a lack of any official recognition that classical formulations are no longer useful. Instead, Freud's writings continue to be widely quoted, and his texts are reinterpreted to support more contemporary ideas.

Thus, if one peruses recent issues of the *International Journal of Psychoanalysis* and the *Journal of the American Psychoanalytic Association,* it quickly becomes clear that only a minority of articles represent a new eclecticism. The movement remains highly conservative, and most papers pay homage to the founder.

In science, theories come and go as new evidence is collected. As Wilson (1998) wittily stated, "[P]rogress in a scientific discipline can be measured by how quickly its founders are forgotten. Yet psychoanalysis retains all previous gods in its pantheon, rather like the multitude of deities worshipped during the Roman Empire" (pp. 182–183).

Students of general medicine or psychology would never be expected to read texts written 50 or a 100 years ago. Today, the concepts in the books of physicians such as Sir William Osler or of psychologists such as William James are of only historical interest. No one would think of taking them seriously as benchmarks of relevance to the present. It is time to put the past behind us and move on.

In summary, the most serious problem with psychoanalysis remains its method of determining truth, that is, its epistemology. However much the field has matured, it continues to suffer from a reliance on clinical inference to support broad conclusions about psychological development. Theory-building on the basis of clinical experience was the basis of Freud's method and became the model for all those who followed him. Those who attempted to revise psychoanalytic theory found it was sufficient to state that they had observed a hitherto undescribed dynamic mechanism. Since the time of Freud, new models of development have proliferated, and much ink has been spilt about their relative merits. We can cut this Gordian knot easily: *None* of the competing theories has ever been based on scientific observation.

Yet as psychoanalysis changes, it has become a moving target for its critics. The model can never be disproved as long as it is open to endless revision. It is fair to acknowledge that by shelving, or even rejecting, some of Freud's most cherished concepts (the central role of sexuality, the Oedipus complex, and the structural theory of the mind) and by replacing these ideas with object relations and attachment theories, psychoanalysis has become more compatible with contemporary psychology. Analysts who are also researchers (Fonagy et al., 1996; Luborsky & Crits-Christoph, 1990; Shapiro & Emde, 1994; Stern, 1985; Vaillant, 1993) have accepted the need to build bridges with science and to expose theories to empirical testing. In the long run, psychoanalysis might even develop a new model, fully consistent with modern developmental psychology and neurobiology (Kandel, 1998, 1999).

But empiricism can also be used as a gloss to cover over an unscientific belief system. Recently, I was asked to be a discussant for a presentation by a leading theoretician and researcher in attachment theory. I raised several problems with this approach and was given a reply along the lines of "Your points are perfectly valid, and I agree that we need more research to determine whether our model is correct." The speaker then went on to speak for another hour explaining how severe personality disorders are caused by a failure of maternal empathy during early childhood, ideas that received an enthusiastic reception from a large audience of clinicians.

One must harbor the suspicion that some psychoanalysts offer lip service to science as a way of maintaining traditional beliefs. The time has come to ask whether the *core* of psychoanalysis is supported by any data. If it is not, it should be replaced by a better theory.

Some analysts have been concerned about this very possibility. For example, Vaillant (1993) acknowledged that the models created by Freud and his successors were built on intuition and clinical inference and admitted that none of their ideas can be called scientific unless they can be proven to have predictive validity. Yet in spite of his research background, Vaillant goes on to present similar arguments to those of Westen in defense of the psychodynamic model. Using the same phrase as Rutter, Vaillant (1993, p. 4), argues for preserving the baby of psychoanalysis even as we discard its bath water. Yet after we remove all speculative elements from the theory, what will remain? The evidence does not yet provide an answer as to whether we will have a healthy baby to save once the bathwater is drained.

The survival of psychoanalysis is best explained by the fact that it addresses phenomena that are difficult to account for using other theoretical systems. Clinicians also feel, understandably, that competing theories do not tell them enough about what to do with patients.

About 15 years ago, I was invited to lecture to a class of medical students about some of the basic concepts in psychiatry. In accordance with my views at that time, I took a strong psychodynamic position, presenting an essentially Freudian model of how psychological symptoms develop. (The coordinator of the course, a neurobiologist, did not invite me back the next year.) When challenged by the students about my theoretical position, I replied that while there were many problems in analytic theory, I could not find a better one.

Like most people, I like to *think* of myself as a free and independent spirit, who comes to his own conclusions. Of course, this is no more true of me than of anyone else. In retrospect, I can see very clearly how my ideas have followed the prevailing zeitgeist. Since then, times have changed and my mind, like many others, has also changed. There are now better alternatives to psychoanalysis than existed in those days. The findings of behavioral genetics have shaken many who believed that parents are all-important for development. Cognitive science provides a viable alternative for the study of mental processes. The entire field of developmental psychopathology has come of age, and can now be thought of as a basic science for clinicians.

☐ Conclusions

We do not have a theory that can explain all the things that psychoanalysis has *claimed* to explain. It will take many decades before we can understand all the interactions between constitution and experience that shape the development of children. At the end of this book, I will make recommendations for how we might begin to carry out this task.

My hope is that psychoanalysis will eventually join the scientific community and accept the standards of empiricism. For this to happen, it must cease to be a separate movement and ideology and develop stronger links with academia. Psychoanalysts could actively support research to test their theories and submit their therapeutic methods to clinical trials. We would then be in a position to find out which parts of this complex theory stand up to the test of data, and which parts do not. Moreover, in this scenario, psychoanalysis would cease to be a separate discipline, and accept incorporation into the science of psychology.

In summary, psychoanalysis has declined, but its ideas live on. Its most influential and basic assumption has been the primacy of childhood. Later in this book, I will examine whether the clinical applications of this model, leading to detailed exploration of childhood experiences in psychotherapy, are actually helpful for patients.

CHAPTER

The Myth of Recovered Memory

Modern psychotherapy is 100 years old. Over time, the mental health professions have matured. Therapists today use much more sophisticated theoretical models. Many of the theories of development described in Chapter 6 are now of only historical interest.

Nonetheless, belief in the crucial role of childhood experiences remains powerful. The continued strength of primacy is dramatically demonstrated by the recovered memory movement. Therapists influenced by this model have again been focusing on a search for childhood trauma. When memories for such events are not available, clinicians still believe they can be recovered from the unconscious. Thus, Freud's claim that psychological symptoms are rooted in early trauma, and that these events are frequently repressed, has been renewed. We have seen a revival of an approach in which therapists search for memories of trauma, that, like hidden abscesses, bore at the psyche from within.

Paradoxically, this return to Freud also reflected disillusionment with psychoanalysis. As the analytic model was revised over time, it came to focus more on intrapsychic conflict and less on real-life events. In the view of several writers (e.g., Masson, 1985; Miller, 1984), psychoanalytic theory took a wrong turn by downgrading reality in favor of fantasy. Restoring central importance to traumatic events and the repression of traumatic memories was seen as a welcome revival of the early Freud.

☐ Child Abuse and Recovered Memories

Research has uncovered many previously hidden facts about the mistreatment of children. It is now indisputable that large numbers of children, many more than had previously been thought, have been exposed to sexual and physical abuse. These findings are the basis for legitimate concern about their health and our need to protect them.

Yet, however important this data is, it can easily be misinterpreted. One problem is that precise figures for prevalence of child maltreatment in the community are difficult to determine, since "abuse" takes many forms. In both American (Finkelhor, Hotaling, Lewis, & Smith, 1990) and Canadian (Badgley, 1984) national surveys, 27% of women and 16% of men reported *some* form of sexual abuse during childhood. However, half of these incidents did not involve physical contact but consisted of either exposure to exhibitionism, or simply a threatening situation. The rate of sexual abuse with contact is much lower, and the rate of serious abuse even lower than that (see Chapter 3). Many writers have confused sexual abuse with incest. The surveys quoted above showed that among the incidents that involved contact, most were single events in which the perpetrator was either a non-family member or a stranger. Molestation by a relative accounts for only about 3% of the incidents of childhood sexual abuse among women. The most damaging scenario, father–daughter incest (Russell, 1986), is even less common.

Actually, the issue that has divided psychotherapists does not concern the reality of child abuse. No responsible person denies the extent of the problem, and all experienced clinicians have seen cases in which abuse constituted a major element in patients' histories. Moreover, there is no reason to doubt the validity of memories reported by patients who have *never* forgotten that such events took place.

The center of the controversy concerns whether traumatic events are usually remembered or more frequently forgotten or repressed. In a widely quoted book, Herman (1992, p. 5) laid down the gauntlet by suggesting that the ordinary response to atrocities is to banish them from consciousness. If this principle were true, then the abuse of children could be even more ubiquitous. Moreover, Herman attributed a very wide range of long-term psychopathological consequences to the impact of child abuse. If we accept this conclusion, then clinical methods should logically return to the early Freud.

Clinical hypotheses can only be proved right or wrong through empirical investigations. But we need to distinguish between two kinds of research questions. The first concerns whether consistent long-term effects result from child abuse and trauma. Investigations addressing this issue (reviewed in Chapter 3) show that child abuse *can* lead to sequelae, but that serious consequences develop only in a minority of those exposed.

The second question, whether traumatic experiences are often repressed, is the subject of the present chapter. I will review the literature on normal and abnormal memory. I will then critically examine the data on repression and dissociation, the assumed mechanisms involved in the loss of memories for traumatic events. I will also show how research contradicts the theoretical ideas behind recovered memories. Finally, I will account for the impact of this movement by examining the roles of suggestion, narratives, and cultural context.

☐ Research on Human Memory

People do not remember events as they happened. A large research literature on the accuracy of memory, starting almost 70 years ago (Bartlett, 1932/1955), shows that recent events are hardly ever recorded in any precise way (Bowers & Hilgard, 1988; Loftus, 1993). The further in the past the original event is, the more likely it is that the memory of it will be distorted.

Memory does not function like a video recorder, laying down a detailed record of every event in our lives. It would not really make sense if that were the case. The brain is faced with constant environmental input, so that what is recorded for future reference requires screening. In spite of the enormous storage capacity of the brain, recording *all* input would be highly inefficient. Like a hard disk on the computer, or a filing cabinet for paper, the mind can easily become overloaded.

Memory systems must therefore be selective. Separate systems exist for short-term and long-term memory. This design protects the long-term system from having to keep permanent records of every event. Moreover, even when long-term memories are laid down, only their most salient elements are encoded. There is really no practical need to keep precise records of every detail of one's life. Thus, memories are overall impressions that are rarely factually precise and include many elements of imaginative reconstruction. What is recorded in the brain is *processed,* so that preexisting cognitive schemata influence the ultimate record of events. Memories are, therefore, *interactions* between actual events and preconceived ideas (Loftus, 1979).

Memory is a highly complex system, with separate mechanisms for remembering a name, a behavioral sequence, everyday events, or childhood events (Schacter, 1996). Researchers have also made a distinction between *explicit* memories, involving the encoding of actual experiences, and *implicit* memories, involving the encoding of skills. These subsystems make use of different neurophysiological pathways. Implicit memories are generally unconscious (Kihlstrom, 1999), but it is not true, as has been sometimes claimed (van der Kolk, 1994), that this system corresponds to the unconscious mind described by Freud.

Some forms of psychopathology, such as PTSD, dramatically affect memory systems. However, PTSD is *not* characterized by amnesia, but by hypermnesia (excessive memory), one of the principal criteria for the disorder in DSM-IV (APA, 1994). Research has consistently shown that traumatic events do not cause amnesia. Instead, attempts at suppression are punctuated by unwanted, troubling, and intrusive memories of traumatic events (Horowitz, 1993).

Infantile amnesia is an interesting phenomenon. Most people cannot remember the events of early childhood. Freud (1917/1955) took this observation as proof of the existence of repression. As it turns out, he was wrong. A wide range of evidence shows that the explanation lies in the immaturity of the brain (Kagan, 1998b; Pope & Hudson, 1995). Without cognitive schema to organize memories, events cannot be recorded in a way that allows them to be retrieved. Given the complexity of long-term memory systems and the enormous amount of neural development that takes place after birth, these conclusions should not be very surprising.

It has sometimes been claimed that traumatic events, when repressed, produce a strong imprint on the brain. As van der Kolk (1994) rather dramatically presented this hypothesis, even when the mind denies the truth, the body remembers. In the same vein, van der Kolk discusses evidence suggesting that traumatic memories may cause changes in neural pathways, such as the hypothalamic-pituitary axis and the hippocampus, and that patients with PTSD show characteristic changes, such as a smaller hippocampus on PET scans. However, these findings do not prove that trauma changes the brain. We do not know at this point whether such findings indicate the effects of trauma, reflect a comorbid condition, or are markers for a biological vulnerability to trauma that can be observed prior to the development of symptoms.

Freud (1896/1962) hypothesized that traumatic events stir up strong affects that must be repressed because they cannot readily be processed. Yet events associated with strong emotion are not remembered any more accurately than those of no emotional significance (Pope, 1997). As Loftus (1979) has documented in experiments, eyewitness testimony is surprisingly inaccurate, because memories reflect as much of what people expect to see as what they actually see. Flashbulb memories (the supposedly photographic recall of dramatic historical events) have also been shown to be highly distorted over time (Bowers & Hilgard, 1988).

In summary, one of the main conclusions that has emerged from research is that no objective method, short of corroborating data, can determine whether any memory is true or false. Moreover, it is surprisingly easy to create false memories. One experimental study (Laurence & Perry, 1983) showed that, once accepted as true by subjects, such "memories" can be reported with enormous conviction. Individuals then add telling details that seem to support the veracity of the story, at least to a naive observer.

Hypnosis does not make recall more accurate. (The idea that it should is based on the video recorder model of memory.) On the contrary, memories obtained under hypnosis are *much* more likely to be false. Many experiments have shown that under hypnosis, one can implant highly detailed, but untrue, memories of past events (Orne, Whitehouse, Dinges, & Orne, 1988).

Therapists' main criticism of these experimental studies of memory is that they do not involve real traumatic events and therefore do not capture the phenomena that clinicians see. But it has never been shown that the mechanisms of memory in therapy patients are any different.

☐ Repression

In his earliest models of psychopathology, Freud had proposed that repressed traumatic events in early childhood are responsible for many symptoms in adults. This concept was first introduced in the book on hysteria by Breuer and Freud (1893/1955), which famously stated that hysterics suffer mainly from reminiscences.

Freud (1896/1962) also hypothesized that when traumatic events cross a stimulus barrier, painful anxiety ensues, and repression is an attempt to defend against this anxiety. When the repression of memories for traumatic events makes them inaccessible in adult life, they can then go on, like hidden abscesses, to be sufficiently toxic to cause symptoms. Freud never gave up these ideas, even though he later downplayed them (Webster, 1996). Thus, psychoanalytic theory continued to encourage therapists to uncover buried memories.

But what happens if one can find no such events? In Freud's view, this does not prove that they never occurred. Instead, memories for these experiences could be repressed and unconscious. In this respect, Freud's unconscious mind became an all-purpose construct that could be used to override any observations that contradict theory. In fact, the concept of repressed memories is a good example of the basic epistemological errors inherent in psychoanalysis (Crews, 1995).

Since Freud, the existence of repression has been taken for granted. Yet researchers have consistently questioned the validity of the construct. Some years ago, J. Singer (1990) published a book based on a large conference of investigators conducting empirical studies of repression. This research literature presents many problems. How does one measure this construct? Can one demonstrate repression experimentally?

As it turns out, there is no easy answer. Some researchers (Luborsky, Crits-Christoph, & Alexander, 1990; Vaillant, 1990) have described a repressive style, that is, a tendency to avoid thinking about problems. But this is not at all what Freud meant when he introduced the word repression. The construct of a repressive style is actually much closer to the idea of *suppression*, conscious avoidance of painful thoughts. Thus, we have to ask why, 100 years after Freud, we still lack convincing proof that the phenomenon of repression even exists.

In the last 10 years, a few researchers have directly examined individuals known to have been traumatized in childhood in order to investigate the possibility of repression of traumatic memories. One report, by Meyer Williams (1994), has been widely quoted as proving the reality of the repression of childhood sexual abuse. In this study, children with documented abuse were interviewed as adults to determine their awareness of these events. The results showed that 38% of these women failed to mention their abuse histories at the time of follow-up.

However, there were several problems with the author's interpretation of her findings (Pope & Hudson, 1995). First, the women were not asked directly about childhood abuse. Moreover, since the design of the Meyer Williams study allowed for no follow-up questions, the findings could, in some cases, have reflected reluctance to discuss these matters with the researchers.

Second, even if the subjects did fail to recall sexual abuse, was this repression or simple forgetting? People forget most things that have happened to them, but this does not necessarily demonstrate a mechanism in which painful thoughts are actively repressed (Brandon, Bookes, Glaser, & Green, 1998). Selective inattention and forgetting of painful memories are observable phenomena that do not require an unconscious mechanism (J. Singer & Sincoff, 1990).

Third, many of these subjects had suffered multiple trauma, and even when they did not recall a specific episode, most remembered *other* incidents of abuse. When these cases are subtracted, only 12% of the subjects remembered no abuse at all.

Finally, among these residual incidents, most occurred before age 5, a time of life for which adults have very few memories of any kind. In summary, Meyer-Williams' study does not present clear evidence demonstrating the repression of childhood traumatic events.

But what if repression does not always occur after abuse, but only develops under special conditions, that is, in children who are abused by caretakers on whom they are dependent and when trauma is chronic rather than acute (Terr, 1991)? Actually, there is no evidence that the mechanisms of dealing with trauma are any different in children. In a study of children followed after a kidnapping on a school bus (Terr, 1988), they tried to suppress the event, but like adults with PTSD, continued to be troubled by it. Moreover, most got the facts wrong, embroidering their memories with many false details.

In summary, no data exists to support the construct of repression. Ten years ago, D. Holmes (1990) summarized the research findings as follows:

One cannot prove the null hypothesis, and therefore we cannot conclude that repression does not exist, but after sixty years of research has failed to reveal evidence for repression, it seems reasonable to question whether continued expenditure of effort on this topic is justified. Regardless of how fascinating the repression hypothesis is, the time may have come to move on. (pp. 98–99)

Most scientific hypotheses, no matter how appealing, normally die a natural death and are replaced by new ideas. In Thomas Huxley's famous phrase, even the most beautiful theory can be slain by one ugly fact. The problem is that the more appealing an idea is, the more difficult it is for people to give it up.

☐ Dissociation

At around the same time as Freud was writing about repression, Janet (1907) introduced a related construct: dissociation (or, in the French original, désagrégation). Janet used this term to describe a more radical form of forgetting, in which entire segments of the mind are cut off from consciousness.

Many decades later, a theory termed neodissociation (Hilgard, 1994) described neurophysiological mechanisms in which brain modules become decoupled. This idea remains controversial (Kirsch & Lynn, 1998). While Hilgard was interested in explaining phenomena seen under hypnosis, we do not know whether similar mechanisms can interfere with memory access in those who have not been hypnotized.

Dissociation is a mechanism that has been invoked to account for certain dramatic clinical phenomena (amnesia and multiple personality). These conditions were first described during Janet's time and have always aroused enormous interest. But until the recent "epidemic" of dissociative disorders, these types of symptoms were rare specimens indeed.

Like repression, the construct of dissociation cannot readily be measured in an accurate or reliable way. The problem has not been solved by the use of self-report measures, such as the Dissociative Experiences Scale (DES; Bernstein & Putnam, 1986). This widely used scale applies the construct of dissociation to a wide variety of phenomena, many of which are not specific to Janet's theory. As a result, the DES may be more a measure of general psychopathology than of dissociative mechanisms (Merskey, 1995). Interview measures of dissociation (e.g., Steinberg, 1994) have even more problems, in that they are validated using a dubious gold standard: the clinical diagnosis of a dissociative disorder.

One reason for the recent interest in dissociation has been its purported relationship with severe trauma. Yet little solid evidence supports this association (Tillman, Nash, & Lerner, 1994). If we do not know what DES scores mean, the fact that they increase in individuals with PTSD does not prove that a dissociative mechanism is involved. There is an even more serious problem. Most of the research that *has* supported a link between dissociation and trauma has been retrospective, often depending on the recovery of memories through hypnosis (Merskey, 1992). The co-occurrence of dissociative phenomena and recovered memories may well be accounted for if both are the products of therapeutic suggestion.

One way to approach this problem is to examine dissociation in nonpatient community samples. An American study (Nash et al., 1993) found only a weak relationship between dissociation and reported trauma, which could be entirely accounted for by coexisting family dysfunction. A large-scale community study in New Zealand (Mulder, Beautrais, Joyce, & Fergusson, 1998) examined DES scores in relation to child abuse. The findings were that dissociative symptoms were strongly related to the presence of a mental disorder, weakly related to a history of physical abuse, and not at all related to a history of sexual abuse.

My own research group has been interested in the problem of understanding the roots of dissociative symptoms. The first set of observations (Zweig-Frank, Paris, & Guzder, 1994) concerned patients with borderline personality disorder. We found that these patients had unusually high levels of dissociation as measured by the DES, but that their scores were better explained by psychiatric diagnosis than by childhood experiences.

This observation led to a second study (Jang, Paris, Zweig-Frank, & Livesley, 1998), in which we conducted a community study of twins who completed the DES. The results established that dissociation has a large heritable component. Moreover, we noted that DES scores intercorrelate with several personality dimensions. Thus, the capacity to dissociate seems to function very much like a personality trait (see Chapter 10).

Dissociation is a fascinating concept that will, no doubt, find a place in the history of psychology. But there is little evidence that this purported mental mechanism plays a crucial role in psychopathology. Moreover, the construct of disorders primarily characterized by dissociation is questionable and has led to specious overdiagnosis, mainly by clinicians who favor these concepts (Merskey, 1992). Until we have more convincing data, it might be better to remove dissociative disorders entirely from the classification system of mental disorders.

☐ Suggestion and Recovered Memories

Recovered memories describe phenomena in which patients seem to remember traumatic events after many years of forgetting them. This phenomenon was central to classical psychoanalysis and remains an important element of psychodynamic therapy. As noted above, these observations have been interpreted as proof of links among trauma, repression, and dissociation. But unless we know that such incidents actually occurred, we can conclude very little.

No research has ever shown that memories of trauma recovered during psychotherapy can be independently confirmed (Pope & Hudson, 1995). One study (Herman & Schatzow, 1987), which is often quoted in support of the verification of recovered memories, is too deeply flawed to prove anything. Careful reading of the paper shows that it describes nothing but *reports* of confirmation from family members, described by members of a support group, most of whom had been encouraged to recover memories of child abuse. (I would like to take this opportunity to confess having quoted Herman and Schatzow repeatedly, before a book by Ofshe and Watters, 1994, convinced me that its conclusions were invalid!)

There is an alternative explanation for recovered memories obtained in the course of therapy. They are the products of fantasy and/or therapist suggestion. To understand how this process might work, we should acknowledge that to some extent, everyone is highly responsive to social cues and expectations. For this reason, suggestibility presents a universal problem in psychotherapy. But some people are more responsive to cues than others. It is these individuals who are most susceptible to methods that search for repressed memories of childhood fantasy.

Children are generally more suggestible than adults. In a series of court cases in which day care workers were mistakenly charged with sexual abuse, children were strongly encouraged by various authorities to accuse them (Pendergrast, 1995). Today, working in day care centers has become a rather hazardous occupation, with some falsely accused persons spending years in prison.

Adults who are highly suggestible were once called "hysterical." Although the use of such terminology is presently considered pejorative, some have argued that the concept of hysteria remains viable (Kihlstrom, 1994; Merskey, 1995; Showalter, 1996). Thus, patients who would have presented with bizarre somatic symptoms a century ago may be similar to those who develop dissociative disorders in the contemporary world.

When suggestible people are exposed to recovered memory therapy techniques, they can produce fantastic tales. Some of these stories have involved satanic ritual abuse—supposed cults in which children are raped and impregnated so that their babies can be killed and eaten (Ofshe & Watters, 1994). Yet in spite of careful investigation by several government bodies, there is absolutely no evidence that any such events have ever occurred (Pope, 1997).

The *reductio ad absurdum* of the recovered memory has involved claims certain patients have made involving more impossible scenarios—alien abductions or memories from past lives. The bias of therapists, which is to believe whatever their patients tell them, has worked a good deal of mischief here. A well-known Harvard psychiatrist (Mack, 1995) ended a distinguished career in professional disgrace by writing a book arguing that aliens are indeed among us, abducting human victims.

Like scriptwriters, therapists can be attracted to the concept of recovered memories because it offers a dramatic scenario. At the same time, the idea that trauma leads to repression has been widely promulgated in the media, drawing much attention from the general public. The influence of its advocates, not to speak of the sales potential of anything written on the subject, has led otherwise reputable publishers to print books on multiple personality disorder and satanic ritual abuse.

No doubt, the intentions of those who created the recovered memory movement were initially benign. Their aim was to underline to therapists the fact that childhood sexual abuse is common and that girls are usually its victims. (Both conclusions are true.) Moreover, the link between child abuse and feminism has led some people to see criticism of recovered memory as if it were a criticism of women's experience. Finally, we live in a time when victimology dominates social thought. Doubters have been attacked for their supposed failure to believe in what patients are telling therapists. Those who question recovered memories of child abuse have even been accused of being in league with its perpetrators.

Recovered memory therapy resembles many efforts at reform, in that it replaced one danger (the failure to investigate trauma) with another (false memories of trauma). A fascinating aspect of these memories concerns their content, which often move from incest to satanic rituals. As suggested by psychoanalysts, the recurrent appearance of the same ideas suggests that human fantasy may have a universal structure.

There is a slippery slope between openness and joining the lunatic fringe. If one is prepared to believe any memory, no matter how absurd, particularly if accompanied by strong emotion, where does one stop? The practitioners of recovered memory therapy failed to understand the strength of mass hysteria. They would have been well advised to read the history of the Salem witch trials. As happened eventually in Salem, the authorities who began the search for satanic rituals must now defend themselves. As the media report massive settlements of litigation against therapists, others have become cautious. Defenders of the movement are now careful to acknowledge the danger of false memories. Yet some of its absurdities have elicited ridicule, weakening the hold of these ideas on the public imagination.

☐ Memories and Narratives

Recovered memories may not be true, but they are always meaningful. Even when remembered events are factually false, they provide *narratives* that people use to make sense of their life experiences. Narratives offer causal explanations for a variety of present difficulties (Kirmayer, 1996). These stories are examples of the attributions (see Chapter 1) that individuals use to explain life events.

How are personal narratives shaped? The way patients tell stories about their lives is influenced by the belief systems of their therapists. Even without overt prompting, suggestion and expectation shapes how people describe their childhood experience. As a result, different patients tell surprisingly similar stories. Showalter (1996) compares the similarity of trauma narratives to the phenomenon of intertextuality in literary criticism, that is, the phenomenon in which the same ideas appear in contemporaneous books.

Most therapists seriously underrate the vast power of suggestion. As a result, patient narratives often seem to appear unbidden to receptive ears. But without making overt suggestions, clinicians send signals that lead patients to provide the data they expect. When patients are unusually suggestible, these cues can determine responses. For example, when transcripts of therapies using recovered memories are examined, one generally finds a large number of leading questions (Loftus, 1993).

False memories also derive from the very context of dynamic psychotherapy, which actively promotes narratives of childhood suffering to account for present difficulties. Moreover, since therapists are trained to be empathic, they usually accept, more or less unconditionally, what patients tell them about their lives. They should be aware that what they hear from patients reflects as much a view of the world as a description of objective reality. The distinction between the way people remember their lives and what may have actually happened has been described as narrative truth versus historical truth (Spence, 1983). In most respects, therapists tend to ignore history in favor of narrative. In understanding emotional problems, perception is often more important than fact. But historical truth remains an important issue in treatment because belief in false memories of trauma can lead to very serious consequences (Pendergrast, 1995).

☐ Memories and Cultural Context

Personal narratives can also be shaped by social forces. Cross-cultural data shows that in most societies, explanations of distress are framed either by religious beliefs or by cultural views on the causes of illness (Dasen, Berry, & Sartorius, 1988). In contemporary society, we are highly sympathetic towards stories of personal suffering. This widely held attitude reinforces the belief that childhood trauma is ubiquitous, that it has a lifelong impact, and that it can frequently be repressed.

The use of recovered memories in psychotherapy reflects current cultural concerns. We can pinpoint five points around which tensions have developed. The first derives from widespread anxiety about the safety of children and a legitimate concern for their welfare. Since child abuse is much more common than had previously been thought (Finkelhor et al., 1990), therapists have been understandably concerned as to whether they have been failing to identify crucial risks for psychopathology.

Second, we live in an age in which nuclear families, or single mothers, have to raise children that would, in previous generations, have been cared for by a bevy of grandparents, aunts, and other members of an extended family. Many working mothers have no choice but to leave their children in day care centers while they work—but that does not mean that they trust caretakers, especially those who are not blood relatives. This is one reason why day care workers have fallen under suspicion for child abuse.

Given that child abuse is a political and social issue, we should not be surprised by the enormous sales of *The Courage to Heal* (Bass & Davis, 1988), a book that purports to explain almost every common symptom occurring in women through repressed incidents of childhood sexual abuse. A few years later, Judith Herman's (1992) book, which presents a similar point of view, albeit in a much more sophisticated way, was acclaimed by a *New York Times* reviewer as the greatest contribution to psychology since Freud. (More accurately, one can say that Herman resembles Freud, in that she begins with preconceived ideas and lacks interest in any data that might disprove them.)

A third factor behind the recovered memory movement is ideological. Psychotherapists are generally sympathetic to the feminist cause. Feminism has done a great deal of good—as shown by epidemiological research (Srole, 1980), increased opportunities and choices for women over several decades have had a measurably positive effect on women's mental health.

On the other hand, Herman (1992) openly presents her theories of trauma as inspired by a political ideology called radical feminism. In this context, it may not be an accident that Gloria Steinem, the editor of *Ms. Magazine*, has been one of the most prominent supporters of clinicians who specialize in treating dissociative disorders.

Feminism can take many forms, and most of its supporters take a more moderate and inclusive position. It is entirely possible to be both a strong feminist and a sceptic about recovered memory (e.g., Showalter, 1996). Unfortunately, some people have difficulty making this distinction and confuse doubt about the validity of recovered memories with a refusal to believe in the reality of the sexual abuse of girls and women, or with a lack of sympathy for feminist ideals.

The fourth factor is less social than universal. It concerns the attraction to a good story, that is, to drama. I remember reading about dissociative disorders and recovered memories years ago and wondering if I would ever see such cases. In comparison, my own practice seemed so dull! Fantasy creates high drama, while reality is often banal.

A love of drama is associated with heightened suggestibility. North, Smith, & Spitznagel (1997) have demonstrated that *all* the famous patients with multiple personality disorder developed symptoms they had previously read about in books. The most celebrated of these patients, Sibyl, once admitted to her substitute psychiatrist (see Borch-Jacobsen, 1997) that she *invented* her series of personalities to please a fascinated therapist.

The fifth source of cultural tension is victimology. It has become fashionable for almost everyone to consider themselves as some kind of victim (Hughes, 1993). Psychoanalysis, in spite of its emphasis on childhood, can be interpreted as holding people ultimately responsible for their difficulties. Yet many contemporary clinicians see their clients as suffering from circumstances beyond their control. Moreover, therapists, who are trained to empathize with patients, have difficulty making moral judgments. At the extreme of this "nonjudgmental" stance, there is no such thing as evil. One psychiatrist (Lewis, 1998) recently wrote a book proposing, based on her interviews with a series of murderers, that people who kill are usually victims of child abuse, who should therefore be treated rather than imprisoned.

☐ Are Recovered Memories Dangerous?

Memory is a sphere in which credulity is a danger and scepticism a virtue. Psychotherapy has been highly vulnerable to faddish treatments in the past (McHugh, 1992). In clinical work, practitioners need to remain cautious and to resist being carried away by zealous enthusiasm. Moreover, the evaluation of any treatment modality requires that it have a plausible basis in theory and that its effectiveness be tested through controlled clinical trials.

The data summarized in this chapter show that the recovery of traumatic memories has little basis in science and also lacks empirical evidence for its purported clinical effectiveness. Yet it is always possible for some patients to benefit from invalid methods of treatment. As Chapter 11 will show, the effectiveness of psychotherapies depends largely on nonspecific factors, so that almost any method that offers patients an explanation of why they fell ill, and a hope for recovery from that illness, can have some degree of success.

But searching for recovered memories in psychotherapy can also have a *negative* impact on patients. As several observers (Crews, 1995; Webster, 1995) have pointed out, these methods are precisely the same as those used by Freud in his early years. The therapist begins with a strong conviction of the importance of childhood sexual trauma and assumes that if such experiences are not remembered, they *must* have been repressed. In many cases, therapists succeed in convincing patients of these beliefs. Hypnosis may be used as an adjunct, with therapy coming to approximate a form of brainwashing.

At present, we do not know for sure whether treatments involving the recovery of traumatic memories can actually do patients harm. Some experts (Kroll, 1995) have described seeing patients who had been damaged by these methods, becoming increasingly regressed and unable to function in the outside world. These potential negative effects need to be researched systematically. In earlier studies of treatment methods based on questionable theories and high charisma, both encounter groups (Yalom & Lieberman, 1973) and EST (Simon, 1978) have been found to be dangerous, particularly for vulnerable individuals.

Another problem results from the unusually high frequency of reports of incestuous abuse produced by patients undergoing recovered memory techniques. Most children who are sexually abused have suffered from the behavior of nonrelatives or relatives who are not their caretakers. But incest is a more dramatic event. When such accusations turn out to be false, the ensuing shattering of families becomes a major side-effect of the method (Pendergrast, 1995). Future observers will see this episode as a *fin-de-siècle* folly inviting ridicule, but it is patients and their families who have had to bear the brunt of the suffering.

☐ Conclusions

There is no special magic in memory. Repression and dissociation are hypothetical mental mechanisms that have not earned substantial research support. There is little evidence that trauma is often forgotten or that recovered memories of trauma are necessarily accurate.

Over the last decade, the issue of recovered memory has polarized psychotherapists. Because of the intensity of the controversy, some prefer to believe that reality must lie between two extremes. One must agree that scientific conclusions can change with new evidence and that research issues cannot usually be resolved without collecting more empirical data. But given our present state of knowledge, attempts at mediation confuse problems of emotion and evidence. It is difficult to be dispassionate when one believes that a method is not only wrong, but possibly dangerous.

The history of the recovered memory movement can also be seen as a warning. It will go down in the history of psychology as one of its greatest scandals, creating a cult that has sometimes threatened to bring the entire practice of psychotherapy into disrepute. The conviction that childhood is the main source of adult symptoms is the ultimate basis of the theories of repression and dissociation. This powerful belief system can lead to serious errors in clinical practice. The concept of recovered memory takes some of the most common but misleading premises underlying psychotherapy, and places them in a distorting mirror.

CHAPTER

8

Childhood, Attachment, and Behavior

This chapter focuses on two theoretical models of the relationship between childhood and adulthood, both of which have had a wide influence on psychology. Attachment theory, although originally derived from psychoanalysis, has developed a strong enough scientific base to join the mainstream of developmental psychology. I will describe the history of the attachment model, address its problems and limitations, and suggest how it might be improved. I will also consider briefly how behaviorism and cognitive-behavioral psychology have viewed the role of childhood in development.

☐ The History of Attachment Theory

John Bowlby was a psychoanalyst whose ideas grew out of the tradition of the British object relations school (see Chapter 6). He was not particularly interested in drives, epigenetic stages, or intrapsychic conflict. Unlike many of his contemporaries, he eschewed complex metapsychological formulations. Instead, he drew on that great British cultural tradition—a sound respect for common sense.

Bowlby, like other analysts, believed that problems in early bonding between mothers and children have a lifelong impact. The attachment model (Bowlby, 1969, 1973, 1980) attempts to account for this relationship. To give him due credit, Bowlby actively encouraged empirical testing of his theory. His books, instead of relying on clinical examples, are replete with references to research findings. Moreover, Bowlby was willing to modify his ideas to accord with emerging empirical data. Thus the model he developed, termed attachment theory, is an amalgam of psychoanalysis and research in developmental psychology. It represents the first serious attempt to create a scientific and testable version of psychoanalytic theory.

Bowlby hypothesized that evolution has created a set of inborn behavioral modules in both mothers and young children designed to promote attachment bonds (Bowlby, 1969). The biological purpose of the attachment system, therefore, is the protection of children, who might otherwise fail to survive. Bowlby further suggested that variations in the quality of attachment largely depend on maternal responses to the child's innate needs.

Bowlby's principal hypothesis was that the quality of the bond between a child and its mother influences all intimate relationships later in life. When the natural mechanisms of the childhood attachment system go awry, lifelong consequences can ensue. In this way, Bowlby made the quality of mothering the central factor in psychological development. The quality of attachment in childhood, good or bad, would generalize to any other situation in which children or adults turn to others to meet their emotional needs. Thus, children who have been securely attached would develop more successful relationships, while those who were insecurely attached would have consistent difficulty with intimacy.

In his earlier writings, Bowlby (1951) had proposed that "maternal deprivation" (the physical or emotional absence of a mother during infancy) causes a wide range of psychopathologies. This assessment was later overturned by Rutter (1972, 1987a), who amassed a large body of data demonstrating that there is no *direct* relationship between maternal absence during the first few years of life and later psychopathology. The negative effects of early maternal deprivation tend to be maintained only when coexisting risk factors are also present and are reversible when these factors are absent.

By taking this new evidence into account, attachment theory matured, developing more complex hypotheses about the relationship between early experience and later behavior. Bowlby was strongly influenced by the observations of family therapists, who saw pathology developing at a systems level. Bowlby's ideas were also influenced by his collaboration with Mary Ainsworth, a developmental psychologist. Instead of hypothesizing that the impact of problems in attachment must always derive from difficulties in early childhood, the model began to put more emphasis on the long-term effects of *continuously* dysfunctional family patterns.

In his last book, Bowlby (1988) explicitly rejected classical psychoanalytic theories. He came to believe that abnormal attachment occurring at *many* stages of development is a risk factor for mental disorders. Thus, the attachment model views the climate of development over the course of childhood as more important than specific events occurring at any one time. This theoretical position is consistent with evidence reviewed in Chapter 3 that cumulative adversities, not single traumatic events, are most associated with psychopathology.

Attachment theory survived the death of Bowlby and continues to be the basis of a large body of active empirical work (Cassidy & Shaver, 1999). Research has been aided by developing standard methods of assessment for attachment styles. Ainsworth (see Ainsworth, Blehar, Waters, & Wall, 1978) studied attachment behavior in young children using the Strange Situation, a procedure designed to observe children's reactions to a series of standardized events: maternal absence, the presence of a stranger, and reunion with the mother. Later, Main (1995) developed the Adult Attachment Interview, designed to assess patterns in later life that closely parallel attachment behaviors in childhood.

These instruments have allowed researchers to study individual differences and to categorize individuals by their attachment styles. The three basic types of attachment in childhood are secure, avoidant, and ambivalent-anxious. Children who are securely attached explore their environment readily, handle separations from the mother well, miss the mother when separated, greet her when reunited, and accept comfort from her when distressed. Insecurely attached children are divided into two subgroups. Those with an avoidant pattern also explore readily, but show little response to separation, avoid the mother when reunited, and seek distance rather than comfort when distressed. Those with an ambivalent-anxious pattern are distressed even when the mother enters the room, become more unsettled when separated, respond with rejection or tantrums when reunited, and are not readily comforted. Later on, a fourth type, the "disorganized" style, was described (Main & Solomon, 1986). Here there is no coherent strategy at all, and the child seems confused or frozen in the Strange Situation.

The Adult Attachment Interview (Hesse, 1999) also identifies four types (secure autonomous, dismissing, preoccupied, and unresolved-disorganized), each of which parallels the four patterns measured in the Strange Situation. Again, the disorganized pattern is most associated with clinical symptomatology, but other variations may or may not lead to dysfunction. Adults with the first three patterns can probably manage to work their way around their styles.

Essentially, adult attachment patterns parallel personality traits (see Chapter 10) and can be understood as manifestations of these trait differences. Moreover, three or four types are probably not enough to account for the full range of individual differences seen in children and adults.

Furthermore, attachment patterns might be more usefully measured dimensionally rather than categorically.

☐ Unresolved Problems in Attachment Theory

The attachment model has several virtues. The model has had a salutary effect in operationalizing psychodynamic theories and exposing them to empirical testing. It offers a better grounded rationale than did psychoanalysis for studying continuities and discontinuities between childhood and adulthood. Attachment theory has therefore had great appeal for researchers. Moreover, since the model links clinical symptoms to developmental psychology, research findings derived from it could be relevant for the treatment of patients.

Yet, in spite of the claims of its proponents, attachment research does *not* provide empirical support for the primacy of childhood. Attachment theory also has serious limitations, and I will outline eight aspects of the model that require further investigation.

Attachment and Temperament

It is difficult to imagine that attachment styles are independent of temperament. In fact, a good deal of research suggests that temperamental abnormalities can interfere with the attachment system, making it more difficult for irritable or shy children to attach to their mothers (Vaughn & Bost, 1999). Temperament is a strong predictor of behavior in the Strange Situation (Kroonenberg, van Dam, von Ijzendoorn, & Mooijart, 1997; Seifer, Schiller, Samereff, Resnick, & Riordan, 1996; Thompson et al., 1988). At the same time, behavioral genetic research (Finkel & Willie, 1999) has shown that attachment styles in children, as measured by the Strange Situation, are moderately heritable, with 25% of the variance accounted for by genetic factors and 75% by unshared environment. (See Chapters 9 and 10 for an explanation of this terminology.)

Attachment theory has not really come to grips with the role of temperament (Rutter, 1995a). The issue is that the attachment system is not simply a reflection of maternal sensitivity to a child. Rather, attachment patterns are interactive. Put simply, difficult children have more difficulty in attaching to their caretakers. As Belsky (1999) suggests, there are temperamentally vulnerable infants who are strongly predisposed to develop secure, avoidant, or resistant attachments, almost regardless of the quality of care they experience. On the other hand, most children have the potential to form different attachment patterns depending on the nature of their environment. This helps to explain why attachment patterns can change as the environment changes, even over relatively short periods (Belksy, 1999).

Attachment and Personality

A second issue concerns whether problems in childhood attachment can account for the development of personality pathology. Personality disorders are complex conditions that are associated with serious abnormalities in intimate relationships. In some ways, these patterns seem to parallel attachment styles, ranging from the detachment seen in the schizoid patient, to the chaos seen in the borderline patient, and the fearful paralysis seen in the avoidant patient. Fonagy et al. (1995) have argued that patients with borderline personality frequently suffer from early abuse and neglect, and that these experiences translate themselves into disorganized adult attachment patterns.

One might easily be persuaded by the parallels between personality disorders in adulthood and the behavior of a difficult child. However, the matter is not that simple, and these relationships are rather tenuous. Patients with borderline personality do not really resemble children. Moreover, even if early adversities count among the risks for personality disorders, their impact can only be understood in the context of a complex matrix of factors (Paris, 1994, 1996c).

Attachment and Intimacy

The assumption that secure attachment in childhood consistently predicts successful intimacy in adulthood has never been proved. Instead, attachment styles are much better understood as alternate game plans. Belsky, Skinberg, & Draper (1991) have argued for a relationship among early experience, sexual behavior, and intimacy. Their hypothesis is that children exposed to early adversity develop a more opportunistic and less stable strategy for mating and reproduction, while children who are raised with greater emotional security are more likely to delay sexual activity and to develop committed relationships. This theory has been partially confirmed by studying relationships between attachment patterns and early puberty. The concept might help to explain recent rising rates of early sexual activity in adolescents. However, we do not have the longitudinal data necessary to confirm these provocative ideas.

Many other factors beyond attachment styles are involved in the development of interpersonal problems in adult life (Rutter, 1995a). There is no justification for the claim that mother love consistently makes people healthy and lovable. One cannot ignore the effects of genes and of environmental factors, inside and outside the family.

Attachment and Psychopathology

Attachment styles are not necessarily pathological. Like personality traits, each type can be adaptive or maladaptive, depending on the circumstances (Kagan, 1989; Richardson, 1995; Rutter, 1995a). Only about 60% of children are "securely" attached, and we should not assume that the other 40% are at risk.

Although secure children are easier for parents to manage, insecure patterns can actually be more effective when a child needs to demand parental attention, as shown by studies of survival in famine conditions (Belsky, 1999). The disorganized type may be an exception and seems to be a pathological variant. Its presence is closely related to clinical symptomatology, yet this style is not very stable over time (van Ijzendoorn, Schiengle, & Bakermans-Kranenbrug, 1999).

Attachment and Mothering

Attachment theory focuses on the role of the mother, to the exclusion of other figures in the child's life. By focusing on the mother–infant bond, to the exclusion of all other influences, attachment theory still reflects its intellectual roots in psychoanalysis. (This bias is far from unique and could also have been observed in much of developmental psychology 10 or 15 years ago.)

Cross-cultural research has shown that attachment patterns are not very different in settings as various as the Israeli Kibbutz and polygamous families in Africa (van Ijzendoorn & Sagi, 1999). It is not at all clear that mothers must always be the primary source of secure attachment.

Throughout most of history, children have been raised by multiple caretakers (Werner, 1984). Mothers raising children by themselves without help from relatives are a recent development. Although Bowlby (1988) claimed he was misunderstood for seeming to support the idea that mothers must stay home with their children, attachment theory tends to favor the idea that infants are programmed to attach to one caretaker.

We also know that the supposedly harmful effects of day care have been highly exaggerated (Belsky & Cassidy, 1994). Essentially, good day care is good for children, and bad day care is bad for them. Attachment theory, by placing excessive focus on problems in mothering, has been misused to make parents feel unjustifiably guilty for any psychological problems in their children.

Moreover, it is doubtful whether most mothers have *ever* been able to provide consistently secure and sensitive rearing for infants. As Belsky (1999) points out, most women during the course of history have been preoccupied with their own survival. As a result, they have rarely been able to provide the kind of undivided and empathic responses to their children that are expected of contemporary middle-class mothers.

Individual Variations in Attachment

The source of individual variations in attachment style is far from fully understood. Bowlby clearly implied that variations between individuals must depend on differences in maternal behavior. The present attachment model continues to give parental qualities much more weight than qualities intrinsic to children.

Yet in one meta-analysis (DeWoolff & van Ijzendoorn, 1997), maternal sensitivity had only a statistical relationship with anxious attachment, accounting for 23% of the variance. As discussed in Chapter 1, accounting for nearly a quarter of the variance in anything is a remarkable achievement in research. However, if three quarters are unaccounted for, we can hardly conclude that attachment styles are only the result of how mothers respond to infants. Moreover, a large proportion of this 23% might reflect reactions by mothers to temperamental differences in their children.

Attachment Across the Generations

The intergenerational transmission of attachment styles is a hypothesis based on the observation that parents who are anxiously attached are more likely to have anxiously attached children. In one study (Fonagy, Steele, & Steele, 1991) attachment behavior in children could even be predicted, at least to some extent, by interviewing mothers during their pregnancy. Yet it is difficult to know how to interpret these relationships. Does the mechanism involve environmental transmission of attitudes from parent to child, as Bowlby thought? Or does it also reflect shared traits between genetically similar members of the same family? Again, ignoring temperament can lead to false conclusions.

Temporal Stability of Attachment

Children who are insecurely attached in childhood tend to remain so in adulthood (Main & Hesse, 1991). However, these continuities arise not in infancy, but later in development. For example, Lewis (1999) found no consistency at all between ratings made in early childhood (age 1) and then repeated in the same subjects at age 18. Kagan (1994) pointed out that it is difficult to determine to what extent continuities result from childhood experiences (such as being raised by parents who fail to offer secure attachment) or from genetic factors (such as temperamental influences that would have continuous effects at all stages of development).

Moreover, attachment styles in childhood are not firmly fixed. The relationship between childhood and adult patterns is, like everything else in development, statistically significant but far from absolutely predictive. As discussed in earlier chapters, longitudinal studies of child development demonstrate both continuities and discontinuities in behavior.

Emotional development offers many opportunities to shift course and experience new forms of interaction.

In summary, while the research generated by attachment theory is an improvement on clinical inference, the model suffers from several flaws. Clinicians who seize on attachment research to rescue primacy are misreading the data.

Reviewing the relation of attachment to childhood problems, Dozier, Storall, & Albus (1999) concluded, "[I]t is unlikely that insecure attachment is either a necessary or a sufficient cause of later disorder, and in some cases it may be an effect of the disorder itself" (p. 484). Similarly, M. T. Greenberg (1999) concluded, "There are relatively few findings regarding the distribution of attachment states of mind among persons with psychiatric disorders" (p. 514).

Attachment theory is the most likely form of psychoanalysis to survive into the next century. However, any conclusions about clinical phenomena drawn from the model must be regarded with caution. In particular, it has not been shown that mother–infant interaction in the first few years of life determines attachment patterns throughout the lifespan. Attachment theory therefore requires major revision. A more powerful and inclusive model would take into account the role of temperament, as well as the influence of a broader range of factors in the environment.

☐ Childhood, Behaviorism, and Cognitive Theory

The belief in the primacy of childhood did not exist in an intellectual vacuum. It was part of a *zeitgeist*, a cultural climate shaping the way people thought about development. In the course of the past century, similar concepts developed out of entirely different psychological traditions. Behavior therapy was actually based on an even more strongly environmental model than was psychoanalysis.

Behaviorism was, in many ways, a uniquely American perspective on development. The idea that differences between people are due to nurture has had a particular appeal for those who left Europe because of a lack of opportunity and who tended to favor the idea that people are capable of achieving anything if they are placed in the right environment.

James Watson, the father of behaviorism, famously stated (1926/1970):

> Give me a dozen healthy infants, well-formed, and my own specified world to bring them up in and I'll guarantee to take any one at random and train him to become any type of specialist I select—doctor, lawyer, artist, merchant-chief, and yes, even beggar-man and thief, regardless of his talents,

penchants, tendencies, abilities, vocations, and race of his ancestors. (p. 104)

Although not all behaviorists shared Watson's overwhelming confidence, these ideas corresponded well to traditional American values. The idea that few behaviors are innate and most are learned remained predominant in social science for many decades. American psychologists of the post-war period (Dollard & Miller, 1950; Hull, 1951/1971) attempted to prove that simple learning principles can explain any complex human behavior.

Behavioral therapy is a psychological treatment based on this theoretical model. Watson, who considered phobias as a useful model for the development of psychopathology, hypothesized that conditioning alone predicts whether children traumatically exposed to a fearful stimulus will develop symptoms. Logically, behavioral treatment for phobia would have to develop methods of reversing this process through deconditioning. As recently as 35 years ago, behavior therapists (e.g., Eysenck & Rachman, 1964) claimed that symptoms are always learned and that learning principles can be used to cure almost any form of pathology.

Today, behavior therapy has become less grandiose and much more focused. Moreover, classical behaviorism has been subsumed by the larger enterprise of cognitive-behavioral therapy. The addition of a cognitive component has led to a very different theoretical model. Cognitive science, based on a large amount of experimental data, provides a better model of how the mind works (Pinker, 1997), one that is much more in accordance with observation than psychoanalysis ever was. Moreover, the theory has led to cognitive-behavioral therapy, a much broader approach to treatment than behaviorism. Cognitive therapy has also, from its inception, encouraged research on its effectiveness (Beck, 1986).

Cognitive theory is unique in that it explicitly takes individual differences into account (Beck & Freeman, 1990). For this reason, the model is particularly consistent with research on temperament. Cognitive theory supports the principle that people are affected differently by the same events because they process them differently. By taking predispositions into account, cognitive behavior therapy overcomes the environmental biases that characterized both psychoanalysis and behavior therapy. In summary, the cognitive model brings nature back into psychology without dispensing with nurture.

The cognitive-behavioral model also has a number of important limitations. We do not have enough information yet to link the mental structures described by the theory with neurobiological processes. As it stands, the model emphasizes thought over emotion, reflecting the relatively primitive state of our psychological theories about emotional development.

The cognitive model is fully compatible with attachment theory, and a fusion of these two approaches might well turn out to be fertile. Cognitive theory has not yet properly explained how interactions between temperament and experience lead children to develop abnormal mental schema. To shed light on this issue, longitudinal studies are needed, generating data that would link cognitive and developmental psychology.

☐ Conclusions

In coming decades, all theories about child development will become both broader and more interactive. Attachment theory needs to take temperament into account, to expand its interest from mother–child interaction to the larger social environment, as well as to examine the cumulative impact of events throughout the course of childhood. Cognitive theory will be broadened by progress in neurobiology, which will help explain the physiological basis of mental structures.

Over the last several chapters, I have examined a series of models that explain psychopathology as the result of early childhood experiences. Most of them have become obsolete. Yet their absence leaves a significant gap. The environment must play an important role in human development. The next section will offer a better way to understand this relationship.

CHILDHOOD AND MENTAL DISORDERS

Part III consists of two chapters presenting a general theory of psychopathology, focusing on the central role of temperament and personality in development.

Chapter 9 discusses the role of genes in personality development and in vulnerability to mental illness. Heritable traits are better predictors of life outcomes than childhood experiences. A general model of psychopathology can be based on interactions between diatheses and stressors.

Chapter 10 outlines the relationship between temperament, personality traits, and psychopathology. Personality, an amalgam of temperament and experience, is a powerful predictor of how children and adults respond to environmental challenges. These individual differences can be illustrated through four basic trait dimensions that lead to unique reactions to adversity.

Genes, Behavior, and Symptoms

There are some natures that have a predisposition to grief, as others have to disease. . . . The causes that have made me wretched would probably not have discomposed, or at least, more than discomposed, another. We are all differently organized: and that I feel acutely is no more my fault (although it is my misfortune) than that another feels not, is his. We did not make ourselves, and if the elements of unhappiness abound more in the nature of one man than another, he is but the more entitled to our pity and our forbearance.
                                              —Lord Byron, quoted in Jamison (1994)

The first part of this book showed that childhood adversity, by itself, does not necessarily cause symptoms in adults. Instead, adverse events are most likely to affect a vulnerable minority and are most often pathogenic when multiple and cumulative.

What is the source of this vulnerability to adversity? This chapter will focus on how genetic variations contribute to the risk for mental disorders.

☐ Genetic Factors and Clinical Practice

Genetics is a very hot topic these days. Almost every morning, we can open the newspaper and read about an exciting new discovery. The Human Genome Project is nearing completion, and the search for candidate genes is at the center of biomedical research. Investigators are hot on the trail of markers for every category of illness. At the same time, behavioral genetic research has shown that personality traits are heritable. Much more than most people would have ever believed, we are a product of our genes.

Yet many psychotherapists remain resistant to genetic explanations of their patients' behavior. This knee-jerk reaction is rooted in the world-view that many clinicians share.

First, therapists receive a training that biases them in favor of nurture over nature. As documented in earlier chapters, many influential theoretical models fail to take biological factors in development into account. Both the psychodynamic and behavioral traditions have seen the organism as a blank slate, with only a grudging and minimal recognition of the role of constitution.

Second, mental health professionals are socially aware. They are wary of genetic explanations that could be used to support the status quo or shift attention away from real social problems.

Third, therapists believe in change. They are reluctant to consider human problems as insoluble or inevitable. They oppose genetic explanations that can make therapists or patients feel hopeless.

Finally, many therapists perceive behavioral genetics in the light of its early history. In the 19th and early 20th centuries, the eugenic movement had a wide intellectual influence, espousing plausible but poorly grounded genetic explanations of behavior. These ideas led to several unpleasant consequences, most particularly the exclusion of specific immigrant groups for their supposed low intellectual capacity (Gould, 1981), and the warehousing of hereditarily tainted psychiatric patients in mental hospitals (Shorter, 1997).

These negative reactions can be understood in historical context, but the scientific understanding of the heritable factors in behavior has matured. Surprisingly, a knowledge of genetics can actually *help* psychotherapists with their work. How might this be so? First, to paraphrase the famous words of the Alcoholics Anonymous prayer, therapists need to know what they *can* change, what they *cannot* change, and have the wisdom to tell the difference. This kind of knowledge helps clinicians to focus their efforts more effectively.

Second, understanding genetics helps clinicians to take individual differences into account. Psychotherapy needs to develop methods specifically targeted to modify temperamental factors in pathology. As the common parlance would have it, we can use different strokes for different folks.

Third, even if symptoms are heritable, this need not mean that they cannot be reversed by environmental changes. Genetic constitution affects everything about us, but hardly ever determines our fate. Genes can be switched on or off, and in most cases, the environment determines whether the genetic code is actually expressed. In medicine, genetic diseases can sometimes be treated successfully simply by changing lifestyles. For example, a susceptibility to coronary artery disease can be countered by diet, exercise, avoiding tobacco, and stress management. Similarly, a vulnerability to depression need not lead to illness when protective environmental factors are present (Post, 1992).

In summary, there need be no real dichotomy between psychotherapy and genetics or neurobiology. Psychotherapy can be the treatment of choice for a wide range of heritable symptoms. Talking to patients, as much as prescribing drugs, changes how the brain functions.

☐ What Is Behavioral Genetics?

Children tend to resemble their parents in intelligence, behavior, and personality. It has also long been an established fact that mental disorders tend to run in families. To what extent are these associations due to genes, and to what extent are they due to learning?

Behavioral genetic methods have used three scientific tools to sort out the roles of heredity and environment. The first is the *twin method*. This involves determining whether monozygotic (identical) twins are more similar for any particular trait than dizygotic (fraternal) twins. The second is the *adoption method*. This procedure involves determining whether adoptees are more similar to their biological parents than to their adoptive parents. Finally, both methods can be combined by studying *twins separated at birth*.

Let us consider these options in reverse order. The last approach, studies of separated twins, is a particularly powerful research tool. When twins turn out to be as similar on a dimension when raised apart than when raised together, there can be little doubt that the trait under study is highly heritable. The problem is that separated twins are very rare.

The Minnesota twin study (Bouchard, Lykken, McGul, Segal, & Tellegen, 1990) was unusual in collecting 56 such cases. The results must count as one of the great turning points in the history of behavioral science. The data confirmed, after decades of controversy, that intelligence is strongly inherited (Bouchard et al., 1990) and that personality traits have a large genetic component (Tellegen et al., 1988). Finally, the Minnesota study showed that specific psychological symptoms, such as criminality and substance abuse, are strongly influenced by genes (Grove, Eckert, Heston, & Bouchard, 1990).

Adoption studies have been more common than research on separated twins. Many children are adopted, providing a natural experiment that separates the effects of heredity and environment. Adoption studies require available and detailed records on both sets of parents. Therefore, much of this research has been carried out in Scandinavia, where people are more easily traced and records are more complete.

Twin studies are, by far, the most common methods in behavioral genetics. About 1 in every 80 births produces a twin pair. Thus, it is possible to collect community samples and then to compare concordances on traits between identical versus fraternal twins. Nonetheless, this method is expensive, and registries of twins from the general population sometimes consist of thousands of pairs.

Even in large twin samples, it may be hard to find sufficient numbers of patients with mental disorders, particularly those with a low prevalence. To measure inheritance of these conditions, researchers can also collect clinical samples in which at least one twin has the condition under study. Obviously, such populations can be difficult to locate.

The greatest success of twin studies has involved the study of normal traits. The essence of the method depends on the observation that whenever concordance is greater between identical than between fraternal twins, the trait under study must be heritable. This conclusion depends on an equal environments assumption, that is, that parents do not systematically raise identical and fraternal twins in markedly different ways. Most researchers consider this assumption a reasonable approximation. Actually, monozygotic twins are treated more similarly, but this is the result of common temperament (Kendler, Neale, Kessler, Heath, & Eaves, 1993a).

The larger the difference between monozygotic and dizygotic concordance, the more heritable must be the trait. Then, using statistical regression methods, heritability can be expressed as a *percentage* of the total variance between individuals. This estimate will vary somewhat in different circumstances. Thus, traits are more or less heritable depending on the environment. When the environment becomes more uniform, as has been the case in Western societies as social class distinctions decrease, genetic differences actually become more important (Lykken, 1995).

Twin methods also allow measurement of the sources of environmental variance in traits. The effects of the environment can be separated by statistical methods into two components: *shared environment* (effects due to growing up in the same family) and *unshared environment* (effects deriving from experiences unique to each individual).

Applying these methods to personality, most traits have heritabilities of about 40% to 50% (Plomin et al., 1997). On the other hand, the shared environment contributes almost *nothing* to the development of personality, and the environmental component in personality is almost entirely unshared. Chapter 10 will examine this surprising discovery in detail.

Finally, behavior genetics allows us to study the way that genes and environment influence each other. These interactions take several forms (Kendler & Eaves, 1986; Rutter, 1991). First, genes bend the twig, making some forms of behavior easier to learn than others. In general, this principle governs how constitution affects learning (Seligman & Hager, 1972). Second, parents treat children differently, depending on their temperament (Lykken, 1995). Third, children shape their environments to accord with temperamental characteristics (Scarr & McCartney, 1983).

In summary, the trajectory of development from childhood into adulthood is strongly influenced by genetic variations. Variance in IQ scores shows an even more powerful genetic component, approaching 70% (Scarr, 1992). The genetic influence on personality is a little less dramatic, but quite considerable.

The idea that personality variations are half genetic has come as a surprise to many clinicians. But it should not shock anyone who has raised a child! Parents bring up their children in more or less the same way but find that each child responds differently, often requiring major modifications of parental strategies.

The results of behavioral genetic studies challenge much of what we thought we knew about the centrality of rearing and family environment. They show the extent to which temperament is a crucial factor in psychological development. They also suggest that the environment for a child consists of a great deal more than its parents.

☐ Genetics and Psychological Symptoms

Genes shape personality and intelligence. They also influence the development of almost every mental disorder. These heritable variations are the primary determinant of the form taken by psychopathology.

These conclusions are supported by a large number of studies using behavioral genetic methods. Interestingly, although family pedigree studies do not separate heredity and environment, whenever illnesses have been found to run in families, twin studies have confirmed that they have a significant genetic component.

I will now very briefly review this literature, touching on a few key points. Readers interested in a more detailed discussion might wish to consult a previously published book (Paris, 1999).

Psychoses

Both twin and adoption studies demonstrate strong genetic predispositions to schizophrenia (Gottesman, 1991). Even more powerful findings emerge for bipolar mood disorder (Gershon & Nurnberger, 1995). Researchers are now actively looking for specific genes linked to both these diseases. If mutations can be found at one or more sites associated with specific psychiatric disorders, then the coming century may see the introduction of gene therapy for the most serious mental illnesses.

These genetic roots for psychotic disorders are now well known. But a wide range of other conditions, seen frequently in practice, also have a significant heritable component.

Depression

All mood disorders are heritable, but some are more heritable than others. Depressions accompanied by melancholia and/or psychosis reflect a large genetic component, but even the garden-variety depressions seen in therapists' offices have genetic predispositions (Kendler, Neale, Kessler, Heath, & Eaves, 1992). If this were not so, then given the stressful nature of human existence, the prevalence of depression would be even higher than it is! Everyone experiences some of these symptoms from time to time, yet even the highest estimates of lifetime prevalence for major depression only reach 20% (Weissman, Bland, Canino, & Faravelli, 1996).

Depression is best understood as the result of interactions between predispositions and stressors. Although losses are often associated with onset (Kendler, Kessler, & Walters, 1995), they are not primary causes. After all, life is full of losses. Even unusually stressful events lead to depression in a minority of those exposed. In the absence of genetic predispositions, life events produce more distress than disorder.

Anxiety

Like depression, anxiety is a universal pattern of response to stress. But clinically significant levels of disturbance are more easily aroused in some individuals than in others. Panic disorder and generalized anxiety disorder both run in families, and twin studies confirm that each of these conditions has a large genetic component (Kendler et al., 1992). Patients with depression often have anxiety disorders, and vice versa (Goldberg & Huxley, 1992). Genetic predispositions for depression overlap those for anxiety, and the environment may determine which type of symptom develops under stress (Kendler, Heath, & Martin, 1987).

PTSD

Trauma is not the *only*, or even necessarily the *main*, cause of PTSD. This conclusion may come as a surprise to some readers. But research shows that most individuals exposed to highly traumatic events, such as combat in wartime (Helzer, Robins, & Wishe, 1979) or random violence in peacetime (North, Smith, & Spitznagel, 1997), do not develop PTSD. Even Holocaust survivors often remain asymptomatic (Eaton et al., 1982).

Research has established that PTSD has a large genetic component. In a study of twins who served in the Vietnam War, True et al. (1993) found that each of the specific symptoms of PTSD is heritable. In the same sample (Lyons et al., 1993), even the level of combat exposure during the war demonstrated heritability, probably reflecting personality traits that influence risk-taking behavior.

Substance Abuse

A large body of research supports the heritability of predispositions to substance abuse (Schuckit et al., 1996). The sons of alcoholic fathers carry a particularly high risk (DeJong, van den Brink, Hartveld, & van der Wielen, 1993; Goodwin, 1985), an association that cannot be explained simply by exposure or by modeling.

Social factors, particularly the use of substances in a context of interpersonal bonding, play a large role in determining the prevalence of these disorders. But these psychosocial influences have their most powerful effects on those who are already genetically predisposed.

Eating Disorders

The two main forms of eating disorder, anorexia nervosa and bulimia nervosa, each have a heritable component (Treasure & Holland, 1995). Anorexia is genetically linked to compulsive personality traits. Bulimia is often related to a predisposition to obesity, but bulimics are heterogeneous, showing some symptoms linked to impulsive personality traits and others linked to depression. Like substance abuse, eating disorders are social phenomena. But social pressures for thinness have a greater effect on those who are predisposed to develop these symptoms.

Disorders Arising in Childhood

Attention-Deficit Hyperactivity Disorder (ADHD) has a large heritable component (Biederman, Faraone, Milberger, & Curtis, 1996; Hechtman, 1994). Patients with attentional and/or hyperactive symptoms demonstrate abnormal findings on brain imaging, and researchers are now searching for genes associated with a vulnerability to ADHD.

Of all the major categories of mental illness, conduct disorder has the weakest heritability and is also unique in demonstrating a large shared environmental component (Cadoret, Yates, Troughton, Woodworth, & Stewart, 1995). This observation can probably be explained by the heterogeneity of the conduct-disordered population (Lykken, 1995). Most delinquent children are raised in dysfunctional families and/or a dysfunctional social environment (Pike & Plomin, 1996). It is therefore not surprising that most cases demonstrate low heritability. However, in a more severe subgroup of conduct-disordered children (those with an early onset, greater severity, and who develop antisocial behavior during adulthood), we observe a much larger genetic component (Rutter, Giller, & Hagele, 1999; Zoccolillo et al., 1992).

Personality Disorders

Genetic variations play an important role in shaping personality traits (see Chapter 10). Thus far, their role in personality disorders has not been as thoroughly researched (Nigg & Goldsmith, 1994). Logically, if disorders are amplifications of traits, they should also be heritable. Thus far, adoption and twin studies have most clearly supported genetic factors in antisocial personality disorder (Paris, 1999). There is also some recent evidence from twin studies for genetic influence on most of the personality disorders described in DSM (Torgersen, 1999).

☐ Genes, Personality, and Symptoms

The observation that normal personality traits, as well as mental disorders, are influenced by genes raises complex theoretical issues. We need to understand the precise mechanisms by which genetic differences shape behavior. DNA may be a magical substance, but it only codes for protein synthesis. How can differences in DNA structure influence the way we think, feel, or behave?

One part of the answer is that personality differences are influenced by individual differences in neurotransmitter activity. For example, a trait called "novelty seeking" may reflect a deficiency in the availability of dopamine in the brain, leading to a need for higher levels of stimulation to achieve a feeling of well-being (Hamer, 1998). Similarly, people with a high level of neuroticism, who tend to have a pessimistic or anxious attitude towards life, may have a deficiency in the availability of serotonin, a transmitter that plays a central role in emotion (Hamer, 1998). Each of these neurobiological variations should also be associated with genetic differences.

At present, the evidence for these hypotheses remains a bit shaky. Some researchers have reported associations between genetic variations and personality traits (Lesch et al., 1996). Although these findings have been prominently reported in the media, other research groups (e.g., Gelertner, Kranzler, Coccaro, Siever, & New, 1998) have not replicated them. (Failures to replicate findings do not usually appear in newspapers!) Nonetheless, we are likely to find more such associations in the future, establishing which ones are real and which ones are artifacts.

Since behavior reflects the interaction of many systems, it is unlikely that there is any simple and direct relationship between traits and neurotransmitter activity. The brain is not a soup whose flavor is determined by neurochemicals. It is an anatomically complex organ with an enormous number of neural connections. The structure and chemistry of the brain is shaped by hereditary factors that are common to everyone. For example, about half of all our genes are assigned to guide the process of neural development. This complexity makes it very unlikely that *single* genes will be found that can account for variations in behavior. Genes work in interaction with each other, and many of them may be required to shape the simplest behavioral patterns. Moreover, it is always worth repeating the principle that the expression of genes depends on the environment.

In summary, *everything is genetic, but nothing is determined.* The heritable factors in mental disorders rarely depend on changes on a single gene. Rather, many genes are involved in every form of behavior. Moreover, genes do not exert direct control over psychological symptoms. Instead, they influence the *threshold* at which symptoms develop in the presence of environmental stress.

Thus, there is no such thing as a gene *for* anxiety or a gene *for* depression. All these predispositions are *complex traits*, the result of interactions between multiple genes. Only a particular combination of genetic changes at many sites creates a predisposition to disorder. This is why mental illnesses are usually not inherited in simple Mendelian patterns. Instead, genes influence behavior and states of mind *indirectly*, by influencing how individuals respond to environmental stressors.

The key concept to keep in mind is that of *gene–environment interaction,* that is, that the effects of genes on behavior only occur in the context of a specific set of environmental conditions. Kendler and Eaves (1987) have described three basic mechanisms governing these interactions. The first type is additive, involving the cumulative effects of genetic and environmental risks. The second type involves genetic differences in environmental *sensitivity*. The third type involves genetic influences on the level of *exposure* to stressful events (Kendler & Eaves, 1986; van Ijzendoorn, 1992). The second and third mechanisms (environmental sensitivity and environmental exposure) both depend on individual differences in personality.

Let us consider some examples of how personality trait profiles influence environmental sensitivity. People differ greatly in the extent to which they experience the same life events as stressful. Those with genetic vulnerabilities are more likely to develop symptoms than those who lack such predispositions.

Neuroticism is one of the most basic dimensions of personality (McCrae & Costa, 1999). This trait tells us, in common parlance, how thin-skinned people are. Those who are most neurotic tend to put a pessimistic or worried spin on life events. They are therefore more sensitive to stress and more likely to develop a variety of psychological symptoms under stressful conditions.

Another example of these interactions has been documented by Blatt (1991), who identified two types of personality structure that increase the susceptibility to depression. The dependent type has an excessive need for the support of significant others and is easily devastated by rejection or loss. The self-critical type has an excessive need for high levels of achievement and is therefore unable to deal with life's inevitable failures. Each of these profiles is associated with higher levels of environmental sensitivity to stress.

The principle that the same environment is different for different people is supported by life events research, which consistently shows that the effects of events depend on how they are processed (Brown & Harris, 1989). Personality traits help account for these differences in the processing of experience. Even siblings growing up in the same family, who are generally treated in much the same way, have unique traits and therefore can end up being almost as different from each other as perfect strangers (Dunn & Plomin, 1990). Contrary to what one might expect, as people get older, the influence of genetics on personality actually becomes stronger (Rutter, 1991).

Let us now consider the relationship of personality to environmental exposure. Individual differences in temperament and personality between children influence not only the severity but even the frequency of negative life events (Kendler & Eaves, 1986; Kendler et al., 1993b). On the one hand, many children are quite resourceful, accessing opportunities and experiences most in accord with their talents and preferences (Scarr & McCartney, 1983). But the other side of this coin is that children with temperamental vulnerabilities are more likely to be exposed to adverse events and also have a reduced resilience to these adversities.

Similar mechanisms operate in adults. For example, an impulsive temperament leads to higher levels of interpersonal conflict, often associated with unstable employment and marital breakdown. Research shows that the frequency of stressful events is influenced by these heritable traits (Kendler et al., 1993b; Thapar & McGuffin, 1996). The list of life events that have a heritable component is long and rather astonishing. It includes marital problems, divorce, the quality of friendships, social supports, problems at work, as well as socioeconomic status and education. These findings clearly contradict the assumption that childhood experience with parents is necessarily the primary determinant of the quality of intimate relationships in adulthood.

Of course, there is no such thing as a gene *for* divorce! Rather, the frequency of marital breakdown is determined, at least in part, by temperamental characteristics. Those with irritable and impulsive traits will be more likely to choose the wrong partner. They will also be more likely to become intolerant of the normal levels of conflict that characterize any marriage.

In summary, genes do not shape symptoms in a vacuum. They affect behavior indirectly by influencing the quality of individual responses to environmental challenges. Genetic effects can therefore not be understood without considering the environment in which they are expressed. At the same time, the nature of the environment itself can be influenced by genetic variability. These interactions underlie the relationship among temperament, personality, and symptoms.

A warning is necessary here. We need to avoid falling into the trap of reductionism, whether biological or psychological. Even if mental disorders are not caused by childhood experiences, it would be equally mistaken to take the contrary, but presently fashionable, position that mental illness is all in the genes. Nor do chemical imbalances account for most psychological symptoms. To understand psychopathology, we need to study interactions between temperament and experience.

Thus, genetic differences do not *directly* determine how people behave, think, or feel. Instead, temperament determines the extent to which people are exposed to adverse events and how people experience and process them. Personality therefore constitutes a missing link in development, a frame joining nature with nurture.

☐ Predisposition-Stress Theory

We are now ready to describe a model of psychopathology to replace the primacy of childhood. This theory will avoid reductionism and be neither purely genetic nor narrowly environmental. Instead, the model will be structured around the interactions between temperament and life experience. The best and most integrative theory of this type is the predisposition-stress (or diathesis-stress) model (Monroe & Simons, 1991), which conceptualizes mental disorders as emerging from a combination of genetic vulnerabilities, constituting *predispositions,* and the influence of life events, constituting *stressors.*

The theory can be described by a set of four general principles. I will outline each of these principles and then provide illustrations.

1. Predispositions can be *necessary* causes of psychopathology, while stressors are usually not. Neither predispositions nor stressors, by themselves, are *sufficient* causes of mental disorders.
2. Differences in predispositions determine the type of disorder that can develop in any particular individual. As a result, different people, when exposed to the same stressor, develop different psychological symptoms.
3. Psychological symptoms develop at a *threshold of liability* reflecting the total weight of predisposition and stress. The weights attached to predispositions and stressors as risks can vary, so that even minor stressors may tip the balance in favor of illness when vulnerabilities are strong, while only severe stress will cause pathology when they are weak.
4. Personality traits reflect these heritable predispositions but do not necessarily produce psychopathology.

Necessary and Sufficient Causes of Psychopathology

Sufficient conditions for disease are those in whose presence a pathological outcome will definitely develop. Actually, it is very rare for any disease in medicine to be caused by a single factor (exposure to certain viruses being a prominent exception). The sufficient conditions for mental disorders are usually a combination of many risk factors, some of which are intrinsic while others are extrinsic.

Necessary conditions are those without which a disorder cannot develop. But the presence of a necessary condition does not mean a disorder necessarily will develop. To consider a common example from medicine, infectious diseases are caused by specific pathogens and cannot develop in their absence. Yet, not uncommonly, these same organisms can live inside the body without causing disease. For example, in the common cold, pathology usually develops when we are at a low level of resistance.

In most cases, psychosocial risks are not necessary conditions for psychopathology. Thus, although depression is common after a loss, it can also develop without any precipitating event. In contrast, biological predispositions *are* truly necessary, since if they are not present, exposure to stressors produces another kind of symptom, depending on individual predispositions. (Or, if the individual is sufficiently resilient, stressors produce no disorder at all.) Therefore, predispositions have a specific relationship to outcome that stressors lack, giving them some degree of primacy in the pathways toward illness and constituting necessary conditions for the development of psychopathology.

Individual Variations and Predispositions

Each individual carries a unique set of predispositions to psychopathology. If stressed sufficiently, everyone has the potential to develop *some* form of symptom (Falconer, 1989). For this reason, it is no longer science fiction to imagine that we will eventually have the option of having our genome read and be told the symptoms to which we will be prone at some point in our lifetime.

The fact that each person, even if exposed to the same stressor, develops different symptoms is nicely demonstrated by research on childhood adversities (Rutter & Rutter, 1993). The same list of risk factors comes up in relation to a variety of outcomes: conduct disorder, attention deficit disorder, or mood and anxiety disorders. This list includes severe marital discord, low social class, large family size, paternal criminality, maternal mental disorder, and foster care placement—adversities that predict the development of many different types of symptoms rather than any one in particular.

In adult populations as well, similar risk factors tend to be associated with a variety of disorders. For example, recent interpersonal losses are at the top of the list in the Life Stress Index, a well-known instrument for assessing the impact of recent events (Rahe, 1995). But these stressors are risks for a wide variety of outcomes: both physical and mental illnesses. To explain why one person becomes depressed after a loss, while another develops a psychosis, a third becomes somatically preoccupied, and a fourth develops a physical illness, we must take predispositions into account.

Strength of Predispositions

Those who are *strongly* predisposed to develop mental disorders may become ill with only a small amount of environmental provocation. This is why disorders such as schizophrenia and bipolar mood disorder, which have high levels of heritability, usually seem to be brought on by minor stressors or by no apparent stress at all.

Those who are *moderately* predisposed to develop mental disorders usually become ill only when exposed to significant stressors. Many common mental disorders that show only moderate levels of heritability fall into this category. Examples include unipolar depression, anxiety disorders, alcoholism, eating disorders, and personality disorders.

Those who are only *minimally* predisposed to develop mental disorders will become ill only when exposed to severe stressors. Some people with a strong constitution may fall ill when faced with severe challenges from the environment. Research on recent life events (Rahe, 1995) shows that the challenges that lead to overt symptoms are usually multiple and cumulative. Moreover, their impact depends on how people interpret them (Brown & Harris, 1989). This explains why most people, even when exposed to a severe stressor, do not develop disorders such as PTSD (Bowman, 1997).

Predispositions and Traits

Individual differences in trait profiles underlie every type of mental disorder. Temperament and personality can therefore be thought of as the matrix, or the culture medium, on which psychopathology grows.

Predispositions do not *cause* disease, but they shape the traits that make illness more or less likely. At the same time, traits are associated with abnormal personality development. In time, the study of personality will establish links between behavioral genetics and molecular genetics. It will then become possible to reclassify mental disorders on the basis of predispositions, many of which will be identified prior to the development of illness.

Until we know more about the causes of mental disorders, the classification of psychological problems must remain arbitrary. Symptoms do cluster together in a way that allows the diagnosis of disorders in patients. Yet the categories in DSM-IV (APA, 1994) are, at best, a useful tool for communication between clinicians and should not be thought of as reflecting absolute reality.

Ultimately, all psychopathology is *dimensional*. This means that illnesses are related to a *spectrum* of possibilities, some of which lead to less serious levels of dysfunction, while others fall within the range of normality. As in quantum physics, where the same entities can be both particles and waves, mental disorders are both categories and dimensions. Even schizophrenia has been shown to be related to milder forms of illness that may only lead to personality disorders or even minor eccentricities (Claridge, 1997; Meehl, 1990).

Similarly, some individuals are more prone to depression and anxiety than others, and these predispositions can be observed during childhood. Children with these vulnerabilities tend to develop *internalizing disorders*. In contrast, other individuals are more prone to act out impulsively, and these predispositions are also observable during childhood. Faced with the same stressors, children with an impulsive temperament tend to develop *externalizing disorders*.

☐ Conclusion

Heredity is powerful but not irresistible. Many genes have to interact to produce a single effect. Some genes may not be turned on until late in development. Moreover, the effects of genes and environment are inseparable. Everything is interactive, and heredity and environment are the yin and yang of development. Only when the *total* weight of genetic and environmental liability passes a given threshold does overt disease develop. Even where genes play a major role, environmental factors must activate them. Similarly, even in disorders in which environment plays the more crucial role, predispositions determine the threshold at which stressors cause symptoms.

At the same time, the environment is not a force acting on passive recipients. Instead, to use a biological metaphor, the personality functions rather like a cell membrane, actively transporting experiences so as to incorporate those it needs and to extrude those it does not.

The predisposition-stress model is in accord with the evidence reviewed in previous chapters about the effects of stressors on children. Adversity strikes hard at the vulnerable, spares those who are resilient, and may even lead to increased resistance to further adversity in a few.

Predisposition-stress theory also explains why childhood experiences, by themselves, do not account for the development of mental disorders. The same experiences are very different for different people. Personality traits, rooted in temperament, are the filter through which all life events are processed. Those who are temperamentally thin-skinned or troublesome are the most likely to have bad things happen to them and the most likely to get upset when they occur. Such individuals are highly sensitive to their environment and have a psychic equilibrium that is easily overturned by the course of life events. Children with a difficult temperament, particularly when associated with traits of irritability and impulsivity, are more likely to experience rejection and hostility, both from parents and from peers. In contrast, those with an easy temperament are less susceptible to adversity and are more likely to elicit support from others when stressful events occur.

Finally, the predisposition-stress model is highly consistent with the ubiquity of resilience. Although we are sometimes inclined to think of children as victims of circumstance, most have real options. A child can minimize exposure to toxic environments and maximize time spent in supportive environments, although the capacity to make these choices also depends on temperament.

In summary, the predisposition-stress model allows an integration between the influence of genes and environment. The next chapter will provide more detail on the role of personality traits as the intermediaries between heredity and experience.

10
CHAPTER

Personality and Psychopathology

☐ What Is Personality?

Situations change, but personality endures. Technically, the term *personality* refers to patterns of behavior, thought, and emotion that are unique to the individual and are consistent in many different contexts. Personality traits, an amalgam of heredity and experience, should be distinguished from *temperament*, the genetic matrix on which traits develop.

Many personality traits can be observed early in life, and there is a large degree of continuity between behavior in childhood and adulthood (Caspi & Roberts, 1999). Over the course of adulthood, traits become much more constant. Longitudinal studies (McCrae & Costa, 1990) show that the continuity of personality increases over the life cycle, so that traits are well established by age 18 and become even more stable after age 30. This continuity is due in part to genes that express themselves later in life and in part to environmental influences that reinforce existing behavioral patterns.

☐ Measuring Personality

Personality is a complex construct. An entire branch of psychology has been devoted to its measurement. Trait psychologists define the "dimensions" of personality through factor analysis of items on self-report questionnaires. These instruments measure a broad and continuous range of trait variations. Since there is no clear boundary between normal and abnormal personality characteristics (Costa & Widiger, 1994; Livesley, Schroeder, Jackson, & Jang, 1994), tests developed to measure normal personality can also be used to study clinical populations.

Psychotherapists might wonder how honest people are when asked to describe their personality in a questionnaire. But the problem becomes even worse when someone else is doing the rating, as when children's temperament is scored from observations of parents or teachers. Some believe that structured interviews provide a better method of assessing personality. After all, experienced clinicians are used to observing behaviors of which patients are only dimly aware. Unfortunately, interviews are labor-intensive and time-consuming. Obtaining corroboration from informants takes even more time. Finally, getting trained observers to agree about how to rate personality traits from interviews is not easy.

Self-report instruments may be "quick and dirty," but they have turned out to be the most useful method for the study of personality. When questionnaires are properly constructed, what adults say about themselves turns out to be reasonably accurate. This conclusion is based on the fact that scores on personality tests are predictive of behaviors in the real world, as well as a wide range of clinical phenomena.

Several different schema have been developed to describe the dimensions of personality. Each cuts into the matrix of traits at a different angle. All share a reasonable level of agreement about the basic elements of personality. The broadest characteristics usually involve needs for stimulation, levels of impulsivity, thresholds for emotional response, strength of reactions to others, and the logic of thought.

I will now briefly review five influential models of personality. Each has advantages, as well as disadvantages, for both research and clinical practice. The goal of demonstrating a broad relationship between personality and psychopathology could be well served by any of them.

The first three models are derived from studies of normal personality, with pathology seen as reflecting extremes on trait dimensions.

Eysenck's Model

Hans Eysenck (1991), a British pioneer in trait psychology, described three personality dimensions: *extraversion, neuroticism,* and *psychoticism.* Extraversion refers to differences in the need for stimulation from other people. Neuroticism describes differences in emotional vulnerability. ("Psychoticism" is a misleading term, and actually describes impulsivity.)

Five Factor Model

Two American trait psychologists, Robert McCrae and Paul Costa, developed a highly influential theory termed the Five Factor Model (FFM; McCrae and Costa, 1999). This model describes five dimensions: *extraversion, neuroticism, openness to experience, agreeableness,* and *conscientiousness.* The first two factors are the same as those described by Eysenck. The third factor, openness, refers to a need for novelty and a capacity to lose oneself or to be highly absorbed. The last two represent different aspects of Eysenck's "psychoticism." Agreeableness refers to the degree to which an individual meets the social expectations of other people, while conscientiousness is the inverse of impulsivity.

Cloninger's Model

An American research psychiatrist, Robert Cloninger, developed a model that has a theoretical grounding in neurobiology. Cloninger, Svrakic, & Pryzbeck (1993) schema describes four dimensions: *novelty seeking, harm avoidance, reward dependence,* and *persistence.* Novelty seeking refers to the need for stimulation. Harm avoidance refers to efforts to avoid the negative consequences of behavior. Reward dependence is similar to agreeableness in the FFM. Persistence is similar to conscientiousness on the FFM.

Among academic personality psychologists, the FFM has been the most popular model. In America, this schema has largely replaced the dimensions described by Eysenck. However, in biological research, Cloninger's system has been more widely used, since its dimensions measure temperamental variations that, at least hypothetically, can be correlated with genetic markers and neurochemical pathways. Although Cloninger et al. (1993) proposed three additional dimensions to measure nonbiological aspects of personality (which he termed "character"), these traits have not been validated by sufficient research data.

In summary, Eysenck, Costa, and Cloninger begin with normality and see pathology as an exaggeration of normal traits. In contrast, two other schema for describing personality begin at the pathological end of the spectrum. Since their dimensions are based on symptoms, they are more or less self-explanatory to clinicians.

Siever's Model

Larry Siever is an American psychiatrist who developed a biological model (Siever & Davis, 1991) describing four personality dimensions: *anxiety, impulsivity, affective instability,* and *cognitive dysfunction.* Each of these traits is assumed to be related to neurochemical variations and to underlie the symptoms of mental disorders—both the symptomatic conditions listed on Axis I of DSM and the personality disorders that are listed on Axis II.

Livesley's Model

John Livesley is a Canadian psychiatrist who developed a model with 18 dimensions (Livesley et al.,1994). These narrow traits can then be combined using factor analysis into four broader dimensions: *inhibitedness, emotional dysregulation, dissocial behavior,* and *compulsivity* (Livesley, Jang, & Vernon, 1998). Genetic influences have been found to operate on both levels. The higher order traits closely resemble four of the dimensions described by the FFM, with inhibitedness paralleling introversion, emotional dysregulation corresponding to neuroticism, dissocial behavior being the opposite of agreeableness, and compulsivity corresponding to conscientiousness. Livesley (1998), in common with the other four theorists, believes that dimensions provide a better description of personality disorders than do the Axis II categories presently defined by DSM.

☐ Personality and Psychopathology

If symptoms result from interactions between predisposition and stress, then psychopathology does not emerge *de novo* as a response to life events. In fact, one can rarely predict symptoms from the nature of a stressor. Different people develop different problems in response to the same life event. Personality traits are one of the main factors determining these reactions.

Ultimately, all psychological symptoms are rooted in personality (Widiger, Verheul, & van den Brink, 1999). To understand why individuals develop a particular set of difficulties, one needs to understand their unique and intrinsic characteristics. For an adequate description of these traits, clinicians must track the trajectory of a lifetime.

This point of view used to be widely held by therapists, albeit in a different context. In the heyday of psychoanalysis, when it was assumed that personality was a result of experiences in early childhood, symptoms were seen as secondary, while personality structure and psychodynamics were seen as primary. Although that approach failed to consider temperament, it at least taught therapists to think about personality.

Today, this piece of clinical wisdom has been largely lost. In practice, patients are usually diagnosed on the basis of presenting symptoms, with a focus on Axis I pathology. Personality is confined to an "Axis II ghetto," where it can conveniently be ignored.

My own discipline of psychiatry has come to be dominated by biological models. Surprisingly, behavioral genetics has had surprisingly little influence on most of my medical colleagues. Instead, the preeminent model is linked to pharmacotherapy, with symptoms seen as reflections of imbalances in levels or activity of neurotransmitters. In this view, the main aim of treatment is to find the right drug, and personality barely comes into the picture.

On the other hand, psychotherapists who attribute symptoms almost entirely to childhood experiences have been equally dogmatic. For example, Herman (1992) wrote an influential book suggesting that impulsive personality disorders should be redefined as "complex post-traumatic stress disorders." In the drama of traumatic experience, personality also plays only a minor role. Herman's volume focuses entirely on environmental factors in development and contains *not one word* about biology or temperament. Inevitably, the model that emerges is simplistic and reductionistic.

We need to redress the lost balance between symptoms and personality. A wide body of evidence shows that personality dimensions have an important effect on the phenomenology, outcome, and treatment of psychological symptoms. This principle has useful applications for the assessment and treatment of most of the patients we see.

Understanding traits is particularly important for patients who meet diagnostic criteria for personality disorders. For example, patients with borderline personality develop different symptoms when they become depressed than do patients who have no personality disorder (Gunderson & Phillips, 1991). Instead of the continuously low mood of a classical melancholia, borderline patients have an environmentally sensitive mood. They react with strong, but changeable, emotions to life events. Their depressions may last for only a few days, or even a few hours. At the same time, in the presence of *any* form of personality disorder, depression is more resistant to therapy (Patience, McGuire, Scott, & Freeman, 1995). This is so whether the treatment offered consists of pharmacotherapy (Soloff, 1993) or psychotherapy (Shea, Pilkonis, & Beckahm, 1990).

☐ The Central Role of Temperament

Temperamental differences can be measured in infancy. At birth, children already vary widely on a number of behavioral dimensions. But these characteristics are not fixed for all time. As discussed in Chapter 2, temperament only becomes truly stable by age 2 or 3. Rothbart and Bates

(1998) describe six dimensions of temperamental variation that can be measured by the time a child is 2 years old and that then remain relatively stable over time: (a) extraversion; (b) anxiety; (c) distress when overstimulated; (d) irritability and anger; (e) agreeableness; (f) maintaining attention. Stability may be greater at the extremes of temperament. Children with unusually high levels of irritability or anxiety are more likely to retain these characteristics as they mature.

Genetic variations are the main source of variations in temperament. This principle has been confirmed by many behavioral genetic studies of temperament, including the Louisville Twin Study (Matheny, 1987), the Colorado Twin Project (Cyphers, Phillips, Fulker, & Mrazek, 1990), the McArthur Longitudinal Twin Study (Plomin, Emde, Braungartm, & Campos, 1993), and a Norwegian twin study (Torgersen & Kringlen, 1978). The results of all these investigations show that temperamental qualities in children that remain stable over time are also heritable.

The influence of temperamental variations on emotional development has been a subject of increasing interest to developmental psychologists (Gross, 1999; Kagan, 1989). However, abnormalities of temperament need not cause mental disorders. Instead, children born with problematical temperaments are at greater *risk* for developing psychological problems. The more intense a trait, the more likely it is to cause dysfunction.

Nearly 40 years ago, Chess and Thomas (1984) began a pioneering prospective investigation to observe and describe temperament. Their New York Longitudinal Study followed a cohort of normal children whose temperamental characteristics had been assessed by direct observations during infancy. The researchers identified three overall types: "easy" children (fortunately, the largest group), "difficult" children (characterized by irritability), and "slow to warm up" children (characterized by slow responses to social interaction).

The last two types parallel the well-known distinction in child psychology between *externalizing* and *internalizing* disorders (Achenbach & McConaughy, 1997). These qualities correspond closely to variations in the broad trait dimensions of adult personality, as well as in attachment styles. Finally, these two basic temperamental types parallel neurophysiological studies (Pickering & Gray, 1999) describing a Behavioral Activation System governing impulsive stimulus-seeking, as well as a Behavioral Inhibition System governing anxiety. This dichotomy between impulsive and anxious temperament will guide much of the forthcoming discussion concerning the relationship between personality and symptoms.

Variations in temperament need not be pathological. Ultimately, these characteristics reflect alternative adaptations to the environment. In an ideal world it is probably better to be an "easy" child. However, in adverse circumstances, irritable children get more attention and are more likely to survive when food is scarce (Buss, 1999). There are also circumstances, such as danger from predators or outsiders, in which a clinging or shy temperament might be a real advantage.

Chess and Thomas (1984) hypothesized that each temperamental type requires a different maternal response. Most mothers will have an easy time with an easy child. A difficult child requires forbearance and limit-setting. A slow-to-warm-up child requires great patience. Parents might raise one child successfully, but fail with another. Thus, whether problems develop depends on the *goodness of fit* between mother and child.

Yet when Chess and Thomas (1990) followed up their cohort into adulthood, temperament was not a strong predictor of psychological problems. There was only some relationship, but not a strong one, between adult symptoms and the "difficult" pattern. Interestingly, the slow-to-warm-up group were no worse off than those who had been easy. In the long run, most children grow out of early shyness. However, since the New York study was conducted on a *normal* group of children, it could not pick up the effects of extreme temperamental variations.

Recently, researchers have followed young children with highly abnormal temperaments into adolescence. Kagan (1994) has followed two cohorts with high levels of shyness or "behavioral inhibition." (I will discuss this study in more detail later in this chapter.) Maziade, Caron, Coté, Boutin, & Thivierge (1991) followed a cohort with unusually high levels of irritability into adolescence. Elevated risks for psychopathology appeared in both these groups. In the behaviorally inhibited adolescents, social phobias and avoidant behaviors developed. Among the irritable adolescents, behavioral disturbances and prepsychotic phenomena were more likely. It will be informative to see what happens to these cohorts as they reach adulthood.

☐ Temperament and Personality

Temperament is the medium on which personality grows. The concept that personality development is rooted in these biological variations has provided a new paradigm for trait psychology (Clark & Watson, 1999). Thus, temperament corresponds to the heritable component found in all behavioral genetic studies of personality traits. No matter which schema we use to describe personality dimensions, this heritable component is consistently large (see reviews in Plomin & Caspi, 1999; Plomin et al., 1997). Moreover, these heritability levels do not depend on self-report— they can also be demonstrated independently by peer measures (Riemann, Angleitner, & Strelau, 1997), teacher ratings, or laboratory observations of children (Plomin & Caspi, 1999).

The role of genes in personality has also been confirmed by all the methods of determining heritability described in Chapter 9. Comparisons between monozygotic and dizygotic twins (e.g., Jang, Livesley, Vernon, & Jackson, 1996; Livesley, Jang, Schroeder, & Jackson, 1993) consistently show that identical twins are much more similar in personality than are fraternal twins. Adoption studies yield somewhat lower estimates of heritability (Plomin & Caspi, 1999), since complex traits involving interactions between many genes are not always transmitted from parent to child. Nonetheless, these investigations show that children are much more similar in personality to their biological than to their adoptive parents. Finally, the heritability of personality was strongly supported by the Minnesota study (Bergeman et al., 1990; Bouchard et al., 1990; Tellegen et al., 1988), with twins reared apart being as similar in personality as those raised in the same family.

In summary, similarities and differences in personality depend more on common genes than on being brought up in any particular family. As discussed in the previous chapter, we can "ball-park" variations in personality as being approximately half due to genes and half due to environment. This applies to almost every trait that has been studied with the possible, but still controversial, exception of agreeableness and positive emotionality (Plomin & Caspi, 1999).

To the extent that personality is heritable, variations in trait dimensions should also be associated with measurable biological markers. Some studies have documented these associations (Coccaro, Siever, & Klar, 1989; Eysenck, 1991; Plomin & Caspi, 1999; Siever & Davis, 1991). Future research should also be able to demonstrate specific gene linkages and associations with personality dimensions. Thus far, a few preliminary findings (e.g., Benjamin, Patterson, Greenberg, Murphy, & Hamer, 1996; Lesch et al., 1996) have been reported, but (as pointed out in the previous chapter) they have not always been replicated. The most likely explanation is that the effects of genes on personality are complex and interactive. As Plomin and Caspi (1999) emphasize, the concept of quantitative trait loci (QTLs) describes complex traits influenced by many different genes. Each genetic locus may account for only a small percentage of the variance, so that only some specific combination can lead to a specific outcome. Eventually, behavioral genetics will be linked to molecular genetics, which will help researchers to know what to look for when studying associations between traits and genes (Plomin & Rutter, 1998).

Finally, additional evidence for the underlying biological nature of personality comes from transcultural research. The same broad trait dimensions have been found to be measurable in cultures all over the world (Eysenck, 1991; McCrae & Costa, 1997).

The heritability of personality provides strong support for the critique of primacy. Temperament, the heritable component of personality, is a major influence in childhood experience, both with family and with peers. This leads to a theoretical point of some clinical significance. The way we raise children does not depend only on our own personality traits. The temperament of a child is a crucial factor in the quality of parenting.

Moreover, genetic factors in personality, as expressed in temperament, do not stop affecting development when childhood ends but continue to have an impact throughout the life cycle. This makes sense when one considers how gene–environment interactions affect exposure to and sensitivity to stressors. Some researchers (Lykken & Tellegen, 1996) have even found evidence that happiness in life is determined, at least in part, by heredity.

Reviewing this literature, Efran, Greene, & Gordon (1998) offered the following beautiful metaphor:

> Temperament and personality are far more biologically determined and less malleable, than radical environmentalism once led us to believe. We are not born with clean slates upon which the environment etches our destinies, but rather we are born with an underlying, genetically coded, emotional imprint that reveals itself throughout our lives, like a photograph slowly materializing in a developing tray. (p. 29)

Yet like other biological "givens," temperamental variations lead to different consequences under different conditions. Life events can shape the traits that emerge from temperament. The influence is cumulative, and it need not be traumatic or dramatic. To give Larkin's fine metaphor (Chapter 5, p. 57) a new twist, the child's environment is like a coral reef, growing steadily but inexorably over time.

Rutter (1987b) suggests that the best model for the process by which the environment shapes personality is *social learning*. This concept derives from a well-known psychological theory (Bandura, 1977, 1999) describing two mechanisms by which family members, as well as other significant figures in the child's life (nonparental authorities and peer groups) can shape a child's behavior. Social learning depends on reinforcements (rewards and punishments), as well as on modeling (imitating the way others behave). Like every other psychological process, these mechanisms are subject to individual variations. Temperament affects how easily a child is reinforced and how ready a child is to learn observed skills. For this reason, the very process of social learning is easier for some children than for others.

☐ Personality and the Unshared Environment

Behavioral genetic methods separate environmental variance affecting a trait into shared and unshared components. In personality, environmental influences are almost entirely unshared. This is probably the most surprising and intriguing finding to emerge from behavioral genetic research. It seems to imply that parents may *not* be the most important influences on a child's personality. Caspi (1998) has described the reaction of developmental psychologists to this finding, ranging from simple disbelief to a search for some explanation that remains consistent with a crucial role for parenting. This is a good example of how "counterintuitive" findings can shape science, and how data can change what we consider to be common sense.

How do researchers account for the central role of unshared environment? Let me list several possible explanations.

The interpretation that most readily comes to mind is that personality is not primarily determined by experiences with parents. Instead, experiences *outside* the nuclear family could be at least as important. Clearly, development is influenced by attachments to extended family members, by socioeconomic circumstances, by culture, by the availability of social networks, and by the cohesiveness of the social community (Cross & Markus, 1999; Paris, 1996c; Rutter, 1989). Perhaps the idea that peer groups and social networks could be more important than parents in shaping personality seems radical. Yet readers who have raised adolescents may not be surprised!

Judith Rich Harris (1998) has written a controversial and fascinating book presenting a detailed argument in support of this thesis, arguing that parenting plays a relatively minor role in personality. Expanding on a previous journal article (Harris, 1995), Harris reviewed a large body of evidence showing a weak influence of parents on their children's development.

It is worth reviewing some of the main findings Harris uses to support her argument:

1. No specific child-rearing practice consistently predicts personality in children. In cases where associations have been reported, they have not been very large. Moreover, since these studies did not control for heritability, genes could easily account for whatever similarities exist between parents and children in personality.
2. Differential parental treatment of children in the same family does not account for personality differences. Even when parents treat children in the same way, their personalities turn out quite differently. Siblings are also rarely similar, most probably due to differences in temperament.
3. The correlation between the personality traits of adopted children and the parents who rear them is zero. There is also no correlation between traits of adopted children and nonadopted children in the same family.

4. Children behave differently in different settings. The way they are raised influences behavior in the home, but not necessarily outside the home. The basic assumption of attachment theory, that the quality of family life determines interpersonal behavior with other people, has not been supported by research.

Harris (1998) goes on to present an alternate model, termed "group socialization," focusing on peer groups as the crucial source of unshared environmental influence. Her view, more radical than anything suggested in this book, is that the influence of families, even over the course of childhood, is a myth—what Harris terms "the nurture assumption."

A second possible explanation of the power of the unshared environment involves gene–environment correlations. Within the same family, similar environments are experienced in different ways by different children. Parents tend to apply generally similar methods to raising their offspring (Plomin et al., 1994; Rowe, 1994). However, they usually find that some children are easier while others are more difficult. For example, most parents prefer a placid child who is easily socialized to an irritable child who requires constant discipline. Many parents will also experience frustration when a child is unusually shy.

Thus, the fact that siblings receive differential treatment from their parents can largely be accounted for by differences in each child's temperament. Traditionally, therapists had believed that children are treated differently by parents for unconscious reasons; for example, they remind their parents of someone else or of some part of themselves. This "scapegoating theory" has been a key principle of family therapy (see Chapter 6). Instead, evidence unequivocally supports the principle that temperament is the primary driving factor in differential treatment. One large-scale study of adolescents (Reiss, Heatherington, & Plomin, 2000) suggests that differences between children in the same family in nonshared environment are, in turn, strongly shaped by genetic differences. At the same time, temperamental variations lead each child to perceive the same family differently (Caspi, 1998). In short, a family that is "good enough" for one child can be inadequate for another (Reiss et al., 1995).

A third possibility that could explain the power of the unshared environment would be if the findings are accurate for normal individuals but do not apply to those who develop mental disorders. As several theorists (Kagan, 1997; Lykken, 1995; Scarr, 1992) have suggested, most children do reasonably well with an "average expectable environment," so that family experiences tend to have minimal effect on their personality. In contrast, those growing up in seriously dysfunctional families would be more affected by the quality of parenting. Moreover, if different children in the same family have different traits, the effects of parental mismanagement would affect those with greater sensitivity and vulnerability, effectively becoming part of the unshared environment.

A fourth mechanism that has been suggested to account for the power of the unshared environment is birth order. In this view, older, younger, and middle siblings each seek a different "niche" in the family (Sulloway, 1996). Older siblings would be more likely to identify with their parents, while younger siblings might be more rebellious. However, these ideas remain controversial, and at present, most evidence suggests that birth order has few consistent effects on personality (Harris, 1998).

Fifth and finally, the term *unshared environment* masks enormous heterogeneity. Which unique experiences have the most impact? Behavioral genetic research needs to study the effects of *specific* life events, to determine how unique adversities interact with unique vulnerabilities.

Can we make a choice between all these possible explanations? At present, we do not have enough evidence to be sure. Very likely, several mechanisms are operative, and there could be complex interactions among them. We will need much more research to disentangle the meaning of environmental factors in development.

I would like, nonetheless, to express a preference. I agree with Harris that we have seriously underestimated the role of the social environment in shaping personality. I have written a book (Paris, 1996c) describing mechanisms by which social factors can shape both normal and abnormal personalities. However, my views about the impact of the family on development differ from those of Harris.

Instead, I closely concur with the position taken by David Lykken, one of the psychologists involved in the Minnesota Twin Study. In his book on antisocial personality disorder, Lykken (1995) emphasizes that parenting is less crucial for the child with a normal temperament but is more important at temperamental extremes. Thus, poor parenting is most likely to damage *vulnerable* children, while good parenting has the capacity to ameliorate temperamental vulnerabilities.

The central role of unshared environment provides clear and strong evidence against the idea that parents are the *primary* influence on a child's personality. Moreover, childhood environments do not influence all children in the same way. As Kagan (1999) points out, most of the time, short of severe abuse and neglect, we should not ask about the consequences of variation in parental practices, neighborhoods, or school environments on the development of children, but how a praticular environment affects a specific temperamental type of child.

The key point here is contained in the phrase *short of severe abuse and neglect*. As documented by research (see Chapter 3), when the environment is *unusually* traumatic, somewhere around a quarter of children develop sequelae. However, if the environment is only *somewhat* defective, which is the situation for most people who seek therapy, the risk is much less. By and large, whether symptoms develop as the result of adversity depends on individual differences in temperament.

Thus, an easy temperament provides a protection against defects in upbringing. In contrast, when an abnormal temperament is combined with family dysfunction, pathology becomes more likely. Similarly, risk factors derived from the unshared environment (inside or outside the family) will have stronger effects on children who are temperamentally vulnerable. These principles closely parallel the predisposition-stress model described in Chapter 9.

□ Personality and Psychopathology

To address the issue of how personality shapes psychopathology, I will avoid the problems associated with the use of DSM diagnoses. These categories tend to overlap with each other, and also fail to capture the individuality of patients. Instead, the discussion in this section will focus on the personality trait dimensions that underlie mental disorders. For this purpose, I will use the model developed by Siever and Davis (1991) describing variations in temperament and personality that define psychopathological clusters cutting across Axis I and Axis II in the DSM system.

Impulsive Personality Dimensions

Impulsivity is the most intensively researched of all personality traits. Higher levels on this dimension lead people to act rapidly in the face of perceived threats, while lower levels lead them to be cautious. Depending on the circumstances, there can be advantages to either strategy. But those who have unusually high levels on this dimension are at risk for a wide range of psychopathologies associated with a loss of impulse control.

Behavioral genetic studies have consistently shown that impulsivity is a heritable trait (Plomin et al., 1997). A large literature (Mann, 1998), including studies on both animals and humans, also suggests that impulsivity is related to levels of neurotransmitters in the brain, most specifically low levels of serotonin activity. This observation helps explain why specific serotonin reuptake inhibitors not only act as antidepressants, but, particularly in higher doses, can have strong anti-impulsive effects (Soloff, 1993).

Problems with impulse control are characteristic of a wide range of mental disorders: impulsive personality disorders (particularly the antisocial and borderline categories) as well as addictions of various kinds (substance abuse, bulimia, pathological gambling). Zanarini (1993) has suggested that all these diagnoses can be thought of as lying on an "impulsive spectrum," sharing common neurobiological mechanisms.

The strongest empirical support for this concept comes from family studies of patients with impulse spectrum disorders. Although specific problems in impulsivity do not necessarily "breed true," individuals with any one disorder within this group are very likely to have relatives with at least one other category. For example, although patients with borderline personality disorder do not often have relatives with this diagnosis, they are likely to have family histories of antisocial personality or substance abuse (Zanarini, 1993).

Personality disorders in the impulsive spectrum also show striking comorbidities. This term refers to the presence of two different disorders in the same patient. Actually, it is arguable that borderline and antisocial personalities might be different versions of the same underlying pathology (Paris, 1977). Borderline patients are largely female and show a larger affective component in their symptoms, as reflected in the fact that their impulsive actions are directed against the self. In contrast, antisocial patients are largely male, and their impulsive actions are directed against others.

The other two disorders in the "B Cluster" of Axis II, histrionic and narcissistic personalities, describe less severe forms of impulsive pathology, with defining features that derive more from problems in interpersonal relationships (Morey & Ochoa, 1989). The differences between these categories also reflect gender. Histrionic patients tend to be female, and their "narcissistic" traits are often related to a concern with sexual attractiveness. In contrast, the diagnosis of narcissistic personality is more often applied to males, whose narcissism is more often associated with grandiose needs for success.

Patterns of comorbidity between Axis I and Axis II also provide good support for the concept of an impulsive spectrum. For example, there is a particularly large comorbidity between substance abuse and antisocial personality (DeJong et al., 1993), as well as a strong association between severe bulimia and borderline personality (Garner & Garfinkel, 1985; Steiger et al., 1991).

If impulsive personality traits are the driving force behind so many different disorders, what determines whether symptoms will consist of criminal activity, substance abuse, overeating, gambling, shoplifting, or slashing wrists and taking overdoses of pills?

There are two possible explanations. One is that each of these behaviors reflects an interaction between impulsivity and some other trait or set of traits. As suggested by Siever and Davis (1991), antisocial pathology corresponds to "pure" impulsivity, while borderline pathology lies at an interface between impulsive and affective dimensions.

The other explanation is more environmental, in that social learning can determine the form of symptoms. A large body of evidence supports this hypothesis. Unlike schizophrenia and mood disorders, which are common all over the world, impulsive disorders show dramatic differences in prevalence between societies, as well as changes in prevalence over time within the same society (Paris, 1996c). It has long been known that alcohol abuse is most common in countries that encourage it (such as France), and much less common in countries that discourage intake (such as Italy). Recent increases in the abuse of alcohol and other substances in North America (Robins & Regier, 1991) have also occurred in European countries, where this behavior was already epidemic, but not in most of Asia (Helzer & Canino, 1992), where serious substance abuse is associated with social shame.

Cross-cultural differences also support the principle that social learning influences personality development (Cross & Markus, 1999). This mechanism also affects the form of impulsive symptoms. Antisocial personality is much rarer in traditional societies such as Taiwan (Hwu, Yeh, & Change, 1989) than in North America or Europe. Borderline personality involves behaviors (such as impulsive overdoses and wrist-slashes) that are becoming increasingly common in highly developed countries, but are rare in traditional societies (Paris, 1994).

Changes in the prevalence of impulsive disorders over time point in the same direction. The prevalence of bulimia nervosa in North America has increased dramatically in recent decades (Garner & Garfinkel, 1985). (The author can remember that as a psychiatric resident 30 years ago, he hardly ever saw a case!) Bulimia now affects a wide spectrum of the female population, which is probably related to cultural factors favoring the pursuit of thinness in young women.

It is also well established that alcoholism and other forms of substance abuse are increasing in prevalence, especially in North America (Robins & Regier, 1991). Recent increases have also been documented for the antisocial category (Robins & Regier), and strong indirect evidence suggests a parallel increase in the prevalence of borderline personality (Paris, 1994).

In summary, although the temperamental factors in impulsivity are well established, it remains to be determined whether the underlying neurobiology is simple (i.e., related to a sluggish central serotonin system) or complex. Impulsivity influences a wide range of psychological symptoms, but the form that psychopathology ultimately takes is determined by other traits, as well as by social learning.

Affective Personality Dimensions

Some people respond with strong emotion to even the mildest stress, while others remain sanguine even in the face of severe stress. Each strategy may be adaptive under different conditions. However, unusually high emotional responsiveness is associated with an increased risk for depression, as well as for those personality disorders with a strong affective component (Siever & Davis, 1991).

Affective instability is not the same as depression. This construct describes a high level of emotional responsiveness to environmental events, as opposed to melancholic depression, in which a low mood is relatively impervious to context. Affective instability leads to very rapid mood swings, with shifts occurring within hours rather than within weeks. In fact, this phenomenon is much more characteristic of personality disorders than of mood disorders (Gunderson & Phillips, 1991).

Linehan's (1993) term for this trait is "emotional vulnerability." She describes a temperamental pattern in which individuals tend to become rapidly aroused and then take a long time to return to normal levels. Linehan hypothesizes that this trait is inherited and that it constitutes a significant risk factor for borderline personality disorder.

The construct of neuroticism is also closely related to the dimension of affective instability. Individuals with high scores on neuroticism scales are more easily aroused and upset by environmental challenges. This trait underlies many mental disorders, including somatization (Kirmayer, Robbins, & Paris, 1994) as well as anxiety and depression (Widiger et al., 1999). Neuroticism also underlies many personality disorders—the borderline category (Costa & Widiger, 1994), as well as disorders in the anxious cluster (Zweig-Frank & Paris, 1995).

Both affective instability (Jang et al., 1996) and neuroticism (Costa & Widiger, 1994) are heritable traits. Although the biological mechanisms associated with these dimensions are not well understood, research on temperament shows that negative emotionality begins early in childhood and remains consistent over time (Caspi & Roberts, 1999).

Affective instability, like impulsivity, takes many different symptomatic forms. One possible explanation depends on interactions with other trait dimensions. Siever and Davis (1991) propose that when impulsivity interacts with affective instability, the result is a mixed clinical picture, which clinicians term borderline personality.

It also seems likely that social learning influences the form taken by affective instability. The example of somatization is instructive. Researchers studying somatoform disorders (Kirmayer et al., 1994) have documented that patients who focus on physical symptoms are unusually vigilant, reacting with alarm to any potential perceived threat in their internal or external environment. But social learning can determine whether people somatize or experience psychic states such as anxiety or depression (Leff, 1988). Moreover, for those who do somatize, the precise form of psychopathology is drawn from a socially determined "symptom pool" (Shorter, 1994).

Symptoms can change over time within the same social setting. Nandi et al. (1968) had observed a high prevalence of conversion symptoms in a village in West Bengal, India. When the researchers returned 20 years later, the society had modernized and, as has been observed in other populations (Leff, 1988), conversion had become rare. Yet at the same time, suicide attempts among young women had become much more common. This finding suggests that affective instability, which had previously taken a somatic channel, was now presenting in a way that clinicians would diagnose as mood disorders and personality disorders.

Anxious Personality Dimensions

Anxious traits lower thresholds for emotional arousal under conditions of potential threat. This points to an overlap with affective instability and neuroticism, and it is therefore not surprising that mood and anxiety disorders are often comorbid.

Nonetheless, anxious traits are associated with unique clinical features. The phenomenology of anxiety often involves a behavioral component with clinging behaviors and a fear of strangers related to Bowlby (1973) as "anxious attachment." Thus, people with anxious traits have strong interpersonal needs that can lead to difficulty in establishing and maintaining intimate relationships.

Anxious attachment probably reflects abnormal temperament (Kagan, 1998). Individuals with this trait are unusually shy and sensitive from birth. This has been shown in a classical study of children with anxious temperament (Kagan, 1994). Inborn differences in the intensity of social anxiety can be operationally defined by a construct termed "behavioral inhibition." Infants who are behaviorally inhibited develop anxiety and withdrawal when presented with unfamiliar social stimuli. Kagan's research showed that this picture is associated with high levels of physiological arousal, leading him to hypothesize that behavioral inhibition is a heritable trait.

Kagan's research group has been following two cohorts, one from childhood to adolescence, and another from infancy onwards. The findings of these prospective studies showed a strong continuity in behavioral inhibition between ages 2 and 7, with three quarters of cases continuing to demonstrate disruptive social anxiety. By age 13, although most of the sample presented only as serious and plodding teenagers, one in eight had overt anxiety symptoms. Follow-up data into adulthood will determine whether these excessively shy children become vulnerable to anxiety disorders, to anxious cluster personality disorders, or to both. All these disorders are comorbid, and patients with one of these usually have a family history for one or more of the others (Paris, 1998a).

Parenting can influence the outcome of an anxious temperament. Although anxious traits are not necessarily, as previously believed, the *result* of parenting styles, family environment can either help or hinder children from overcoming them. Kagan (1994) found evidence in support of traditional clinical observations concerning parental overprotection. The more parents exposed their anxious children to social situations, the more likely it was that their social anxiety would improve. If, on the other hand, parents responded to their children's anxiety with anxious responses of their own, the problem sometimes became worse.

These observations support a theory proposed by Bowlby (1973): One reason why attachment styles are intergenerationally transmitted is that anxious parents make their children anxious. However, overprotective behavior is also described by patients with a variety of different psychological symptoms (Parker, 1983). Parents may be particularly likely to be overprotective when raising children with an anxious temperament, but children with these difficulties may respond to overprotection by becoming even more anxious.

The outcome of anxious temperament can also be influenced by interactions with other traits. For example, a combination of anxiety and affective instability can be associated with a predisposition to anxiety disorders and/or depression.

Finally, the social context shapes the symptomatic sequelae of anxious traits. In cultures where relationships are largely confined to the family and where submission to authority is normative, such characteristics may be less problematical. Even so, traits reaching extreme levels can cause psychological distress. For example, Japanese populations have a very high prevalence of social phobia (Kirmayer, 1985) and may be more likely to develop anxious cluster personality disorders (Paris, 1998a).

Cognitive Personality Dimensions

Traits associated with defective cognition reflect heritable neurobiological abnormalities. Patients with schizophrenia often have relatives with other, less severe conditions, lying in a "schizophrenic spectrum" (Gottesman, 1991). Similar observations apply to twin pairs: If an affected member has schizophrenia, the unaffected member will have schizoid personality traits. Patients with schizotypal personality disorder exhibit some of the same biological markers as schizophrenics, even though most never develop frank psychotic symptoms (Holzman, 1996). Schizoid and paranoid personality disorders lie in the same spectrum (Paris, 1996c). Lesser degrees of cognitive dysfunction can take nonpathological forms (Claridge, 1997).

Problems in cognitive function also emerge as part of the clinical picture of other mental disorders. For example, borderline personality disorder presents with a combination of all three dimensions: impulsivity, affective instability, and cognitive instability. In his follow-up research on children with irritable temperament, Maziade et al. (1990) found an increased risk for psychosis during adolescence. Children with attention deficit disorder, conduct disorder, and borderline pathology of childhood show neuropsychological and neurophysiological abnormalities that reflect deficits in "executive function" that resemble those seen in patients falling in the schizophrenic spectrum (Paris, Zelkowitz, Guzder, & Joseph, 1999).

Thus, the cognitive dimension of personality can produce phenomena ranging from eccentricity to personality disorder to psychosis. Interactions with other traits might explain why these temperamental variations can produce such widely varying effects. Those with impulsivity might develop borderline personality, while those with temperamental anxiety might develop schizoid personality.

Traits leading to social eccentricity also have different effects in different social contexts. Modern societies, with their high demands for performance in occupational and social settings, may be increasing the levels of psychopathology associated with cognitive dysfunction (Paris, 1996c).

☐ Conclusion

Personality is the construct that explains why different people, faced with the same stressors, develop completely different symptoms. Personality is strongly rooted in temperament—"as the twig is bent, so is the tree."

Each trait profile is associated with a liability for a specific set of mental disorders, so that personality strongly influences which set of symptoms can develop in any individual. Within that set, whether one develops one disorder or another will depend on a number of factors: intensity of the trait, interactions with other traits, cumulative liability derived from the weight of psychosocial stressors, social learning, gender, and social context.

PART

IV

CHILDHOOD AND TREATMENT

Part IV consists of two chapters examining how the understanding of childhood experiences affects clinical practice.

Chapter 11 reviews the evidence about what works in psychotherapy. The most important factors relate to the therapist's ability to establish an alliance, and the patient's ability to work effectively on present problems. In contrast, there is little evidence that interpretations linking the past, or the transference, with the present influence therapy outcome.

Chapter 12 concerns how best to customize therapy for patients. Psychodynamic formulations, based on the primacy of childhood, are inadequate, and need to be replaced by a broader theory that takes temperament into account. The clinical implications of this approach are best understood through differences on four trait dimensions.

CHAPTER

Childhood in Psychotherapy

This chapter will review evidence that casts doubt on whether exploring childhood experiences is essential in psychotherapy. If the theory of primacy is wrong, then understanding childhood may not be the royal road to recovery from psychological symptoms, and establishing links between early and later experiences need not be crucial to therapeutic success.

I will begin by examining what research shows about the main factors that make psychotherapy work. (Since this literature is so vast, I will generally rely on reviews in standard texts, which contain evaluations and meta-analyses of hundreds of studies.) I will then focus on the more specific issue of whether interpretations making links between past and present are a major factor in therapy. I will also review studies of transference interpretations, since these interventions are predicated on the idea that patients repeat childhood experiences in relationships with therapists. I will then show that the data supports an alternate view of the mechanisms behind the success of psychotherapy. The chapter concludes by considering why research has failed to affect the practice of dynamically oriented therapy.

☐ What Research Tells Us About Psychotherapy

Eight broad principles about psychotherapy emerge from the research literature:

1. Psychotherapy is an effective form of treatment.
2. No single method of therapy is more effective than any other.
3. Outcome depends more on patients than on therapists.
4. All types of treatment work through common mechanisms.
5. Therapeutic relationships are more important than specific techniques.
6. Successful therapy focuses on solving problems in the present.
7. The length of therapy does not determine outcome.
8. Long-term therapy is not specific for personality disorders.

☐ Research on Therapeutic Outcome

Is Psychotherapy Effective?

First, the good news! An enormous amount of research demonstrates that psychotherapy works and that it is broadly effective in a variety of patients. These conclusions have been most clearly supported by a method termed *meta-analysis*, which combines findings from many different studies. Twenty years ago, Smith et al. (1980), reviewing the results of a particularly large-scale meta-analysis, concluded: "Psychotherapy benefits people of all ages as reliably as school educates them, medicine cures them, or business turns a profit" (pp. 183–184). Research over the last two decades, whether from single studies or from further meta-analyses, consistently supports this conclusion (see reviews in Lambert & Bergin, 1994; Wampold, Mondin, Moody, Stich, & Benson, 1997).

Do Different Forms of Therapy Yield Different Results?

Although psychotherapy helps most patients, research provides scant support for the idea that *specific* methods make a large difference in outcome (Hubble, Duncan, & Miller, 1999). Comparative trials of contrasting methods on similar samples of patients, for example, behavior therapy versus psychodynamic therapy (Sloane, 1975) or cognitive-behavioral therapy versus interpersonal therapy (Elkin, Shea, Watkins, & Imber, 1989), show either no differences at all or only minor differences. With a few exceptions, therapeutic outcomes are about the same whether the method used is psychodynamic, cognitive, behavioral, or interpersonal. Nor is there any evidence that therapy is more likely to fail with any particular method.

Many years ago, Rosenzweig (1936) suggested that comparisons between different forms of therapy tend to elicit a Dodo bird verdict. (Rosenzweig was quoting the dodo's line from *Alice in Wonderland*: All have won and all shall have prizes.) Forty years later, reviewing a large series of comparative trials of different types of therapy, Luborsky, Singer, & Luborsky (1975) found that the evidence supported, even more strongly, the Dodo bird verdict. Twenty-five years further on, reviews of the literature (Ahn, 1997; Hubble et al., 1999; Wampold et al., 1997) have concluded that there is no reason to modify this judgment, with the possible exception of some behavioral techniques for anxiety disorders.

The absence of effects specific to any method is troubling for clinicians who have been trained in specific approaches that they believe to be uniquely effective. Yet the data are indisputable. But these results also lead to a further conclusion: Psychotherapy does not work the way we think it does.

Do Specific or Nonspecific Factors Determine Outcome?

If different forms of therapy yield similar results, then techniques are less crucial than we think. Moreover, common mechanisms must be involved in all therapeutic methods. These "nonspecific factors" (Strupp & Hadley, 1979) are the most important mechanisms behind the success of psychotherapy. They are only nonspecific because we have not yet learned how to specify them!

Research strongly supports a crucial role for common factors. Whatever the favorite theory of the therapist, patients tend to improve when offered a relationship that provides them with understanding and empathy (Hubble et al., 1999). This type of relationship helps patients to regain morale (Frank & Frank, 1991). At the same time, it is also the best grounding for the other primary task of therapy: problem-solving. It is therefore not surprising that therapists who establish the most positive relationships with patients obtain the best results.

Are Therapists or Patients More Important for Outcome?

Orlinsky, Grawe, & Parks (1994), in an extensive review of this issue, concluded that therapist factors are not as strong predictors of treatment outcome as patient factors. Levels of functioning prior to treatment are the best predictors of success (Lambert & Bergin, 1994).

These findings might be discouraging in the sense that patients who are already healthier do best in therapy. As Horwitz (1974) ironically described the situation, the rich get richer and the poor get poorer! On the other hand, these results can also be seen as encouraging, in the sense that the therapist's task is to catalyze self-healing (Hubble et al., 1999).

Even more galling to practitioners who have spent many years perfecting their craft is that there is little evidence that experience makes a large difference in outcome. In a famous study that was, ironically, specifically designed to *prove* the value of experience, Strupp and Hadley (1979) assigned patients randomly to highly experienced therapists or to sympathetic college professors. The results of treatment were no different in the two groups. The generalizability of this study was limited by the fact that the patients had only minor difficulties and that therapy was brief. Yet a lack of any large impact of experience has been confirmed in many other studies, including one (Propst, Paris, & Rosberger, 1994) in which I was a member of the research team.

These findings do not show that all therapists are interchangeable. The data does demonstrate that some therapists are much better than others (see Orlinsky et al., 1994). But the largest differences between practitioners seem to be the result of natural talent, rather than length of professional experience or training. It is probable, however, that training can amplify a therapist's inborn skills.

The Centrality of the Therapeutic Relationship

To understand the implications of these findings, we need a theory that makes common or nonspecific factors in therapy central. Frank and Frank (1991) suggest that patients come to therapy feeling hopeless and demoralized and that treatment works by restoring hope and morale. This model accords with observations reported by Howard, Kopta, Krause, & Orlinsky (1986), which demonstrate that the most rapid improvement occurs in the very early stages of therapy.

If the effects of nonspecific factors are crucial, we should try to maximize them. In fact, the common factors in therapy are no mystery. Most studies have shown that the most important elements are a well-defined contract with a strong alliance, an atmosphere of openness, the provision of validation for the patient's inner experience, and a focus on current life problems and relationships (Orlinsky et al., 1994).

The centrality of common factors contradicts the assumption that therapists should be primarily interested in understanding childhood experiences. Perhaps exploring the past gives therapist and patient something to do while waiting for nonspecific factors to take effect!

The Role of Problem-Solving

A strong alliance is usually a necessary, but not a sufficient, cause for recovery. There is more to treatment than the experience of being understood. Psychotherapy is also a learning process. Frank and Frank (1991) suggested that after initial increases in morale, patients become incrementally better over the succeeding months as they learn new behavioral skills. In other words, therapists need to teach patients new ways to solve old problems.

The question is how to go about this process of education. A vast area of investigation, termed process research, has examined the complex question of how patients learn new skills. Each type of treatment has its own theory about how this happens. Dynamic therapists modify defenses and interpret repetitions of the past. Cognitive therapists modify dysfunctional cognitions and suggest behavioral strategies. Yet few specific interventions have been shown to be consistently associated with outcome. As Orlinsky et al. (1994, p. 292) concluded from their review, focusing on current difficulties and feelings is what usually works best in any form of therapy. By and large, the more treatment focuses on problems in living, particularly difficulties in current interpersonal relationships, the more successful it is likely to be.

Does Length of Therapy Influence Outcome?

Almost all psychotherapy research has been conducted on short-term treatment. Hardly any systematic research exists on treatments lasting more than 1 year.

We know the limits of short-term therapy. At least 25% of patients fail to respond to interventions with durations up to 6 months (Howard et al., 1986). But this does not prove that longer treatments should be prescribed for these cases. In fact, therapy, whether brief or long, can entirely fail to help certain individuals, particularly those with personality disorders (Paris, 1998b).

We need empirical evidence that long-term therapy produces outcomes that are not possible using short-term interventions. Yet only a few studies have addressed this question. Brief courses of therapy are known to be highly effective for acute depression (Elkin et al., 1989), and a very wide range of symptoms can remit in the first few months of therapy (Howard et al., 1986).

Kopta, Howard, Lowry, & Bentler (1994) carried out a very rare study, examining treatments lasting for more than a year. Some patients with personality problems eventually improved with longer periods of treatment. The authors were sufficiently impressed with these findings to suggest that they might support changing policies of managed care, so as to allow payment for long-term therapy in selected cases. However, this conclusion was unjustified. Longer therapies have not been shown to be cost-effective. Even in Kopta et al.'s study, when psychotherapy lasted 1 or 2 years, over half of the patients with personality pathology failed to respond to treatment at all, and the level of improvement in the other half was far from dramatic.

Another question that needs to be addressed is whether mechanisms of change are different in long-term therapy. It is possible that nonspecific effects, however much they dominate the picture in brief interventions, are less important in long-term psychotherapy. Alternatively, it is possible that however gradual their effects, common factors remain important.

One approach to whether long-term therapy operates through unique mechanisms is simply to ask patients about their subjective experiences. In a classic study of long-term psychodynamic therapy by Strupp, Fox, and Lesser (1969), when patients and therapists were interviewed about what had helped in a series of successful treatments, they gave strikingly different answers. The patients spoke most frequently of the experience of being heard and understood, and emphasized the positive quality of their relationships with therapists. Yet much of the time, they could not remember the specific content of their sessions. The therapists, in contrast, spoke of specific interventions and interpretations that they believed had made a crucial difference in outcome. Understandably, they attributed improvement to the correct application of their own theoretical models. Judging from the research literature, it seems likely that on this issue, patients are right and therapists are wrong.

Is Long-Term Therapy Effective for Personality Disorders?

Although symptoms often resolve within a few months, long-term therapy is often viewed as indicated for a different purpose: as a treatment that goes beyond symptoms, aiming to change personality structure (Gunderson, 1985). Thus, open-ended therapy, with its broader goals, might not depend on a simple restoration of morale. Intuitively, support seems insufficient for treating patients with dysfunctional interpersonal relationships. Thus, one crucial test of whether long-term therapy works in a unique way would be to examine its efficacy for patients with personality disorders.

Very few studies have directly addressed this question (see review in Paris, 1998b). The most ambitious attempt to determine the value of psychodynamic therapy in this population was a study carried out in the 1960s at the Menninger Clinic. The findings showed that patients with higher initial ego strength (i.e., better levels of premorbid functioning) did best (Kernberg, Coyne, Appelbaum, Horwitz, & Voth, 1972). However, in spite of lengthy treatment, a large number of these patients ended up functioning quite marginally (R. Wallerstein, 1986).

Several of the findings in the Menninger study contradicted the predictions of the research team. Many patients with low ego strength did surprisingly well if they developed a strong working alliance, suggesting that they may have benefited most from supportive aspects of treatment (Horwitz, 1974). Unfortunately, the design of the study made it difficult to draw firm conclusions, since the treated sample lacked a comparison group receiving no treatment or another form of therapy.

The most encouraging findings on the treatment of patients with personality disorders have emerged from Linehan's (1993) dialectical behavior therapy (DBT) for borderline personality. This method is an eclectic adaptation of cognitive-behavioral therapy and consists of highly active interventions designed to teach patients how to control strong emotions, as well as to control impulses to act out. Linehan showed, in a comparative trial with supportive treatment, that DBT can be effective within a 1-year time span in controlling impulsivity, particularly in reducing self-destructive behaviors.

Given the rarity of differences in comparative studies of therapies, this was an impressive result. However, the long-range value of Linehan's approach remains unknown. The original group of treated patients, who received DBT over a decade ago, were followed up only a year later, so that we do not know whether treatment was effective in the long term. Moreover, although Linehan has recommended a longer course of therapy than the modules provided in her research, it is not known whether continuing treatment past the 12 months provided in her original study would actually have accomplished more.

In spite of these limitations, we can applaud the success of DBT in a population of patients noted for being refractory to almost every form of treatment. How were these results obtained? One likely explanation is that Linehan developed a method that capitalizes on nonspecific factors. Her approach focuses constantly on validation of the patient's experience and also uses innovative techniques to get patients to focus on solving current life problems. Another point of interest is the theoretical background of the method, which is based on a predisposition-stress model. DBT specifically aims to modify the effects of an abnormal temperament.

Psychotherapy Research: A Summary

To summarize the implications of all the empirical studies reviewed above: *Psychotherapy works because therapists listen and patients learn.* The most effective factors in psychotherapy derive from a strong therapeutic alliance

and from a problem-solving approach. Evidently, the conduct of psychotherapy is more commonsensical and less complicated than it seems. Thus,
a researcher's advice to a practitioner might parallel Spock's (1946) famous advice to mothers: You know more than you think you know.

☐ Research on the Exploration of Childhood Experience in Therapy

The influence of the psychoanalytic movement led generations of therapists to believe that the key to successful therapy involves the accurate
reconstruction of childhood experiences. *Interpretation* is a term describing this process: explaining the present through events in the past, and
demonstrating these connections to patients. Freud (1900/1953),
semijocularly quoting scripture, proclaimed that psychoanalysis depends
on the principle that the truth shall make you free. The entire apparatus
of psychoanalytic therapy, free association, dream interpretation, analysis of resistance, and removal of repression, was designed to parallel the
methods of archaeology, digging up buried evidence of a long lost past.

Different versions of psychodynamic theory lead to different approaches
to the exploration of the past. For example, some therapists (e.g., Herman,
1992) focus on exploring memories of childhood trauma. Others (Bowlby,
1973; Kohut, 1970) tend to explore memories of emotional neglect, reconstructing family climates that failed to meet basic needs.

No matter what the focus, we need to know whether the exploration
of childhood actually makes a difference in results. In an era of evidence-
based practice, it is insufficient to justify theories through clinical experience or to convince one's colleagues through charisma and rhetoric. More
and more, practitioners demand to see evidence in support of theory. Is
there solid empirical data to demonstrate whether accurate interpretations actually lead to more successful therapy?

This question can be answered succinctly. *There is no such data.* This is
not for lack of trying! Several researchers have attempted to document a
relationship between interpretations and outcome. The expected conclusions have simply not emerged.

It could be argued, of course, that research has, thus far, not been sophisticated enough to provide an adequate and fair test for psychodynamic theory. Yet in spite of the attempts of many therapist-researchers
(e.g, Luborsky & Crits-Cristoph, 1990; Westen, 1998) to support psychoanalytic principles with evidence, the results remain inconclusive. Some
say that psychodynamic therapy has not yet had its day in court. But in my
view, the burden of proof lies with those who believe in this model, use it in
their practice, and continue to teach it to new generations of students.

Let us examine what evidence we have about the value of interpretations in therapy. Although earlier studies of process were too methodologically flawed to draw any conclusions, psychotherapy research has become increasingly sophisticated. Although no studies have directly measured the effectiveness of exploring childhood experiences in therapy, the issue has been addressed indirectly.

Luborsky and Crits-Christoph (1990) conducted the most carefully designed studies testing the value of psychodynamic methods. Their research showed that patients are more likely to improve when therapists consistently follow the themes of what patients say in a session. Raters were trained to assess these themes using a measure termed the Core Conflict Relationship Schema (CCRT).

Luborsky and Crits-Christoph's (1990) research has been widely quoted. But these observations do not prove that interpretations work. One might equally conclude that the CCRT measures nonspecific factors. Simply put, therapists do better when they listen accurately to what patients say.

Psychodynamically trained therapists often have the subjective impression that their interpretations are having significant impact. This occurs when patients accept interpretations, even expanding on the therapist's comments, providing what Langs (1973) has called "clinical confirmation." But as Frank and Frank (1991) point out, the reason why so many different theoretical models tend to help patients is that each of them provides *some* explanation of distress. When patients agree with a therapist's interpretation, that in itself proves little. A large body of research (see Dawes, 1994) suggests that patients tend to adjust what they say to conform to the theoretical views of their therapists. In this respect, free associations are far from free.

Another line of research that could potentially support the value of exploring childhood experience concerns transference interpretations. The principle here is to teach patients how past experiences determine the present by observing this process in the crucible of an intense and dependent relationship with the therapist. Problems in this relationship provide a "here and now" experience through which relearning can take place. In theory, the ideal interpretation connects present problems to childhood experience and/or transference phenomena that are unconscious repetitions of these experiences, creating a "triangle of insight" (Malan, 1979).

Piper, Joyce, Azim, & McCullum (1991) examined whether patients became more cooperative after transference interventions, using audiotaped transcripts of sessions. Patients were divided into two groups, those with better or worse interpersonal relationships prior to treatment. The first group did seem to benefit from interpreting transference. However, the differences in outcome were not very striking, and it is difficult to be sure whether these specific interventions were the factors that led to improvement. Actually, these results tend to confirm the findings of the Menninger study, in that patients who are well-functioning do best in dynamic therapy.

However, most patients practitioners see patients with serious problems in their interpersonal relationships. In the Piper et al. study, for this second group, interpretations were counter-productive and disorganizing. The higher the frequency of comments about the therapeutic relationship, the poorer was the outcome. Piper et al. suggested that one possible explanation is that therapists may sometimes make interpretations out of desperation, particularly when there are weaknesses or ruptures in the therapeutic alliance.

Another study by Piper, Joyce, McCallum, and Azim (1998) sheds further light on the dangers of relying too much on interpretation in psychotherapy. The research examined the prediction of therapeutic dropouts in two forms of time-limited therapy. The results showed that more patients leave treatment when therapists apply more transference interpretations. One possibility is that patients who come for psychotherapy are already suffering from emotional dysregulation, so that comments about transference only increase their distress, driving them out of therapy before they have the chance to contain their emotions. Chapter 12 will introduce the idea that discussing difficult emotions can be particularly problematic for patients with personality disorders, particularly those with underlying traits of affective lability.

Other investigations of transference have yielded similar results. Horowitz, Marmar, Weiss, DeWitt, & Rosenbaum (1984) found no relationship between the use of transference interpretations and outcome in short-term therapy. One study that did report positive findings (McCullough et al., 1991) examined only 16 patients, with results that could have been attributable to nonspecific factors.

It is possible that while transference interpretations can be problematical in short-term therapy, they could be more useful in long-term therapy and are best reserved for that setting. However, we have no data to support using them in long-term treatment either. Again, the burden of proof lies with those who insist that using transference is crucial for outcome.

In summary, we have no evidence that transference interpretations are, as Freud described them, pure gold, or even that they are all that useful. The method seems helpful for a few, neutral for most, and negative for others. Moreover, transference can be an easy way out of trouble. Telling patients who are frustrated with the way a session is going that they are really angry at someone else in their past is unempathic. Overuse of this type of comment may account for the high drop-out rate for psychodynamic treatment in neurotic patients (Piper et al., 1998), as well as even higher rates in patients with personality disorders (Gunderson et al., 1989).

It is not even clear that childhood experiences are the main explanation for the phenomena called transference. Patients do tend to react in the same way to therapists as to other important people in their lives. But personality traits, by their very definition, describe the fact that people have similar reactions in similar contexts. Are these patterns transferred from early relationships with parents or are they only another manifestation of temperament?

In conclusion, interpretations linking the present to the past, or to the transference, are of unproven value in psychotherapy. It remains possible that future research findings could change this judgment. As the witticism goes, absence of evidence is not evidence of absence. But grandiose claims about the value of interpretative interventions, often associated with a devaluation of nonspecific factors, are not supported by empirical evidence. Until data appears to the contrary, the psychotherapy research literature only provides further support for the conclusion that the primacy of childhood is a myth.

☐ Why Primacy Remains Popular Among Psychotherapists

Psychotherapy works, but the understanding of childhood is not the main mechanism behind its success. After a century of practice, research has failed to confirm Freud's ideas about the mechanisms determining recovery in psychological treatment.

Some therapists believe that these issues are too difficult to operationalize in systematic empirical designs. But I would argue that psychological services need to be as evidence-based as drug therapy. Practice must become rooted in data drawn from clinical trials. Moreover, Freud (1916/1963) had explicitly stated that the value of his method could be demonstrated by its therapeutic effects on patients. By this very standard, psychoanalysis has failed badly. To quote Kandel (1999):

> The decline in the use of psychoanalytic therapy is most attributable to causes outside psychoanalysis: the proliferation of different forms of short-term psychotherapy . . . the emergence of pharmacotherapy, and the economic impact of managed care. But one important cause derives from psychoanalysis itself. One full century after its founding, psychoanalysis still has not made the required effort to obtain objective evidence to convince an increasingly sceptical medical profession that it is a more effective mode of therapy than placebo. (p. 521)

Why then does the psychoanalytic model, rooted in the theory of primacy, retain such a hold on clinicians? I will suggest three possible explanations: belief in narrative, toleration of cognitive dissonance, and the need to account for failure.

The Belief in Narrative

While science encourages doubt, clinical practice requires belief. Theories impose order on the chaos of the therapeutic encounter. Whether or not they are true, explanations that can make sense of problems will always be appealing.

Psychotherapy is not designed to determine historical truth (Spence, 1983). Working together on problems only requires that patients and therapists share the same beliefs. Those who provide the service and those who receive it sort themselves out in accordance with these commonalities.

Clinicians who believe that psychological problems originate in childhood experiences tend to treat patients who already subscribe to the same ideas. Those who share a belief system may be considered good patients and given approving labels such as "psychological-minded," or insightful. Other patients are unwilling to hold their families to blame for their troubles and may not accept the primacy of childhood. Today, many patients prefer to believe that their difficulties are accounted for by chemical imbalances. Those who choose relatively concrete explanations for their troubles may be labelled alexithymic (Sifneos, 1996). Or, in the parlance of 12-step programs, they are in denial. Such individuals do not end up in dynamic therapy and will seek out other forms of treatment.

The result of this sorting process is the emergence of shared historical narratives that support common beliefs. Patients who accept dynamic psychotherapy and stay in this form of treatment provide active and continuous confirmation for the theories held by their therapists. Since the primary task of therapy involves empathic listening, it is difficult to remain sceptical for long. For this reason alone, clinicians tend to believe in the veracity of narratives.

Sometimes practitioners find it difficult to believe that so many different people can tell the same story, seemingly without significant prompting. They are impressed by the narratives that emerge in therapy and come to regard them as valid reflections of historical truth. In this way, psychotherapy has an intrinsic tendency to validate its own theories. Therapy shapes anecdotes and memories into a dramatic story. The narratives that emerge become plausible accounts for the trajectory of a patient's life.

In addition, therapists do not always recognize how strongly what people say in therapy is influenced by their culture. Many of those who seek therapy are immersed in what can be called *the culture of primacy*. For those who live within this culture, behavior always has a historical explanation. Thus, whether someone is a drug addict, a criminal, or has committed suicide, one must search for causes that lie in the quality of their upbringing. Patients who believe in these ideas are most likely to be considered good therapy candidates.

With a little practice, it is often possible to make striking connections between the present and the past. The problem is that even when these links are plausible, they are just as likely to be wrong as to be right. Yet clinicians will resist discarding methods in which they have been trained. Many therapists are *emotionally* committed to the culture of primacy. This is particularly so for those who have themselves undergone psychoanalysis. To give up such deeply rooted beliefs is almost equivalent to losing one's personal identity.

A rejection of childhood primacy should not in any way lead us to ignore personal histories. Understanding the past will always play an important role in psychotherapy. Historical contexts provide frames for identifying patterns of behavior and for determining which strategies for change are most likely to be effective (Paris, 1998b). Cognitive-behavioral therapists (Beck & Freeman, 1990; Linehan, 1993) are also interested in these issues.

Moreover, responsiveness to personal histories is experienced by patients as empathic. This is the factor that patients report to be most associated with a good outcome (Strupp, Fox, & Lesser, 1969), and empathy also makes it easier for patients to change their behavior. When people feel understood, they are more prepared to listen to good advice, however carefully couched that advice is in therapeutic neutrality.

A distinction needs to be made, however, between understanding life histories and seeing early experiences as the main determinant of current problems. At least for some people, focusing too much on the past has its dangers. Most experienced therapists have had patients who are virtuosos in producing past–present links yet are still unable to change. Many of these individuals also fail to make serious commitments in their lives. When the present is empty, the past rushes in to fill the vacuum.

Toleration for Cognitive Dissonance

If the theory of primacy is wrong, then it should not really be surprising that therapies based on this model are no more effective than their competitors. Yet even if psychotherapy does not work through interpretations, its best practitioners depend on them less than one might expect. As clinicians mature, they learn to do what works. They develop their craft and practice in a way that brings the best results. Without changing theoretical orientation, most therapists eventually spend less time exploring the past.

The best therapists are not usually theoreticians. They have a high tolerance for cognitive dissonance (i.e., the contradiction between belief and observation). Clinicians who have the most talent benefit from experience. With time, they understand patients more rapidly. This helps them to work with troubled people and to help them change. Over time, these therapists learn to build a strong alliance and to make effective use of nonspecific factors. Consistently successful practice draws more and more on common factors, the nonspecific elements described by the literature as most associated with positive outcomes.

Thus, no matter what theory one uses, therapists will spend most of their time focusing on current problems. Psychodynamic therapy has a model for this process, termed "working-through." This construct has often been invoked to explain why interpretations do not necessarily lead to short-term behavioral change (Wachtel, 1994). Much of the work of therapy consists of unlearning maladaptive behaviors and learning more adaptive ones. Working-through has also been used to explain why long-term psychotherapy has to be so long. However much one understands one's psyche, dysfunctional patterns of behavior developed over long periods of time have to be unlearned, followed by relearning new and more adaptive patterns. These mechanisms parallel, albeit in a less systematic way, the principles of behavior therapy.

Every therapist devotes a great deal of time to identifying maladaptive behaviors. Psychodynamic clinicians are saying to their patients, over and over again—you react to people as if they were your parents, and that's why you can't see how you might deal with them differently. Or, as Ronald Reagan famously said to Jimmy Carter in the 1980 Presidential debate, "There you go again!" Psychodynamic therapists can reduce their cognitive dissonance by interpreting these patterns as repetitions of childhood experiences. Yet even when patients respond positively to such interventions, they may be helped more by the confrontation than by the insight.

Accounting for Failure

Science aims to be an *open* system, in which the real test of an idea comes when it fails to explain observations. In the view of one philosopher (Popper, 1968), the basic criterion for a scientific enterprise is the rejection of hypotheses when data fails to support them. Disciplines that rely on clinical inference fail to meet this standard. Although psychoanalysis has always claimed to be a science, it has not generated the empirical research needed to test its hypotheses.

In contrast, *closed* systems are characterized by fixed beliefs and are designed to accommodate failure. Religious cults that incorrectly announce the end of the world reduce cognitive dissonance simply by rescheduling the event. Similar considerations apply to the world-embracing but failed theory of "scientific socialism."

Failure challenges the belief systems of psychotherapists. Ideally, our inability to obtain the results we hoped for should stimulate us to question and revise basic assumptions. But there are always ways to explain away unpleasant phenomena. In classical psychoanalysis, when patients refused to agree with a therapist's interpretation, this did not prove that the intervention was wrong. Failure was often seen as reflecting bad timing or resistance. The same intervention might still hit the mark if introduced at a later stage. (This might be particularly likely to happen if the patient aims to please, and learns what the therapist wants.)

Similarly, when patients failed to get better, psychoanalysts rarely concluded that their method was wrong. Lack of response only proved the strength of defenses, or even of a "negative therapeutic reaction" in which the patient aims to defeat the therapist. In summary, failure was accounted for not by mistaken theories and inappropriate interventions, but by technical errors in the application of an essentially correct model.

These rationalizations are still used by therapists to maintain the belief that personal narrative is a key that can unlock psychopathology. Once one assumes that patients get better only when the therapist offers the right interpretation, a failure to improve may only reflect the therapist's inability to make the right intervention. To find out which interpretation actually is right, a clinician must develop ever more profound insight into the nature of childhood experience.

Even worse, if results are not satisfactory, it is not the method that is at fault but the person applying the method. Psychodynamically oriented therapists have been trained to wonder what is wrong with *them* if their patients are not doing well. Why have they failed to find out enough about the patient's past? Were they insufficiently trained? Do they need to learn a different theoretical model? Should they attend more conferences, read more books, or get supervision from a senior therapist? Or are their own personal reactions to patients getting in the way? In other words, have they failed to understand their countertransference? If not, should they seek personal therapy for themselves? All these questions undermine self-confidence without producing better results.

Finally, the most common explanation of the failure of patients to progress in psychotherapy is that change takes time. This can be a good principle, but it can also be used as an excuse. No matter how long treatment has already lasted, its duration can be deemed insufficient. The result is interminable therapy.

Existing data does not support the idea that therapeutic impasses are usually or necessarily the fault of therapists. Instead, serious difficulties are most often due to patient factors. Those with low levels of functioning are not particularly suitable for dynamic therapy and should usually not be offered this approach.

If clinicians were more familiar with the research literature, they would stop worrying about whether they have sufficiently explored childhood experiences and get on with their job. When treatment does not work, they would understand the intrinsic limits of what any form of psychotherapy can do for certain patients. It is hard enough to stop patients from blaming themselves for every failure. Therapists should be trained to avoid the same problem.

☐ Conclusion

The practice of psychotherapy demands skill in understanding inner experiences and in teaching people new ways of solving old problems. But there is little evidence that success depends on explaining the present by the past. Instead, patients get better when offered a new environment in which they can grow and heal. In this sense, therapy can be thought of as a practical application of resilience.

The discipline of psychotherapy has suffered from its failure to base its practice on scientific empiricism. As a result, there has been no basis on which to judge the value of different methods. Moreover, therapy has splintered into innumerable "schools," each claiming to have the most effective approach. Such phenomena are associated with immature science or with nonscience (Kuhn, 1970).

Therapists should not be prescribing the same form of treatment for patients with widely varying problems. Nor should different clinicians offer patients radically different forms of treatment for the same problem. Instead, we should aim to develop a universal psychotherapy, which can then be adapted to fit the needs of each individual patient.

12

Temperament and Psychotherapy

Psychotherapy is not a suit than can be tailored to fit all sizes. Instead, treatments need to be *customized*. Again, different folks need different strokes. In the past, therapists were trained to make psychodynamic formulations, and this method became the standard way to customize treatment. This chapter will critique this approach and will argue that an understanding of individual differences in temperament provide a better way.

☐ Psychodynamic Formulations

Therapists have always recognized the need to provide treatment that fits the specific needs of consumers. In the past, they were trained to use a method termed *psychodynamic formulation*. This approach is deeply rooted in the theory of primacy. Formulations are a practical exercise that account for adult symptoms by childhood experiences, describing parallels between past events and present conflicts. As an example of the method, let us consider a prototypical case, based on a common clinical presentation.

> A 28-year old woman appears in the clinic with a mixture of depressive and anxious symptoms. She is tearful, has trouble sleeping, and wakes up in the morning feeling anxious and light-headed, accompanied by cardiac palpitations. These difficulties began a month previously when her boyfriend of 2 years suddenly ended their relationship.
>
> When the history is taken, it emerges that the patient was an only child who was raised by a single mother. Her father had abandoned the family

when she was an infant and never returned to visit her. Although her mother had initially been able to cope after the separation, she had been treated for depression when the patient was an adolescent. The patient, who describes herself as having been a shy child, has been very devoted to her mother and is still living at home. She has only one close female friend. The relationship with the boyfriend was her first. She had no idea that there were any problems prior to its dissolution.

What might a classical psychodynamic formulation of this case look like? Most likely, it would focus on the impact of the patient's childhood experiences on her present difficulties. The most obvious issue is loss. To have been abandoned by a father, particularly at an age when one is particularly vulnerable, could have produced complex and troubling emotional responses. A formulation would therefore suggest that this early loss has been reevoked by the recent loss of the boyfriend. Inevitably, the patient would have sought a substitute father in any man she loved. Then, as in her childhood, she was abandoned by a man in circumstances beyond her control.

All these conclusions are at least plausible. As discussed in Chapter 3, stressors in the present tend to be more difficult for those who have suffered past traumas. But this type of formulation provides only a partial explanation of the clinical picture. It fails to answer two crucial questions: (a) Are the factors invoked either necessary or sufficient to cause illness in the patient? (b) Does the formulation explain why the illness took this particular symptomatic form?

First, let us examine the precipitating circumstances of the patient's symptoms. Many are upset when abandoned by a longstanding lover, yet few come to clinical attention. Even among those who have lost a father, distress is more common than disorder. Most people fail to develop major symptomatology after a loss and eventually get over the experience. Sometimes people even feel better at the end of a love affair!

Second, there is little research evidence that people who are abandoned by their fathers in childhood are statistically more likely to develop psychological symptoms as adults. Significant risks associated with early losses depend on complex and cascading pathways, involving many intervening variables.

Third, we cannot artificially isolate one influence from all others. In addition to the assumption that the lost lover represented the abandoning father, the patient grew up with a mother who had to cope on her own, who eventually became depressed, and who was emotionally unavailable. Of course, a good formulation should take this into account. But how do we know that other factors did not play an equally important role? Life trajectories are enormously complex, and one could easily multiply any list of hypotheses. (Readers of the psychodynamic literature will recognize how often writers do just that!) How can we reasonably choose among all these possibilities?

Fourth, the formulation fails to take the patient's temperament and personality into consideration. To what extent did her shyness and avoidance make her vulnerable to depression? Might she have reacted differently if she had a different trait profile? Would, for example, a woman with an impulsive character have developed fewer neurotic symptoms, but more "acting out" following a similar loss?

Fifth, the formulation fails to consider the role of biological predispositions to mental disorder. Psychodynamics do not explain why patients develop different symptoms. To what extent is the specificity of the clinical picture determined by an inherited vulnerability to mood and/or anxiety disorders? We know that mental illnesses are rooted in diatheses, but we do not routinely include this in formulations.

Sixth, the formulation fails to consider the social context in which the patient has been living. In dealing with losses, the strength of social networks can make the crucial difference between normal grief and clinical depression.

Thus, this classical formulation is remarkably inadequate. What are its implications for treatment? Therapy would probably make links between past and present, so as to demonstrate to the patient how her reaction to the loss of the boyfriend represents a repetition in her mind of an earlier abandonment. If the patient has trouble leaving a short-term treatment or is anxious about her attachment in long-term treatment, such reactions will be interpreted as transference.

It is entirely possible that the patient will improve as a result of this approach. After all, many people who seek therapy after a loss tend to get better. But the mechanism of improvement need not be a specific response to interpretations. It is more likely that success depends on an amalgam of naturalistic healing, the support of a safe relationship with a therapist, and the use of the alliance to develop better skills in establishing and managing intimate relationships.

In summary, formulations that explain the present through the past are not entirely wrong; they are only half-truths. Pathways to pathology are much more complex than these narratives suggest. Moreover, formulations that fail to take individual differences into account can be simplistic and misleading.

The example discussed above is a general prototype, although it describes a scenario that most therapists will recognize from their practice. Now let us now consider two real cases, both taken from the psychotherapy literature.

The first example involves a patient with borderline personality. This case was described in a book by a clinician-researcher with a strong psychodynamic orientation, who has developed an interpersonal theory of personality disorders (L. Benjamin, 1993).

> A woman in her 30s made cuts on her arms and abdomen whenever she was stressed. . . . She would also binge until her stomach hurt intensely. . . . She suffered from dissociative episodes and could not remember what happened for extended periods of time. She had many hospitalizations, usually for suicidality precipitated by her therapist's vacations. . . .
>
> Her mother was perfectionistic and competent, and maintained excellent order in the house. The patient's mother expected the patient to perform perfectly, and then claimed the daughter's successes for her own. The patient was angry with her mother and felt close to her father, who was alcoholic. During adolescence, she had assumed responsibility for trying to control his drinking, but he paid her no attention because she was not a boy. Alone after school, she suffered painful sexual abuse and beatings from an older brother on a daily basis. When she attempted to get help from her mother, she was told that she probably did something to start it.
>
> The patient felt she had no identity. Although she had significant educational and professional accomplishments, they counted for nothing because her mother expected them anyway. Her father acknowledged nothing from a female. She felt the only way she could be unique was to be sick; this denied her mother's mandate to be perfect. (Benjamin, 1993, p. 128)

This type of formulation is by no means unusual in the literature. Yet it suffers from several serious problems. The evidence does suggest that the patient came from a dysfunctional family. However, we need to ask how these specific adversities, distressing as they probably were, explain the development of a condition as serious as borderline personality disorder. Is there a valid cause and effect relationship between the patient's childhood and her adult symptoms? For example, we learn that the patient's mother was compulsive and unloving. Yet many such mothers produce compulsive children remarkably like themselves. Without an impulsive temperament, this patient would probably not have developed along these pathways.

Later, Benjamin (1993, p. 129) claims that the patient is revenging herself on her mother by being sick. This type of statement is found fairly frequently in psychodynamic writings. The concept is that patients become sick because their sickness serves a purpose. Alternatively, patients are the victims of their parents' projections or are carriers of a family member's sickness. One wonders whether people who suffer from a mental disorder have any right at all to be ill!

The formulation also puts a great deal of emphasis on maternal neglect. We also learn that the father rejected the patient. Although this information is based entirely on self-report, let us assume, for argument's sake, that the perceptions are historically accurate. We would still need to know *why* she was not loved and why her brother was preferred to her. Could it be, for example, that she had a difficult temperament and that her parents could not accommodate it? This type of vulnerability could well have interfered with goodness of fit.

Paternal alcoholism is a well-known risk factor for many forms of pathology. However, most people who grow up in this type of family environment do not develop personality disorders—or any disorder at all. On the other hand, shared impulsive traits between father and daughter might well be relevant to the development of borderline personality.

Sexual abuse from a sibling is known to be a risk for pathological sequelae. But, as shown in Chapter 3, such experiences have only a statistical relationship to psychopathology in adulthood. Most people with such a history are distressed, but few are seriously disordered. Abuse, by itself, does not account for the depth of pathology described in this patient.

In summary, Benjamin (1993) has described a series of early experiences, each of which has a plausible relationship to borderline pathology. But none of the risk factors presented, by themselves, are sufficient to explain the wide range of symptoms seen in the patient. Borderline personality disorder (which happens to be my main research interest) is best described from a "multidimensional" approach, integrating biological, psychological, and social factors (Paris, 1994). A more general lesson is that without considering temperament, neither the extent nor the particular form taken by psychopathology can be explained. Every aspect of this formulation would have benefited from a consideration of the specific interaction of trauma and neglect with impulsive temperament.

Let us now consider a second case drawn from the clinical literature. This one involves the treatment of a child, as described in an article published in a leading psychoanalytic journal (Gilmore, 1995).

Gilmore treated a 6-year-old girl in psychoanalysis for an intense and insistent belief that she wanted to and could become a boy. The patient was having many conflicts with her adoptive mother, played in an aggressive way, and was only interested in boy toys and male sports.

The following excerpt gives the flavour of the author's approach to formulation:

> In the case presented here, the early traumatic loss of the foster mother heightened my patient's intolerance of separations, her sensitivity to her mother's approval, and her fears of her instinctual life, which she apparently experienced as directly threatening to her mother. In an atmosphere coloured by the mother's sense of failure as a woman, her envious resentment of females with childbearing capacity, and her father's inability to rejoice in the femininity of his wife and daughter, these predilections promoted her rejection of her gender role and her wish to disavow her gender identity. Her wish to be a boy and to have a penis were organizing fantasies that achieved a compromise among conflicting elements in her early experience. (Gilmore, 1995, p. 57)

This example does not illustrate theories about the impact of childhood on adulthood, but it certainly exemplifies primacy. The author applies the principle that problems in later childhood must derive from experiences even earlier in life, beginning in infancy.

Several problems are notable in the formulation. First, it makes no attempt to consider the role of temperament. This issue might be highly relevant in an adoptee, although we have no information about the biological parents. Second, the traumatic experiences most important in the child's life are assumed to occur very early. The author focuses on the supposed trauma of being rejected by a biological mother, passed on to a foster mother, and then to an adoptive parent. Yet, there is no research evidence that adoption, by itself, should be thought of as a risk factor for problems, either in childhood or later in development (M. A. Singer et al., 1998).

Moreover, Gilmore's formulation proposes that the child's femininity presented a threat to the adoptive mother, who is assumed to feel inadequate because of her infertility. (It is not stated whether the mother agreed with this idea!) Thus, the child's problems are seen as a result of aberrant parental behavior: the failure of both parents to respond to her properly, as well as the effects of the parents' own intrapsychic problems. Supposition is piled on supposition, and a high level of metapsychological speculation is imposed on the clinical material.

The article goes on to describe a successful psychoanalysis of 7 years' duration, ending when the child reaches puberty at age 13. The author assumes that the therapist's psychodynamic understanding and capacity to interpret underlying conflicts were the key factors in improvement. The possibility that, like many other girls, the patient simply outgrew her tomboy stage, or that doing so was made somewhat easier by the presence of a sympathetic female therapist, is never considered.

The formulations in both these published cases range from the plausible to the fantastic. In neither case were the theoretical models rooted in evidence. What is particularly instructive is how primacy is applied—the therapists simply assumed that specific combinations of life events must be associated with each and every symptom constellation. Such formulations would be more acceptable if they were presented more tentatively. They would also come closer to accounting for psychological symptoms if they were expanded to take other psychosocial adversities, as well as temperamental factors, into account.

☐ Temperament and Formulation

If psychodynamic formulations do not provide a Michelin guide to therapy, what *can* we use to guide clinical interventions? In this section, I will suggest an alternate type of formulation that addresses individual differences in temperament. This book has emphasized that interactions between personality and adversity are essential to understanding the etiology of mental disorders. This chapter will propose ways in which these interactions can also serve as the basis of treatment planning.

Therapists apply models they believe in. But the failure to take temperament and personality into consideration may be the cause of some of the common frustrations they face. Patients, with what may seem like stubbornness, refuse to make use of our helpful interventions. Many of these difficulties can be accounted for by personality and temperament. Patients who are unusually irritable or impulsive may not readily be able to follow certain types of structures and will either complain about therapy or drop out early. Patients who are unusually shy or compulsive may find it easier to talk to a sympathetic therapist than to undertake the actions needed to change their lives.

The idea that the techniques of psychotherapy can be adapted to different temperamental types is not new. Many years ago, Burks and Rubinstein (1979) suggested applying the temperamental theory of Chess and Thomas (1984) to clinical situations. They described ways to help patients understand their temperament and to make behavioral changes consistent with these profiles. The authors administered temperamental questionnaires at the beginning of treatment, shared the results with patients, and taught them to approach their problems in the light of this information. Burks and Rubinstein also suggested strategies to provide "goodness of fit" in therapy for patients who have unusually difficult temperaments.

Researchers and clinicians interested in personality disorders have also suggested methods designed to modify the behavioral consequences of temperament. Beck and Freeman (1990) described how to individualize cognitive-behavioral therapy for each category of personality disorder listed on Axis II of DSM. Similarly, Stone (1993), an eclectic psychoanalyst with an interest in constitution, described methods of temperamental modification for patients with personality disorders. Linehan (1993), a cognitive-behavioral therapist, hypothesized that an abnormal temperament is a necessary cause of borderline personality disorder. She proposed that the unusual emotional vulnerability of these patients requires therapists to develop strategies to teach them better internal control for emotional reactions to life events.

Psychotherapists may be aware of the large genetic component in personality but are not sure how to apply this knowledge in practice. One common error is the assumption that psychotherapy is primarily useful for problems of environmental origin, while genetic problems have to be treated with drugs. This is far from the case! A large body of research supports the effectiveness of psychosocial and psychoeducational interventions, even in disorders as genetically determined as schizophrenia (Hogarty, Anderson, Reiss, & Kornblith, 1991). The converse is also true, since drugs help many patients with milder, reactive forms of depression that are environmentally driven.

An insightful paper (Efran et al., 1998) by three family therapists attempted to come to grips with the implications of behavioral genetics for clinical practice. They described an intellectual odyssey that closely mirrors my own (see the Introduction to this book). In spite of having been trained in radical environmentalism during the 1960s, the authors gradually came to appreciate the primacy of genetics in human development. They summarize their conclusions as follows:

> If even half of it is confirmed, the therapy field is in for a major paradigm shift that will rewrite our job descriptions. At a minimum, the new genetic discoveries will soon require therapists to distinguish what their clients can change from what they can't, recognize the limits of adaptability, and concentrate their efforts where they will do the most good. However, news of this impending paradigm shift does not yet seem to have registered on most therapists' radar screens. (p. 38)

Efran and colleagues (1998) go on to suggest how psychotherapists can take genetic research into account. First and foremost, they need to stop blaming parents for their children's problems. Second, therapists working with parents should help them to provide children with the right environment for their temperament: consistent structure and limits for the impulsive child and gradual social exposure for the anxious child. Third, therapists working with adults need to help them to find niches in adult life that are suitable for their temperament.

In summary, an ideal clinical formulation should assess temperament and then place the impact of life events, in both childhood and adulthood, in that context. In a book on the treatment of personality disorders (Paris, 1998b), I argued that each personality type needs a different therapeutic method and that the purpose of treatment is to teach patients better ways of making trait profiles work for them (and not against them). But *every* patient has a unique personality profile. In this chapter, I will suggest that similar principles apply to the broader range of patients seen in clinical practice.

The personality schema described in Chapter 10 (the four personality dimensions described by Siever and Davis, 1991) is a useful guide to temperamental variations. I will therefore apply the same theoretical framework to the planning of clinical interventions.

☐ Impulsive Personality Dimensions

Impulsive spectrum disorders are a group of conditions in which the inability to control behavior is a central issue. As discussed in Chapter 10, all these diagnoses (substance abuse, addictive disorders of other kinds, and impulsive personality disorders) share a common genetic matrix and a common etiology and are highly comorbid.

Understanding the personality traits behind these various disorders can help to plan effective clinical management. Individuals with impulsive traits have an unusual need for structure and control. The experience of families, teachers, and peers all confirm this principle. Although almost everyone works best in some form of structure, it is almost an absolute requirement for individuals with high levels of impulsivity.

The effects of impulsive traits can be apparent in early childhood. These children are difficult to manage for any parent, and when their behavioral problems are not controlled, they are vulnerable to developing the symptoms of conduct disorder (Lykken, 1995). The literature on the causes of conduct disorder (as well as on its frequent adult outcome, antisocial personality) points to an etiology based on interactions between temperamental impulsivity and ineffective parenting styles.

Many of these children grow up in families that either do not provide discipline or that discipline inconsistently (Cadoret et al., 1995; Robins, 1966). Interactions between temperament and family structure create a vicious circle in which ineffective parenting amplifies impulsivity, while continued impulsive behaviors evoke even more ineffective responses. Clinicians working with these families (e.g., Kazdin, 1997) have advocated parental training to provide these children with a kind of tough love, in which the consequences of behavior are clear and are followed with consistency.

Impulsive patients present a similar challenge to psychotherapists. Their greater need for structure helps explain why psychotherapies based on unstructured techniques, such as free association and therapeutic silence, are so often problematical in this population. Impulsive patients usually need to control behavior prior to understanding their inner world.

Substance abuse is an excellent example of this principle. Therapists who work with alcoholics know from experience how they can use an unhappy childhood as an excuse for continuing the same behavior. The most effective approaches involve giving priority to behavioral control. For example, it has been consistently shown that addictions respond best to methods of the type pioneered by Alcoholic Anonymous (Frances & Miller, 1991). The AA program contains many useful elements. It provides structure and control through meetings and sponsors. It also returns the responsibility for drinking to patients (through the paradox of admitting that alcohol use is beyond their control).

The treatment of other addictions, whether they involve drugs, gambling, or eating, is subject to similar principles. Bulimia nervosa is a good example. A large body of evidence shows that effective management of these symptoms requires much more than expressive psychotherapy. Bulimic patients also need to be in programs that teach them both behavioral control and changed attitudes toward eating and body image (Garner & Garfinkel, 1985).

Impulsive personality disorders have long been a subject of fascination and frustration for psychotherapists. Very few clinicians treat patients with a diagnosis of antisocial personality disorder (ASPD). Most efforts at treating this population have taken place in forensic settings, where impulsivity can be safely controlled. But results are rarely stable after discharge from these units. Research suggests that ASPD hardly ever responds to treatment in any form, with real change requiring something akin to a religious conversion (Paris, 1996c; Yochelson & Samenow, 1976).

Patients with borderline personality disorder are also notorious for their capacity to frustrate clinicians. Often, borderline patients present clinicians with unresolvable dilemmas, such as frightening and controlling their therapists with threats of suicide. But these patients demonstrate impulsivity in almost every area of their lives. Unfortunately, in this population, the response to psychotherapy, which requires a fair degree of reflection and patience, reflects these impulsive traits. When offered open-ended therapy, patients with borderline personality often fail to respond (Paris, 1994) or drop out entirely (Gunderson et al., 1989).

One possible explanation of these observations is that psychodynamic methods, in which patients are expected to talk about their inner world with only intermittent feedback from the therapist, are more suitable for people who can control their behavior but offer insufficient structure to contain serious impulsivity.

Some therapists (e.g., Kernberg, 1984) have recommended hospitalizing impulsive patients in order to conduct therapy in an environment in which acting-out is restricted. But this approach also runs the danger of being counterproductive. It is practically impossible to contain impulsivity, even on a ward. Moreover, in-patient settings in which patients spend hours talking to nursing staff about their problems, encourage a high level of expressiveness accompanied by inconsistent reinforcements, which may actually increase impulsive behaviors (Dawson & MacMillan, 1993).

Psychodynamic theory describes acting-out as a defense against painful affects. (Linehan's, 1993, DBT draws on similar ideas.) But expressing one's feelings is rarely sufficient, by itself, to control impulsivity. For example, borderline patients have unusually intense emotions that can escalate into affective storms that lead to impulsive actions. Encouraging these patients to express these emotions may lead to more, not less impulsivity. This may be one explanation for the negative effects of interpretation in low-functioning clinical populations (see Chapter 11).

Keeping highly impulsive patients in psychotherapy is difficult. In this light, the fact that patients with borderline personality rarely drop out from Linehan's (1993) method of treatment represents a unique accomplishment. The explanation may be that DBT is a highly structured method with strong elements of validation, which targets impulsivity using cognitive and behavioral strategies specifically designed to contain and delay action.

At the highest levels of impulsivity, patients are at risk for dropping out of treatment. At more moderate levels, one sometimes sees the contrary problem: interminability. For example, in patients with narcissistic personality disorder (NPD), the central problem is grandiosity. In spite of this trait (and probably because of it), narcissistic patients suffer from chronic and surprisingly intense levels of dysphoria (Torgersen, 1995). Although patients with NPD are not as impulsive as those with ASPD or borderline personality disorder, their style is much more action-oriented than reflective. Due to dysfunctional intimate relationships, NPD patients may use therapy to avoid change. They can become overly attached to a therapy situation that provides them with a haven against a hostile world, or attracted to a situation in which the minutiae of their inner world are the subject of consistent attention. Unfortunately, while enjoying therapy for its own sake, they may be doing little to modify the maladaptive relationships causing their distress. Therefore, effective treatment of this population requires consistent (but tactful) confrontations (Paris, 1998b).

In summary, patients with impulsive spectrum disorders need a more structured treatment approach. The most successful therapies teach them how to control their actions and tolerate the dysphoric states that underlie these actions. Impulsive patients also need to develop better judgment and more adaptive strategies for handling relationships.

☐ Affective Personality Dimensions

The disorders in which the dimension of affective lability plays a central role include dysthymia, nonmelancholic unipolar depression, as well as some impulsive spectrum and anxious spectrum personality disorders. These conditions tend to occur together, so that dysthymia, as opposed to acute depression, is very frequently accompanied by a personality disorder (Pepper et al., 1995).

Affective lability is qualitatively different from clinical depression (Gunderson & Phillips, 1991). The primary characteristic of people with these traits is an unusual sensitivity to the environment. Every bad thing that happens affects them badly. They have difficulty controlling their emotions or in stepping back from feelings so as modulate them. These phenomena closely correspond to the personality dimension of neuroticism (see Chapter 10).

Affective lability accompanied by impulsivity is a potent brew. Individuals with this profile have powerful emotions, and they manage them through action. This pattern can be best seen in borderline personality disorder, in which interactions between affective lability and impulsivity lead to a runaway positive feedback loop in which the actions used to deal with affective lability lead to negative consequences that only increase dysphoria.

The crucial point about patients with affective lability is that they do not necessarily feel better when they express their feelings. In Freud's (1916/1963) hydraulic model, unexpressed emotions were thought to build up an internal mental pressure producing potentially pathological consequences. Similarly, the construct of alexithymia (Sifneos, 1996) implies that people who have trouble expressing feelings are particularly likely to develop certain types of symptoms (psychosomatic illness or substance abuse) which function as equivalents for emotional states. In this light, the most important question about these patients would be whether emotions are properly communicated.

The edifice of traditional psychotherapy has been built on the principle that expressing one's feelings is central to healing. This idea has also worked its way into popular culture. It has become a received wisdom among educated people that those who are upset usually need to share their feelings and talk them out.

These principles are no doubt suitable for *some* people. But they are not necessarily appropriate or useful for managing affective lability. To help people with these traits, we need to think about how emotions are *processed*. Emotional processing is a central construct in psychological models of human emotion (Magai & McFadden, 1996). These theoretical developments have paralleled the development of cognitive therapy, a model in which the internal processing of experience plays a primary role.

The practical implication is that the first step in dealing with dysphoric emotions need not always involve communicating feelings. Most of us like to feel understood by significant others—we can all relate to the ubiquitous need to tell about our day. But, like everything else in human psychology, these needs are subject to individual differences.

People with high levels of introversion can sometimes do perfectly well in life without discussing their feelings on a regular basis. Problems arise when dysphoric reactions pile up and reach a threshold at which symptoms appear. For this reason, introverted individuals often benefit from identifying their emotions at an earlier stage. Therapists, who may be somewhat introverted themselves, can easily empathize with this sort of problem. In contrast, people with high levels of extraversion have emotions that are easily verbalized but mercurial. Their way of expressing feelings suffers from a lack of preliminary reflection.

Thus, depending on one's traits, there are adaptive and nonadaptive ways of communicating emotions. Individuals who are affectively labile present a special problem. In these patients, talking can too often be premature. Without a preliminary attempt at processing, emotions are raw, and feelings need time to ripen. As suggested by Linehan (1993), it may be better to sort out one's reactions first, by identifying what they are, and understanding the impact of the events that have elicited them. Thus, people with affective lability may do better to either distract themselves or simply allow time to pass, so as to avoid feeling overwhelmed, before expressing how they feel.

These techniques parallel many of the methods used by cognitive therapists to teach patients how to handle intense emotions. Beck's (1986) cognitive therapy for depression is a good example. In this view, normal sadness only turns into depression when an individual feels inadequate and helpless. In therapy, the rational part of the mind is mobilized to break these links between cognition and feeling.

Linehan's (1993) DBT applies similar cognitive techniques to the affective instability in borderline personality disorder. Borderline patients often complain that unless they can find comfort, they must act out in order to avoid feeling overwhelmed by dysphoria. Linehan teaches them to learn how to wait, to distract themselves, and to be more confident that solutions to the problems that upset them can be found.

In summary, identifying patients as having affectively labile traits leads therapists to plan somewhat different approaches to treatment. We need to be cautious about encouraging simple expressions of affect in every patient. A good cry does not necessarily make for a good session! The affectively labile patient can easily become lost in his or her own emotions. Empathy must also be provided with a light touch. Without being unnecessarily critical, the emphasis can shift from the feeling itself to dealing with the situations that evoked the feeling.

☐ Anxious Personality Dimensions

Anxious traits and anxious temperament play a major role in anxiety disorders and anxious cluster personality disorders (Paris, 1998a). Intense trait anxiety also interferes with the process of psychotherapy. Like individuals with impulsive traits, those with behavioral inhibition are tempted to become more attached to the *process* of treatment than to its content. Afraid of intimacy and of the possibility of rejection, they are often motivated to maintain a safe relationship with a therapist but slow to generalize this experience to other situations or to translate insight into life change.

Parenting and psychotherapy present strikingly parallel problems. In the case of temperamental anxiety, overprotection creates a feedback loop that intensifies the problem. Kagan (1994) suggests that parents can help a child with an anxious temperament by encouraging exposure to stressful situations. In the same way, therapists must also avoid being overprotective by preventing the treatment setting from becoming too safe an environment, and by actively encouraging new behaviors outside the treatment. Therapists who keep patients indefinitely in treatment are behaving like anxious mothers.

The consequences of supporting this negative feedback loop are real. In the face of stress, patients with avoidant traits tend to withdraw, those with dependent traits tend to cling, and those with compulsive traits tend to procrastinate. Avoidance, dependence, and procrastination all tend to breed more of the same behaviors by blocking the exposure mechanisms that reverse them.

For this reason, psychodynamic interpretations, intended to elucidate the historical factors that have amplified anxious traits, may be insufficient for patients with this form of temperament. In these populations, cognitive and behavioral interventions leading to the development of new behavioral repertoires are usually necessary. This conclusion, central to the practice of cognitive-behavioral therapy (Beck & Freeman, 1990), has also been supported by many psychoanalysts (e.g., Wachtel, 1994).

Finally, in patients with anxious traits, therapists need to reconsider the practice of responding to impasses by lengthening treatment. Doing so is not a rational response to patients of any temperament and may be particularly problematical in patients with anxious traits. As I have discussed elsewhere (Paris, 1998b), continuous treatment is not the only or the best response to the persistence of character pathology. Instead, therapists might consider introducing models making use of an intermittent course of treatment, with planned interruptions punctuated by focused interventions.

☐ Cognitive Personality Dimensions

Patterns of cognitive impairment are rarely treated with psychotherapy alone. However, patients who fall in the schizophrenic spectrum, but who are not psychotic, can be seriously disabled by their difficulty in understanding their interpersonal environment. These individuals do not always think clearly and frequently misinterpret environmental cues. They need to be taught a wide variety of skills allowing them to sort out real from imagined dangers, as well as to see the world from the point of view of other people.

The best documented approach to this population was developed for overt schizophrenia (Hogarty et al., 1991), but its methods are likely to be applicable to individuals with disorders in the schizophrenic spectrum. They involve interventions aiming at psychosocial rehabilitation that primarily aim to help seriously ill patients find a social role, most particularly to hold some form of employment.

Schizophrenic spectrum disorders have to be distinguished from anxious personality disorders, in which patients have an intense desire for human relationships but are too frightened to seek them out. Patients with cognitive problems usually cannot tolerate close relationships, because these situations involve so many inherent ambiguities. They often become loners. Some can successfully manage a life on the margins of society. Others will become distressed, and tend not to seek help, even when symptomatic. When these patients present clinically, the goals will usually focus on social rehabilitation.

☐ Examples of Interactive Temperamental Formulations

I will now apply the principles discussed in this chapter, giving examples of interactive formulations that take both temperament and experience into account. To illustrate my ideas, and to provide a general paradigm, I will make use of two typical clinical examples, one involving an impulsive spectrum disorder, and the other involving an anxious spectrum disorder.

Impulsive Spectrum

Case History

Angela was a 25-year-old university student who presented to a clinic complaining of suicidal ideas, auditory hallucinations, and chronic mood swings. All of these symptoms had been present for nearly 10 years. She presented to therapy after the break-up of a relationship with a man.

Angela's mother had often described her as a holy terror who she had experienced as difficult to handle. From the earliest years of her childhood, she had been an unusually active and defiant child, but with a special charm that protected her from the consequences of her actions. Her older sister, in contrast, was a reserved and highly focused child who never gave her parents a moment's worry. Her father was an alcoholic who had succeeded in hiding his substance abuse from his employers, but who functioned poorly in his roles as husband and parent. As a result, her mother was mildly but chronically depressed.

During Angela's childhood, she was often moody, and known for having a short fuse. But she did well in school, was reasonably popular, and had no observable psychological symptoms. Angela first developed severe problems in early adolescence. She hung around with a bad crowd, began drug use, and entered into sexual promiscuity, all before the age of 14. Angela formed relationships with conduct-disordered boys of her own age or with older boys who were attracted by her sexual availability. Her parents were concerned about Angela but unable to control her, and their own marriage became strained by quarrels about their prodigal daughter. Fortunately, Angela was able to place her schoolwork in a separate compartment. For example, although she tried every known drug at least once, she did not become seriously addicted and kept her use of substances limited to weekends. As a result, she was about to finish university, only somewhat behind schedule.

Formulation

This patient presented with complex difficulties that cannot be accounted for simply. Temperamentally, she had been a difficult child. Moreover, a first-degree relative (her father) also had an impulsive spectrum disorder. The crucial effect of her temperament vulnerability is demonstrated by the dramatic contrast between the patient and her sister. Yet this alone cannot fully account for the severity of her pathology.

Nor do the psychological risk factors experienced by this patient, by themselves, explain her symptoms. Certainly, a family with an alcoholic father and depressed mother is not an ideal environment in which to raise a child. Moreover, Angela lacked the firm structure and discipline that are so important for children with impulsive traits. In addition, she associated herself with a peer group that encouraged substance abuse and lived in a society where this kind of behavior was tolerated. Thus, adolescence presented a crisis that Angela was unable to master. Many of the events that followed can be seen as resulting from this vicious circle.

On the other hand, many children grow up in similar families and do not develop anything like the level of disorder that Angela had. Interactions between temperament and experience allow the emergence of at least a credible relation between cause and effect.

Implications of the Formulation for Therapy

Formulating Angela's problems as the result of interactions between temperamental factors (impulsivity and irritability) and experiential factors (dysfunctional family and pathological peer group) provides the beginning of a framework for undertaking therapy with this patient. The therapist would need to help Angela develop greater capacity for self-observation, allowing her to understand her inner emotional life and to learn ways, other than acting out, to deal with them.

Substance abuse is often a complicating factor in patients with impulsive spectrum disorders, requiring referral to specialized programs. In this case, given the intermittent nature of Angela's drug use, psychotherapy alone might be sufficient to control the problem. In addition, the presence of high ego strength in specific areas of her life (most particularly school) is a positive prognostic sign.

Anxious Spectrum

Case History

Barbara was a 22-year-old university student who presented for therapy with panic attacks. Barbara had also experienced serious difficulties with intimacy. Two years previously, after being dropped by her first boyfriend, she had given up seeing men entirely.

Barbara grew up in an immigrant family. Her parents were hard-working, and highly focused on financial success. Both father and mother spent long hours in the family store, and they were usually too tired to spend much time with Barbara when they were home. Her mother had also had panic attacks when she was young and was later treated by a family doctor for low mood and insomnia with antidepressants.

Barbara was a shy and awkward child who had always had trouble making friends. Her younger brother, an outgoing and popular boy, was something of a jock; successful in several sports during high school, he had recently been admitted to engineering school. Her mother stated that Barbara was a slow feeder, who smiled much later than her brother. Her parents did not encourage her to overcome this difficulty and were somewhat overprotective in their attitudes about having a daughter grow up in North America. She never discussed inner feelings with her parents, and her excellence at school was sufficient success for them.

As an adolescent, much the same pattern continued. She went to a high school that emphasized academic achievement and provided minimal support for social development. Thus, Barbara had little experience with the opposite sex until she met Julian in her first year of university. They went out for 2 years, and when Barbara fell in love with him, she was sure that they would eventually marry. When Julian announced that he "needed space" and wanted to see other women, Barbara was crushed. It was at that point she began to have panic attacks. Although she kept a few old friends, she became increasingly reluctant to socialize with people she did not know. She only sought help at the point when her symptoms began to interfere with her academic work.

Formulation

Like Angela, Barbara presented with complex problems. Temperamentally, she had been a slow-to-warm-up child. Moreover, a first-degree relative (her mother) also developed an anxious spectrum disorder.

Barbara's parents had not provided her with sufficient help for her temperamental vulnerability. There was, again, a striking contrast in temperament between the patient and a sibling. If Barbara had been more like her brother, she would not have needed as much family support and would have built a wider social network that would have made her less vulnerable to deficiencies in parenting. Greater involvement with peers, as well as a more structured environment for social development, might have helped her to overcome the deficiencies of her family.

In the end, a combination of temperamental vulnerability, failure of needed psychosocial supports to overcome that vulnerability, and a disappointment in love led to overt symptoms, eventually producing a disabling level of social anxiety.

Implications of the Formulation for Therapy

Formulating Barbara's problems as a result of interactions between temperamental factors (anxious traits and behavioral inhibition) and experiential factors (unsupportive parents) could provide the beginning of a framework for undertaking therapy with this patient. It is, of course, likely that Barbara would respond to medical treatment for her panic attacks. However, drugs do not consistently reverse severely avoidant behavioral patterns. The therapist would need to help Barbara to expose herself to the social situations that frighten her and to learn strategies that would allow her to tolerate the inevitable rejections in both intimate and nonintimate encounters.

☐ Communicating Formulations to Patients

The previous chapter suggested that therapy works by developing a positive relationship that can be used for problem-solving. But after emphasizing common factors in therapy and criticizing the idea that interpretations are a crucial factor in outcome, I can hardly suggest that *my* type of formulations must always be accurate. Moreover, we do not know whether providing better explanations really leads to better results.

Nonetheless, I will suggest a few tentative clinical guidelines that follow from my approach. I recommend that formulations by therapists should be *shared* with patients. Moreover, in today's world, clinicians no longer communicate their conclusions in an *ex cathedra* manner. Instead, modern therapists usually consider themselves to be consultants to, and partners with, their patients. Sharing formulations encourages needed feedback to modify the therapist's ideas.

Formulations using an interactive model also allow for a different type of interpretation. In patients with impulsive disorders, the therapist communicates an understanding of temperament and then interprets the effects of life events in that context. Here is a typical comment a therapist might make to such a patient:

> Given your naturally active way of dealing with problems, you haven't always understood what you feel inside. This makes it hard for you to deal with what happens to you in life. When you were growing up, it would have helped if someone could have shown you how to manage your feelings and solve your problems. You often end up doing things you regret, instead of looking first at how you feel inside and then figuring out a way to solve a problem.

Similarly, patients with an anxious temperament might be told:

> You were born shy and have always had problems with shyness. You are sensitive to rejection, as we know from your experiences as a child and from your present social problems. When you don't feel accepted, you tend to withdraw from people. When you were growing up, you lacked someone to help you master these feelings. Now you avoid the situations that scare you instead of accepting your feelings and learning how to get past them.

Such examples are in accord with three broad principles developed in this chapter. First, they acknowledge the value of personal narrative, but place the impact of life events in a temperamental context. Second, they focus on problem-solving in the present. Third, sharing one's ideas with patients has the goal of establishing a formulation that will be common to both parties in the therapeutic encounter.

☐ Conclusion

Temperament, not history, is a guide for customizing psychotherapy. Interactive formulations assess the impact of life events in the context of temperament. By understanding individual differences, therapists are more likely to find the right approach for each patient and to devise strategies that more accurately and specifically target problems.

V

IMPLICATIONS

Part V consists of two chapters examining some of the broader implications of the ideas presented earlier in the book.

Chapter 13 concerns how primacy affects our views about raising children. Parents have been made unnecessarily anxious about the consequences of mismanaging their offspring, and held guilty for any problems that arise later in life. The ingredients of successful and unsuccessful parenting depend on responses to temperamental differences.

Chapter 14 reviews what we do and don't know about the impact of childhood on later life and how we might go about finding out. The book concludes by placing childhood in the context of history, suggesting how a different view of its impact can lead to a new perspective on the human condition.

CHAPTER

Parenting

☐ Why Therapists Are Not Experts on Life

Mental health professionals are treated with ambivalent respect. When I tell other people what I do for a living, it is not unusual to get responses such as, Oh, you're a psychiatrist—well what do you think about——?, with the blank being filled in with a recent and celebrated crime story or the sexual practices of the rich and famous. In a less benign vein, if I challenge some conventional wisdom, I may get the comment, How can you possibly say a thing like that—after all, you're a *psychiatrist*.

As I get older, I gain knowledge but become increasingly cautious about pontificating. Professionals can easily fall into a flattering trap, pretending to an expertise to which they are not entitled. Therapists have been known to offer advice on social policies, the prevention of crime, or the secret of marital happiness. The most common example concerns the proper way to raise children.

Therapists do have professional knowledge about the risk factors for psychopathology. This expertise allows them to define parenting styles that increase the likelihood that children will get into difficulty. It is highly probable that abuse and gross neglect of children is bad for them. It is possible that overt parental discord and family breakdown can do children some degree of harm. One can also say with authority that children with an abnormal temperament need special care. Clinicians can therefore play a role in educating the public about what *not* to do with their children.

183

I am *not* saying that parents don't matter. Instead, I am proposing an interactive view of how families affect development. Parents have more leeway to go wrong with some children, and less with others. But the focus of this chapter is whether mental health professionals have enough expert knowledge to advise parents how to raise *normal* children. Our understanding of the extremes of temperament and adversity does not tell us how to behave with the average child. If anything, too much advice from clinicians about the rights and wrongs of parenting can be counter-productive.

☐ The Best Is the Enemy of the Good

To translate this saying back to its French original: *Le meilleur est l'ennemi du bon*. Those who insist on perfection in life risk becoming paralyzed and unproductive. Parents who try to have a perfect family and to raise children perfectly are almost surely bound to be disappointed.

Marriage provides a good example of this principle. Amato and Booth (1997) report that marital satisfaction is much lower than it was in previous generations. Why should this be so, in a time when people choose their own partners and marry for love?

The explanation is that people expect too much from marriage. In the past, husbands and wives worked together to raise children. Their bond was as much a union of families as of individuals. Today, people expect to find profound happiness with their partners and are intolerant of the inevitable disillusionment when intimate relationships prove less than perfect. Amato and Booth (1997) found that the majority of dissolved marriages are not a necessary escape from severe discord and abuse, but result from reactions to feelings of dissatisfaction.

Thus, in married life, the best is very much the enemy of the good. Moreover, changing partners is hardly the road to bliss. Research shows that remarriages following divorce are even more unstable than first marriages (Riley, 1991). In a famous phrase, Samuel Johnson described a second marriage as the triumph of hope over experience.

Attempts to raise perfect children is equally doomed. As we have seen, every child is born with a unique temperament, and these characteristics can influence the environment. By and large, empirical evidence supports the common belief that providing love and support, as well as encouraging the independence of the growing child, is beneficial for development. But the bad effects of bad parenting are much more dramatic than the good effects of good parenting.

The most important thing that parents can do for their children is to avoid doing things that are known to be harmful. In short, *we know how to ruin children, but not how to raise them.*

In clinical practice, therapists have a responsibility to advise patients against unwise actions but are usually more tentative when suggesting new behaviors. Similarly, it is more effective to warn parents to stop doing negative things than to tell them how to raise their children. Not surprisingly, most of the programs developed to train parents (e.g., Gordon, 1970) are primarily designed to teach control and discipline. These interventions have been shown to be effective in the short term (Brestan & Eyberg, 1998), but their long-term effectiveness is uncertain (Kazdin, 1997).

If there is no absolutely right way to raise children, therapists should be careful about providing feedback to patients that explicitly or implicitly blames their parents. In the past, these interventions have done a great deal of harm. Notoriously, clinicians blamed mothers for any and all disorders, ranging from schizophrenia to attention deficit disorder. Parents were made to suffer lifelong guilt, while therapists have rarely been held responsible for evoking such feelings. Recovered memory therapies take these matters to an extreme, encouraging patients to confront, or even to divorce, parents who are believed to have abused them—to break with their families to protect themselves against further toxicity (Prendergast, 1995).

If we were to choose a villain in this drama, we could not do better than Bruno Bettelheim. A therapist known for work with troubled children, Bettelheim's wider influence derived from a series of best-selling books. A recent biography (Pollak, 1997) documents a number of troubling facts about this man, including the fact that he invented data to prove the purported success of his methods. But the most relevant issue concerns Bettelheim's attitude towards parents. Like many therapists of his time, he blamed mothers for a wide range of disturbances in children, even in conditions, such as autistic disorder, that are now known to be almost entirely organic in origin.

Bettelheim was not working in a vacuum—he only amplified ideas that were already well ingrained in psychology and popular culture. Fortunately, these ideas, however current they were in the previous generation, have become a historical curiosity. We now know that young children, or even infants, cannot easily be molded by their mothers. Thus, when children develop mental disorders, their parents should be declared *not guilty*—at least until proved otherwise.

☐ Benjamin Spock and the Art of Parenting

We live in an era when many people mistrust the opinions of their parents. Mothers and fathers in our culture have become anxious about doing the wrong thing. But unlike previous generations, they have little faith in the wisdom of the past. In the context of this lack of received knowledge, parents are hungry for expert help. They look for advice from newspapers, magazines, and television. The child care section of any bookstore is filled with volumes on every conceivable aspect of parenting.

Moreover, many people, under the influence of either their own psychotherapy or prevailing cultural ideas, believe that their own psychological problems must be the result of incompetent rearing during childhood. When such individuals have children of their own, they are determined to avoid making the same mistakes. These concerns further feed the demands of contemporary parents for expert advice.

Over the last 50 years, Benjamin Spock (1946) has been the most frequently relied upon authority on the best way to raise children. Although different editions of his work prescribed somewhat different nostrums, generations of parents (myself included) found support and comfort in his famous book.

Spock was a prominent doctor who was read by parents in the belief that he gave them access to the latest *scientific* advice on raising children. But Spock had little training in formal research, and his book was more influenced by ideology than by evidence. Moreover, Spock was very much a child of his time (Maier, 1998). Raised in the early part of the 20th century, he rejected earlier traditions in favor of an approach strongly grounded in psychoanalytic theory.

Sound common sense underlay many of Spock's practical suggestions. He also tuned in to some of the most profound themes from contemporary culture, including: the loss of tradition as a guide to living and the resulting fear that children can easily be damaged by their parents. Famously, he reassured mothers that they knew more about raising children than they thought they knew and that they should trust their own instincts.

Spock's ideas most closely parallel the principles of attachment theory. His view was that children are bound to be happier when parents are empathic and loving. This might be true during childhood, but there is no evidence that children raised according to Spock do better as adults than those raised under older paradigms, such as "spare the rod and spoil the child."

By present standards, Spock did not actually recommend an overly permissive approach to child-rearing. He has been unfairly blamed for producing a generation of spoiled children, the so-called baby boomers. Actually, if there has been any real increase in cultural narcissism, it is much more likely to be due to other, much more powerful economic and social forces, such as unprecedented levels of affluence, the breakdown of extended families and community ties, and a decline in the influence of organized religion.

Moreover, it remains doubtful whether parents' gratification of children's needs in early childhood affects later character development. Parenting does not create personality, but only amplifies existing characteristics. Thus, narcissistic traits in children might be exaggerated by overindulgent parents. But this is hardly the same thing as assuming that any child raised according to Spock's principles will end up seeking membership in the "me generation."

Spock's success was due to a unique combination of down-to-earth practicality and a theoretical model that conformed to the received wisdom of his time. Modern psychoanalysts (Winnicott, Bowlby, Erikson, and Kohut) have all emphasized the importance of protecting the bond between child and mother, proposing that problems in this relationship can be the primary source of later psychopathology. But Spock's strong emphasis on mothering came under attack. Feminists accused him of making women feel guilty about focusing on their careers. Even in a time when most women work, the question of what constitutes adequate day care remains controversial, and a new generation of advisors to mothers (e.g., Leach, 1984) have continued to raise anxiety about its dangers.

☐ Parenting and Temperament

We cannot determine the effectiveness of parenting without considering the nature of the child. Different approaches are appropriate for different children. The same parental behavior can be successful or unsuccessful, depending on individual differences in temperament.

In children with constitutional vulnerabilities, some specific rearing practices can become problematical. Thus, inconsistent discipline amplifies impulsivity, even though this parenting style will not have dramatically negative effects on a shy or compulsive child. Similarly, overprotection amplifies behavioral inhibition, even though this parenting style will not have major effects on a child with impulsive traits.

The quality of parenting is more important in raising children with temperamental vulnerabilities than in raising children with easier temperaments. This is one of the main reasons why siblings raised in the same home, and who are exposed to a similar parental environment, can each turn out to be perfectly normal or seriously pathological.

Applying the Chess and Thomas (1984) classification, a child with an easy temperament is likely to compensate for minor degrees of neglect and to be resilient to short-term traumatic experiences. But a child with a difficult temperament who is not handled with sufficient discipline, attention, and tough love can enter a vicious circle in which defiance and rejection feed on each other. A child with a slow-to-warm-up temperament who is not exposed to social interactions can enter a vicious circle in which anxiety and overprotection feed on each other.

☐ Parenting in the Light of Research on Child Development

Research on the genetic and environmental factors in personality and psychopathology leads to a new perspective on parenting. Although parenting is important, it is only one of several factors influencing development, and not necessarily the primary driving factor (Kendler, 1995). Genes shape behavioral differences between children, and the most important environmental influences are unshared. Thus, personality is not necessarily a consequence of growing up in a particular family, and psychological symptoms cannot be accounted for by parenting practices alone (Kendler, 1996). The way we raise children has a more consistent impact on inner feelings than behavior and explains more about distress than about disorder.

In effect, research is telling us something we knew all along. Ultimately, what children become is not under our control. Therefore, parents should be less anxious about their task. They should stop worrying that the smallest mistake can ruin a child's life.

The goodness of fit model (see Chapter 10) has been supported by research. Thus, the task of parenting is different for each child. Lykken (1995) compared individual differences in temperament to differences between breeds in animals. For example, a dog-owner who purchases a bull terrier has a very different task from one who buys a cocker spaniel. Lykken compares the bull terriers to temperamentally impulsive children: If properly reared, they can be lovable, but if badly reared, they can be uncontrollable.

Thus, parents need to recognize individuality and develop strategies for care that resonate with that uniqueness. If they have an impulsive, overactive, or irritable child, they will have to spend extra time providing structure and control. If they have a shy, anxious child, they will have to take extra care to provide socializing experiences.

The principles I have recommended for psychotherapy (Chapter 12) are essentially the same as those I am suggesting for parents. There is no size to fit all. Therapists need to accept that the problems patients have are the result of both constitution and experience; this knowledge will help them to avoid making facile formulations, particularly those blaming parents for everything that has gone wrong. Similarly, parents need to accept that, even with the best intentions, they cannot produce ideal results in their children. When a child is troubled, parents are better advised to focus on what can be done rather than what should have been done.

☐ Happiness, Unhappiness, and Chaos

The idea that happiness or unhappiness in life is determined by whether childhood was happy or unhappy is a cultural shibboleth. It is entirely possible, and actually quite common, for people with unhappy childhoods to be happy later in life. It is also possible, and equally common, for people with happy childhoods to go off the rails at crucial times during their adult development (Myers & Diener, 1995). Parents cannot determine whether their children will be happy. Life is not predictable enough for that to be possible. Some evidence also suggests that the capacity for happiness itself is, at least partly, genetic (Hamer, 1998; Lykken & Tellegen, 1996). Thus there are several ways in which happiness can be just a matter of good luck. Moreover, as with any trait, a capacity for happiness is useful in some circumstances and not in others. If life presents few challenges, it is more adaptive to be optimistic and to put a positive spin on events. Yet when life is difficult, a pessimist, who is always prepared for adversity, may fare better.

Development does not stop, as Freud supposed, with sexual maturity. Adults continue to change throughout the life cycle (Harris, 1998; Vaillant, 1977). Moreover, the life events that drive these changes are often unpredictable (Lewis, 1997). Ultimately, the course of human life is chaotic. We would like to believe that the past determines the present, because doing so makes some sense out of the universe. But life events only bend the twig and do not determine the final shape of the tree.

Most scientists believe that the future is unknowable. In biology, the history of life on earth does not lead inevitably to the triumph of intelligence. In fact, the evolution of our own species may be nothing but a fortunate accident (Gould, 1989). The course of evolution is shaped by unpredictability and chaos, and survival is as much a matter of chance as of design.

It is easy to see parallels with the task of raising children. Parents need to give up their fantasies of control and to accept that psychological development is nondeterministic. Finally, the fact that we can never predict the quality of a human life from childhood experiences is actually quite fortunate.

☐ Conclusion

We do not need to ask whether parents matter. There can be no doubt that they do. It is better to treat children with kindness than with cruelty. At the very least, the quality of upbringing is important in the short term and has an influence on continuing relationships between parents and their adult children.

The real question concerns whether failures of parenting necessarily cause serious and irreversible damage. The answer is that defective parenting is sometimes a contributing factor to mental illness, but it is not, by itself, its primary cause. Nor is parenting the primary source of personality traits or of whether an adult child will be happy or unhappy.

To reiterate, parents can damage children, but rearing practices make the most difference for temperamentally vulnerable children. Most children remain resilient, both to the mistakes of their parents and to a broad range of adversities. Thus, the book of life is not determined by its first chapter. Parents should therefore be more forgiving of themselves for inevitable failings. Life has a complex trajectory that, even late in its course, allows for correction.

The fact that we can never predict the quality of a human life from childhood experiences is fortunate indeed. Who would want to be deprived of the opportunity to make one's life productive, in spite of the circumstances under which it began?

What We Do and Don't Know About Childhood

☐ The Limits of Knowledge

The state of scientific knowledge is always provisional. Since received wisdoms have so often been proved wrong, one should never trust claims to absolute truth. Arguing for a negative, as this book has done, can sometimes be hazardous. The limits of knowledge also reflect the narrow lens of existing theoretical models. The choice of which observations to make has to be made on the basis of current ideas. When theories change, phenomena that were previously invisible can come to light.

Conclusions must be provisional when data is incomplete. I have summarized the present state of research on the relationship of childhood to adulthood. My overall conclusion is that given the lack of evidence, the primacy of childhood must be judged a myth. Yet we lack firm answers to almost all the crucial questions. We can feel fairly secure that most of the broad linkages claimed in the past are, at the very least, overdrawn. It remains possible that further studies might discover subtle relationships between early experience and adulthood. Yet even if this should turn out to be the case, I predict that any such findings will have to be understood in the context of interactions with temperament.

☐ Ten Unanswered Questions About Childhood

In the course of this book, I have described many issues that require further research. The developmental model I have outlined here can only be considered a draft for a future, more comprehensive theory. I would therefore like to focus on 10 questions that are in particular need of further investigation.

What Mechanisms Account for Continuities and Discontinuities in Development?

Development is marked as much by discontinuity as by continuity. Temperament can be observed early in childhood, and these characteristics are predictive, at least on a statistical basis, of later psychological problems. However, children also change a great deal over time, sometimes in unpredictable ways.

In 1963, the British Broadcasting Corporation televised a program, given the name *7 Up*, on a group of 7-year-old children drawn from different social backgrounds. The children were later interviewed at ages 14 and 21. The producers then decided that it would be useful to follow these children into adulthood, and this cohort has, with some attrition, been reinterviewed every 7 years, producing new programs called *28 Up, 35 Up,* and *42 Up*.

This BBC follow-up study does not rate very high from a scientific point of view—the sample was small and unrepresentative, and the assessments were entirely unsystematic. However, the continuities and discontinuities in the lives of the participants give the series a sense of drama that have led to a cult following. Some of the more advantaged children have led predictably advantaged lives. Yet some of the disadvantaged children have also done amazingly well in life. One of the participants, who had been an unusually happy child, later fell victim to mental illness.

Clearly, life holds many surprises. Continuities are always easier to understand, yet we need to know more about discontinuities. To what extent is temperament modified by experience? Or, as seems to be the case for some mental disorders, can genetic vulnerabilities remain invisible throughout childhood, and then be switched on at some later point?

What Is the Contribution of Heredity to the Development of Personality?

Genes account for about half of the variance in personality. But this is nothing but an approximation. The true figures could be higher or lower, and they could also be different for different traits.

The findings of behavioral genetic research also do not tell us *which* genes are involved with *which* traits. If we knew the answer to this question, we would have a much better way of classifying personality and of predicting the later course of its development. Thus, mapping individual differences in traits that are consistently associated with variations in the genome would create a classification rooted in biology, replacing the rough and ready dimensions we use now, based on the factor analysis of self-report questionnaires.

Can We Better Define, Describe, and Quantify the Concept of Temperament?

At present, temperament can only be operationalized through behavioral observations. If it were rooted in biological data, we could establish useful links between behavior and biological markers, and between behavior and genetic variations.

It is not science fiction to imagine a time when every child will have its genome read soon after birth. Although genes can only tell us about *tendencies*, not outcomes, information about these variations will become the basis of a new and more useful classification of temperament in children.

What Factors Shape the Influence of Unshared Environment on Personality?

In Chapter 10, I described several possible explanations of the nature of the unshared environment, the component of experience that most influences personality. But to say that the environment is unshared is only to acknowledge ignorance. This term describes a vast variety of life experiences of many different kinds. We need to make this construct more precise, dividing it into portions that will be more coherent and more specific. Thus, research can allow us to study the effect of *specific* life events, while controlling for heritable influences. Behavioral genetic methods should also be linked to the methods of molecular genetics, providing direct access to the mechanisms of interaction between genetic vulnerability and experiential adversity (Plomin & Rutter, 1998).

Are There Any Adverse Events that Consistently Produce Sequelae When They Occur Early in Childhood?

I have promised to remain doubtful—even about my own doubts! I can not therefore exclude the possibility that the principle of primacy might still apply under *some* conditions. For example, it is possible that severe neglect or gross mistreatment over long periods of early childhood might have sequelae different from the normal trauma that children survive. As suggested in Chapter 4, researchers await with anticipation the results of long-term outcome studies for Romanian orphans who experienced very extreme conditions early in childhood.

Do Adversities Ever Produce Irreversible Effects?

Single events are extremely unlikely to produce sequelae that cannot normalize over time. Yet with respect to severe and cumulative adversities, the question of irreversibility remains open. The effects of neglectful care for young children can usually be reversed by changing their environment for the better. However, the older the child is, and the longer the child has been exposed to mistreatment, the more difficult it is to reverse these sequelae.

The explanation of this observation is not obvious. Can it be accounted for by reactions that become automatized? In other words, can children be so stressed for so long that they cease to trust anyone and close down emotionally? Is there a biological effect to stress, mediated by hormonal effects on the brain? Do these effects apply to every child, or does abnormal temperament play a role in the recovery from adversity? Do critical periods play any role at all?

These questions remain unanswered. Studies of high-risk populations are the best way to address them.

What Are the Mechanisms Behind Resilience?

I have shown that children are generally resilient to adversity. But why are some children so much more resilient than others?

Chapter 4 described research findings bearing on this issue, but we need to know much more. Which temperamental qualities help children deal with stress? What kinds of life experiences provide them with significant protection against adverse events? Again, we need more prospective studies of children at risk to answer these questions.

How Are Children of Different Temperamental Types Affected by Adversity?

I have suggested mechanisms through which adverse events may have specific effects on children with different temperamental propensities.

Thus, the irritable child is more prone to conflict and rejection, by both parents and peers, while the abnormally shy child is prone to parental overprotection and peer group rejection. It follows that the different types of adverse life events described in Chapter 3 (trauma, neglect, family dysfunction, family breakdown) may have entirely different effects in different children.

However plausible these ideas, they require proof. Again, we can only address this issue by carrying out large-scale longitudinal studies of children, preferably using twin designs to control for genetic factors.

Can Understanding Temperament Lead to More Effective Psychotherapy?

I suggested in Chapter 12 how temperamental models can help therapists to understand patients better. But, as I emphasized in my critique of the psychodynamic model, theories are not a sufficient basis for conducting treatment. I have not *proved* that my idea is actually more effective in helping patients recover from their symptoms. I may find this approach more plausible (and more consistent with other knowledge) than other models. But I must apply the same criteria to my own ideas as I have to those of others. I need to be cautious and avoid claiming to know for sure whether my ideas have practical value. Only clinical trials, systematically comparing different methods, can answer such questions.

What Are the Best Strategies for Managing Children at Temperamental Risk?

Chapter 13 criticized many received wisdoms about parenting. I have also suggested that parents who raise a child with a problematical temperament need to do more than just "fly by the seat of their pants." Research suggests specific strategies for managing the irritable child and the behaviorally inhibited child. Yet we do not know how consistently effective these approaches are or whether they remain effective over time. Of particular importance is that we do not know whether parents who have difficulty in managing a difficult child can be effectively taught new techniques.

☐ How Can We Answer These Questions?

Years ago, when I first began to do research, I expressed frustration to a colleague about the fact that I could not find a way to test my deeper clinical insights about patients. He informed me that while the most important questions are not the most easily researchable, the most researchable questions are not necessarily the most important!

This conclusion was amusing, in a cynical way—but it was not quite correct. More accurately, we can say that trivial questions are easier to answer, while the most important problems in psychology will require many decades of effort. I will now make a recommendation for a method that has the capacity to address these complex issues.

The most reliable source of information on how early experience shapes adult life involves *prospective longitudinal studies of children in community populations*. Relationships between risks and outcomes reported in retrospective studies of clinical samples are often misleading. Chapters 3 and 4 described the results of existing long-term prospective investigations of children. But we have only a relatively small number of such investigations. The explanation is that they are expensive, time-consuming, and must be led by investigators with a reasonably long life expectancy of their own.

Nonetheless, prospective studies are irreplaceable. They will be particularly helpful in addressing the problem of determining whether continuities over time reflect temperament, life experience, or both. Several strategies are needed to address these crucial distinctions, which even most existing prospective studies of children have not been designed to make.

1. We need to factor out the relative roles of genetics and environment in personality development. To do so, researchers should ideally follow large samples of identical and fraternal twins over time.
2. Since this is not always possible, children in prospective studies should be genotyped. As the human genome is accurately mapped, and as technology makes the reading of the genetic map easier, this method will be used more and more commonly.
3. Children should be studied from infancy onwards. The earlier the observations, the better will be the baseline of temperamental measures.
4. Regular assessments of parenting behavior should be made over the course of childhood.
5. Measurement of the influence of factors outside the family (social class, quality of schools, peer groups, community influences) should be included in the design.
6. Studies should be done on more than one site to eliminate bias due to the idiosyncrasies of different samples.

☐ Research and Public Education

I have presented a series of ambitious ideas for further investigation. Can we ever find the financing to carry out such expensive research? I know this would be difficult, but do not think it impossible. Experience suggests that scientific support follows sufficient public awareness of a problem. We need to raise public consciousness about the importance of studying children in order to gain the information we need to prevent and treat mental illness.

Several major mental disorders have shown a dramatic increase in prevalence since the Second World War, most particularly in young people (Rutter & Smith, 1995): substance abuse, suicidal depression, eating disorders, conduct disorder, as well as antisocial and borderline personality disorders. These changes in prevalence reflect social changes. Even though most children continue to grow up normally and successfully, childhood has become more stressful.

In this context, prospective research could tell us something of absolutely crucial importance. Which children are most vulnerable to the demands of contemporary life? Prevention of psychological problems often goes to waste because it is applied to everyone, even those who are most unlikely to develop serious difficulties. If we could identify the most vulnerable populations, we could better focus our efforts.

Support for research on cancer, AIDS, or other diseases was not based on answers, but on unanswered questions. We need to tell the public the importance of finding out why more young people are developing serious psychological symptoms. We also need to stop pretending to an expertise we lack and claiming that we know all the answers. Mental health professionals can educate the public about what we do and don't know about childhood.

☐ The History of Childhood

Being a child has never been easy. In prehistoric times, most children died early, usually from disease, sometimes from predation. From what we know of hunter-gatherer societies, it seems likely that parents, who were themselves busy surviving, could not always attend to the emotional needs of their offspring.

The picture in historical times is based on better data, but is no more elevating (DeMause, 1974). The rich often arranged to have their children raised by wet nurses and nannies, spending little time with them. The poor had more children than they could support, giving them away to foundling homes, where most of them perished.

The contemporary idea that mothers should focus on supporting the emotional life of each child would have seemed very strange at most points of history. Children have generally not been raised by mothers alone, but in extended families and communities. In hunter-gatherer and agricultural societies, they were expected to work from an early age and to help their families survive. Even the concept of adolescence did not exist until modern times, when children began to undergo long periods of education.

These conditions often exposed children to adversities that many people today would call abuse or neglect. Yet somehow, children were either raised or managed to raise themselves. In spite of the lives most children led, we have no reason to believe that mental illness was any more common in the past. Clearly, developmental models, such as attachment theory, that claim to have discovered universal principles of raising children or that claim that children can be damaged by relatively minor empathic failures, are lacking in historical perspective.

From both a physical and an economic point of view, children today have better lives than they could have expected through most of history. We live in an age of enormous affluence, and most of us can look forward to a lengthy lifespan. If it is *still* difficult to be a child, this has nothing to do with the quality of parenting! We should not accept the cliché that troubled children are necessarily victims of malignant or unresponsive parenting. The main problems faced by contemporary children have to do with the effects of social mobility and individualism. Children today can be much more isolated from their communities, and may have difficulty accessing the supports they need outside the family. Adolescents and young adults suffer from an important additional burden, in that they have to find their own occupations and their own intimate attachments (Paris, 1996c).

We need to think differently about human nature. Children are not puppets of circumstance. In a world of opportunity, some succeed, while others fall by the wayside. Part of the explanation lies in luck. Part of the explanation lies in families. Yet, more than we have previously believed, character is destiny.

☐ Adversity, Tragedy, and Hope

Understanding the impact of individual differences in temperament and personality helps us to avoid seeing people as victims. Instead, life can take on a *tragic* dimension. This concept is not quite the one we see in Greek tragedy, which suggested that men must submit to a fate predetermined by the gods. Rather, it closely corresponds to the tragedies of Shakespeare, which are based on the idea that while life is full of adversity, character determines fate.

Almost a century ago, an English critic (Bradley, 1906/1955) argued that the power of the greatest Shakespearian tragedies depends on interactions between flaws in the character of its heroes and the impact of unexpected events. The best and most famous example is Hamlet. If Hamlet's parents had been happily married, melancholy and indecision might never have created serious problems for him. Tragedy arises when Hamlet is challenged by adversity and finds himself temperamentally unsuited to deal with it. At the end of Act I, he states: "The time is out of joint. Oh cursed spite/That I was ever born to set it right." Later in the play, as Hamlet learns to face adversity with resolve and courage, he states: "The readiness is all."

Samuel Johnson once remarked that those who know Shakespeare will find little to surprise them in the world. Although patients in therapy are not necessarily heroic, their dilemmas in life can be surprisingly similar to those described in classical drama. Tragedies arise at the interface between personality and experience. Since events have no absolute meaning independent of how we perceive, process, and experience them, people are not victims of circumstance, but have the power to determine their own fate.

☐ Determinism and Free Will

The primacy of childhood is based on outdated scientific notions. Two hundred years ago, Laplace, a noted French astronomer, claimed that if only he knew the coordinates of every heavenly body, he would be in a position to predict with precision the future history of the entire universe. This level of determinism was extreme, but it described accurately the philosophy of the 19th century, the same climate of opinion that shaped the ideas of Sigmund Freud.

Early in the 20th century, quantum theory overthrew determinism in physics. For a long time, it appeared that this change applied only at the micro level. More recently, it has become apparent that even at the macro level, precise prediction will always be impossible, since small changes in initial conditions influence ultimate outcome (Gleick, 1987). It is now considered impossible to predict the weather with more than statistical accuracy, and the half-humorous claim has been made that the fluttering of a single butterfly can cause hurricanes on the other side of the earth. Similarly, there is no linear path between life events or between different periods of the life cycle. This revised scientific philosophy can usefully inform the study of child development. No one can predict the future.

☐ Conclusion

It is time to summarize. Overthrowing the myths of childhood can lead to an increased respect for humanism and free will. We can stop blaming life's difficulty on our upbringing and our parents. We are all marked by personal histories. Even more so, we are shaped by socioeconomic back-grounds. Yet neither families nor social class prevent us from achieving personal goals. We have unique temperaments and unique talents, and we can find ways to make these characteristics work for us.

We can benefit from understanding the past but need not spend our lives grieving over the losses and defects of childhood. If the future is not determined, we are empowered. At every stage of development, life is full of adversity. Yet the world remains full of choice and possibility.

REFERENCES

Achenbach, T. M., & McConaughy, S. H. (1997). *Empirically based assessment of child and adolescent psychopathology: Practical applications* (2nd ed.). Thousand Oaks, CA: Sage.

Ackerman, N., (1966). *Treating the troubled family*. New York: Basic.

Adler, G. (1985). *Borderline psychopathology and its treatment*. New York: Jason Aronson.

Ahn, H. (1997). A meta-analysis of outcome studies comparing bona fide psychotherapies: Empirically, "all must have prizes". *Psychological Bulletin, 122,* 203–215.

Ainsworth, M. D., Blehar, M. C., Waters, E., & Wall, S. (1978). *Patterns of attachment*. Hillsdale, NJ: Erlbaum.

Amato, P. R., & Booth, A. (1997). *A generation at risk*. Cambridge, MA: Harvard University Press.

American Psychiatric Association. (1980). *Diagnostic and statistical manual of mental disorders* (3rd ed.). Washington, DC: Author.

American Psychiatric Association. (1994). *Diagnostic and statistical manual of mental disorders* (4th ed.). Washington DC: Author.

Anthony, E. J. (1987). Risk, vulnerability and resilience: An overview. In E. J. Anthony & B. J. Cohler (Eds.), *The invulnerable child* (pp. 3–48). New York: Guilford.

Badgley, R. F. (1984). *Report of committee on sexual offences against children*. Ottawa, Canada: Supply and Services Canada.

Bandura, A. (1977). *Social learning theory*. Englewood Cliffs, NJ: Prentice-Hall.

Bandura, A. (1999). Social cognitive theory of personality. In L. A. Pervin & O. P. John (Eds.), *Handbook of personality: Theory and research* (2nd ed., pp. 154–196). New York: Guilford.

Bartlett, F. C. (1932/1995). *Remembering: A study in experimental and social psychology*. New York: Cambridge University Press.

Bass, E., & Davis, L. (1988). *The courage to heal*. New York: Harper and Row.

Bateson, G., Jackson, D., Haley, J., & Weakland, J. (1956). Towards a theory of schizophrenia. *Behavioral Science, 1,* 251–255.

Beck, T. A. (1986). *Cognitive therapy and the emotional disorders*. New York: Basic Books.

Beck, A. T., & Freeman, A. (1990). *Cognitive therapy of personality disorders*. New York: Guilford.

Beitchman, J. H., Zucker, K. J., Hood, J. E., DaCosta, G. A., Akman, D., & Cassavia, E. (1992). A review of the long-term effects of child sexual abuse. *Child Abuse and Neglect, 16,* 101–118.

Belsky, J. (1999). Modern evolutionary theory and patterns of attachment. In J. Cassidy & P. R. Shaver (Eds.), *Handbook of attachment: Theory, research and clinical aspects* (pp. 141–161). New York: Guilford.

Belsky, J., & Cassidy, J. (1994). Attachment: Theory and evidence. In M. Rutter & D. Hays (Eds.), *Development through life: A handbook for clinicians* (pp. 373–402). Oxford, England: Blackwell.

Belsky, J., Steinberg, L., & Draper, P. (1991). Childhood experience, interpersonal development, and reproductive strategy: An evolutionary theory of socialization. *Child Development, 62,* 647–670.

Benjamin, J., Patterson, C., Greenberg, B. D., Murphy, D. L., & Hamer, D. L. (1996). Population and familial association between the D4 receptor gene and measures of novelty seeking. *Nature Genetics, 12,* 81–84.

Benjamin, L. (1993). *Interpersonal diagnosis and treatment of personality disorders: A structural approach.* New York: Guilford.

Bergeman, C. S., Chipuer, H. M., Plomin, R., Pedersen, N. L., McClearn, G. E., Nesselroade, J. R., Costa, P. T., & McCrae, R. R. (1993). Genetic and environmental effects on openness to experience, agreeableness, and conscientiousness: An adoption/twin study. *Journal of Personality, 61,* 158–179.

Bernstein, E. M., & Putnam, F. W. (l986). Development, reliability, and validity of a dissociation scale. *Journal of Nervous & Mental Diseases, 174,* 727–734.

Bettelheim, B. (1967). *The empty fortress.* New York: Free Press.

Biederman, J., Faraone, S. V., Milberger, S., & Curtis, S. (1996). Predictors of persistence and remission of ADHD into adolescence. *Journal of the American Academy of Child and Adolescent Psychiatry, 35,* 343–351.

Blatt S. J. (1991). A cognitive morphology of psychopathology. *Journal of Nervous & Mental Diseases, 79,* 449–458.

Borch-Jacobsen, M. (1997). Sybil—the making of a disease: An interview with Dr. Herbert Spiegel. *New York Review of Books, 44,* 60–64.

Bouchard, T. J., Lykken, D. T., McGue, M., Segal, N. L., & Tellegen, A. (1990). Sources of human psychological differences: The Minnesota study of twins reared apart. *Science, 250,* 223–228.

Bowers, K. S., & Hilgard, E. R. (1988). Some complexities in understanding memory. In H. M. Pettinati (Ed.), *Hypnosis and memory* (pp. 3–17). New York: Guilford.

Bowlby, J. (1951). *Maternal care and mental health.* WHO Monograph Series 2. Geneva: World Health Organization.

Bowlby, J. (1969). *Attachment.* London: Hogarth Press.

Bowlby, J. (1973). *Separation.* London: Hogarth Press.

Bowlby, J. (1980). *Loss.* London: Hogarth Press.

Bowlby, J. (1988). *A secure base: The clinical application of attachment theory.* London: Routledge & Kegan Paul.

Bowman, M. (1997). *Individual differences in post-traumatic response.* Mahwah, NJ: Erlbaum.

Bradley, A. (1906/1955). *Shakespearian tragedy.* New York: Meridian.

Brandon, S., Bookes, J., Glaser, D., & Green, R. (1998). Recovered memories of childhood sexual abuse: Implications for clinical practice. *British Journal of Psychiatry, 172,* 296–307.

Brestan, E. V., & Eyberg, S. M. (1998). Effective psychosocial treatments of conduct-disordered children and adolescents. *Journal of Clinical Child Psychology, 27,* 138–145.

Breuer, J., & Freud, S. (1893/1955). Studies on hysteria. In *The standard edition of the psychological works of Sigmund Freud* (Vol.II, pp. 1–39). London: Hogarth.

Brown, G. W., & Harris, T. (1989). *Life events and illness.* New York: Guilford.

Browne, A., & Finkelhor, D. (1986). Impact of child sexual abuse: A review of the literature. *Psychological Bulletin, 99,* 66–77.

Bruer, J. (1999). *The myth of the first three years.* New York: Free Press.

Burks, J., & Rubenstein, M. (1979). *Temperament styles in adult interaction.* New York: Brunner/Mazel.

Buss, D. M. (1999). Human nature and individual differences: The evolution of human personality. In L. A. Pervin & O. P. John (Eds.), *Handbook of personality: Theory and research* (2nd ed., pp. 31–56). New York: Guilford.

Cadoret, R. J., Yates, W. R., Troughton, E., Woodworth, G., & Stewart, M. A. (1995). Genetic environmental interaction in the genesis of aggressivity and conduct disorders. *Archives of General Psychiatry, 52,* 916–924.

Caspi, A. (1998). Personality development across the life course. In W. Damon (Editor in-chief), N. Eisenberg (Volume Editor), *Handbook of child psychology* (Vol. 3, 5th ed., pp. 311–388). New York: Wiley.

Caspi, A., Elder, G. H., & Herbener, E. S. (1990). Childhood personality and the prediction of life course problems. In L. Robins & M. Rutter (Eds.), *Straight and devious pathways from childhood to adulthood* (pp. 13–35). New York: Cambridge University Press.

Caspi, A., Moffitt, T. E., Newman, D. L., & Silva, P. A. (1996). Behavioral observations at age three predict adult psychiatric disorders: Longitudinal evidence from a birth cohort. *Archives of General Psychiatry, 53,* 1033–1039.

Caspi, A., & Roberts, B. W. (1999). Personality change and continuity across the lifetime. In L. A. Pervin & O. P. John (Eds.), *Handbook of personality: Theory and research* (2nd ed., pp. 300–326). New York: Guilford.

Cassavia, E. (1992). A review of the long-term effects of child sexual abuse. *Child Abuse and Neglect, 16,* 101–118.

Cassidy, J., & Shaver, P. R. (1999). *Handbook of attachment: Theory, research and clinical aspects.* New York: Guilford.

Cherlin, A. J., Furstenberg, F. F., Chase-Lansdale, P., Lindsay, K., & Kiernan, K. (1991). Longitudinal studies of effects of divorce on children in Great Britain and the United States. *Science, 252,* 1386–1389.

Chess, S., & Thomas, A. (1984). *Origins and evolution of behavior disorders.* New York: Brunner/Mazel.

Chess S., & Thomas, A. (l990). The New York longitudinal study: The young adult periods. *Canadian Journal of Psychiatry, 35,* 557–561.

Clark, L. A., & Watson, D. (1999). Temperament: a new paradigm for trait psychology. In L. A. Pervin & O. P. John (Eds.), *Handbook of personality: Theory and research* (2nd ed., pp. 399–423). New York: Guilford.

Claridge, G. (1997). *Schizotypy.* Cambridge, England: Cambridge University Press.

Clarke, A., & Clarke, A. (1979). *Early experience and behavior.* New York: Free Press.

Cloninger, C. R., Svrakic, D. M., & Pryzbeck, T. R. (1993). A psychobiological model of temperament and character. *Archives of General Psychiatry, 50,* 975–990.

Coccaro, E. F., Siever, L. J., & Klar, H. M. (l989). Serotonergic studies in patients with affective and personality disorders. *Archives of General Psychiatry, 46,* 587–599.

Cohen, J. (1990). Things I have learned (so far). *American Psychologist, 45,* 1304–1312.

Cohen, P., & Cohen, J. (1996). *Life values and adolescent mental health.* Mahwah, NJ: Erlbaum.

Cohler, B. J., Stott, F., & Musick, J.S. (1995). Adversity, vulnerability, and resilience: Cultural and developmental perspectives. In D. Cicchetti & D. J. Cohen (Eds.), *Developmental psychopathology, Vol. 2: Risk, disorder, and adaptation* (pp. 753–800). New York: Wiley.

Coie, J. D., & Dodge, K. A. (1998). Aggression and antisocial behavior. In W. Damon (Editor-in-chief) & N. Eisenberg (Volume Editor), *Handbook of child psychology* (Vol. 3, 5th ed., pp. 779–862). New York: Wiley.

Costa, P. T., & Widiger, T. A. (Eds.). (1994). *Personality disorders and the five-factor model of personality.* Washington, DC: American Psychological Association.

Crews, F. (1995). *The memory wars.* New York: New York Review of Books.

Cross, S. E., & Markus, H. R. (1999). The cultural constitution of personality. In L. A. Pervin & O. P. John (Eds.), *Handbook of personality: Theory and research* (2nd ed., pp. 387–398). New York: Guilford.

Cummings, E. M. (1996). Marital conflict and children's functioning. *Social Development, 3,* 16–36.

Cyphers, L. A., Phillips, K., Fulker, D. W., & Mrazek, D.A. (1990). Twin temperament during the transition from infancy to early childhood. *Journal of the American Academy of Child and Adolescent Psychiatry, 29,* 393–397.

Dasen P., Berry, J. W., & Sartorius, N. (1988). *Health and cross-cultural psychology.* Newberry Park, CA: Sage.

Dawes, R. M. (1994). *House of cards: Psychology and psychotherapy built on myth.* New York: Free Press.

Dawson, D., & MacMillan, H. L. (1993). *Relationship management of the borderline patient: From understanding to treatment.* New York: Brunner/Mazel.

Deater-Deckard, K., Dodge, K. A., Bates, J. E., & Pettit, G. S. (1998). Multiple risk factors in the development of externalizing behavior problems: Group and individual differences. *Development & Psychopathology, 10,* 469–493.

Degler, C. N. (1991). *In search of human nature: The decline and revival of Darwinism in American social thought.* New York: Oxford University Press.

DeJong, C. A., van den Brink, M., Harteveld, F. M., & van der Wielen, E. G. (1993). Personality disorders in alcoholics and drug addicts. *Comprehensive Psychiatry, 34,* 87–94.

DeMause, L. (1974). *A history of childhood.* New York: Psychohistory Press.

DeMause, L. (1982). *Foundations of psychohistory.* New York: Creative Roots.

DeSalvo, L. (1989). *Virginia Woolf : The impact of childhood sexual abuse on her life and work.* Boston: Beacon Press.

Deutsch, M. (1960). The pathetic fallacy: An observer error in social perception. *Journal of Personality, 28,* 317–322.

DeWoolff, M. S., & van IJzendoorn, M. H. (1997). Sensitivity and attachment. *Child Development, 68,* 571–591.

Dollard, J., & Miller, N. E. (1950). *Personality and psychotherapy.* New York: McGraw Hill.

Dolnick, E. (1998). *Madness on the couch.* New York: Simon & Schuster.

Downey, G., & Coyne, J. C. (1990). Children of depressed parents: An integrative review. *Psychology Bulletin, 108,* 50–76.

Dozier, M., Stovall, K. C., & Albus, K. E. (1999). Attachment and psychopathology in adulthood. In J. Cassidy & P. R. Shaver (Eds.), *Handbook of attachment: Theory, research and clinical aspects* (pp. 497–519). New York: Guilford.

Dunn, J., & Plomin, R. (1990). *Separate lives: Why siblings are so different.* New York: Basic Books.

Durham, W. H. (1992). *Co-evolution: Genes, culture, and human diversity.* Stanford, CA: Stanford University Press.

Eaton, W. W., Sigal, J. J., & Weinfeld, M. (1982). Impairment of holocaust survivors after 33 years. *American Journal of Psychiatry, 139,* 773–777.

Efran, J. S., Greene, M. A., & Gordon, D. E. (1998). Lessons of the new genetics. *Family Therapy Networker, 22,* 26–32.

Elkin, I., Shea, T., Watkins, J. T., & Imber, S. D. (1989). National Institute of Mental Health Treatment of Depression Collaborative Research Program: General effectiveness of treatments. *Archives of General Psychiatry, 46,* 971–982.

Erikson, E. (1950). *Childhood and society.* New York: Norton.

Erikson, E. (1959). *Young man Luther.* New York: Norton.

Erikson, E. (1969). *Gandhi's truth.* New York: Norton.

Eysenck, H. J. (1991). Genetic and environmental contributions to individual differences: The three major dimensions of personality. *Journal of Personality, 58,* 245–261.

Eysenck, H. J., & Rachman, S. (1964). *Causes and cure of neurosis.* San Diego: Edits.

Falconer, D. S. (1989). *Introduction to quantitative genetics.* Essex, England: Longman.

Farber, S., & Green, M. (1993). *Hollywood on the couch.* New York: William Morrow.

Farrington, D. P. (1988). Studying changes within individuals: The causes of offending. In M. Rutter (Ed.), *Studies of psychosocial risk: The power of longitudinal data* (pp. 158–183). New York: Cambridge University Press.

Fergusson, D. M., Lynskey, M. T., & Horwood, J. (1996a). Childhood sexual abuse and psychiatric disorder in young adulthood I. Prevalence of sexual abuse and factors associated with sexual abuse. *Journal of the American Academy of Child and Adolescent Psychiatry, 34,* 1355–1364.

Fergusson, D. M., Lynskey, M. T., & Horwood, J. (1996b). Childhood sexual abuse and psychiatric disorder in young adulthood II. Psychiatric outcomes of childhood sexual abuse. *Journal of the American Academy of Child and Adolescent Psychiatry, 34,* 1365–1374.

Finkel, D., & Willie, D. (1999, April). *Behavioral genetic analysis of the relationship between attachment and temperament.* Paper presented at the Society for Research in Child Development, Albuquerque, NM.

Finkelhor D., Hotaling G., Lewis, I. A., & Smith, C. (1990). Sexual abuse in a national survey of adult men and women: Prevalence characteristics and risk factors. *Child Abuse and Neglect, 14,* 19–28.

Fisher, S., & Greenberg, R. (1996). *Freud scientifically appraised: Testing the theories and therapy.* New York: Wiley.

Fonagy, P., Leigh, T., Steele, M., Steele, H., Kennedy, R., Mattoon, G., Target, M. M., & Gerber, A. (1996). The relation of attachment status, psychiatric classification, and response to psychotherapy. *Journal of Consulting and Clinical Psychology, 64,* 22–31.

Fonagy, P., Steele, M., & Steele, H. (1991). Maternal representations of attachment during pregnancy predict infant-mother interactions at one year of age. *Child Development, 62,* 891–905.

Fonagy, P., Steele, M., Steele, H., Leigh, T., Kennedy, R., Mattoon, G., & Target, M. M. (1995). Attachment, the reflective self, and borderline states. In S. Goldberg, R. Muir, & J. Kerr (Eds.), *Attachment theory: Social, developmental and clinical perspectives* (pp. 233–278). Hillsdale, NJ: Analytic Press.

Frances, R. J., & Miller, S. I. (Eds.). (1991). *Clinical textbook of addictive disorders.* New York: Guilford.

Frank, J. D., & Frank, J. B. (1991). *Persuasion and healing* (3rd ed.). Baltimore: Johns Hopkins University Press.

Freud, A. (1937). *The ego and mechanisms of defense.* London: Hogarth.

Freud, S. (1896/1962). The aetiology of hysteria. In J. Strachey (Ed.), *The standard edition of the psychological works of Sigmund Freud* (Vol. 3, pp. 191–224). London: Hogarth Press.

Freud, S. (1900/1953). The interpretation of dreams. In J. Strachey (Ed.), *The standard edition of the psychological works of Sigmund Freud* (Vol. 5, pp. 3–223). London: Hogarth Press.

Freud, S. (1905/1953). Three contributions to the theory of sexuality. In J. Strachey (Ed.), *The standard edition of the psychological works of Sigmund Freud* (Vol. 7, pp. 135–231). London: Hogarth Press.

Freud, S. (1916/1963). A general introduction to psychoanalysis. In J. Strachey (Ed.), *The standard edition of the psychological works of Sigmund Freud* (Vol. 15, pp. 3–448; Vol. 16, pp. 243–449). London: Hogarth Press.

Freud, S. (1917/1955). A childhood memory from Dichtung und Warheit. In J. Strachey (Ed.), *The standard edition of the psychological works of Sigmund Freud* (Vol. 17, pp. 145–146). London: Hogarth Press.

Freud, S. (1918/1955). A case of obsessional neurosis. In J. Strachey (Ed.), *The standard edition of the psychological works of Sigmund Freud* (Vol. 17, pp. 23–122). London: Hogarth Press.

Freud, S. (1920/1955). The psychogenesis of a case of homosexuality in a woman. In J. Strachey (Ed.), *The standard edition of the psychological works of Sigmund Freud* (Vol. 18, pp. 145–174). London: Hogarth Press.

Gabbard, G. (1995). *Psychodynamics in clinical practice: DSM-IV edition.* Washington DC: American Psychiatric Press.

Gabbard, G. O., & Gabbard, K. (1999). *Psychiatry and the cinema* (2nd ed.). Washington, DC: American Psychiatric Press.

Garmezy, N., & Masten, A. S. (1994). Chronic adversities. In M. Rutter & L.Hersov (Eds.) *Child and adolescent psychiatry: Modern approaches* (3rd ed., pp. 191–208). London: Blackwell.

Garner, D. M., & Garfinkel, P. E. (1985). *Handbook of psychotherapy for anorexia nervosa and bulimia.* New York: Guilford.

Gelertner, J., Kranzler, H., Coccaro, E. F., Siever, L. J., & New, A. S. (1998). Serotonin transporter gene polymorphism and personality measures in African American and European American subjects. *American Journal of Psychiatry, 155,* 1332–1338.

Gellner, E. (1993). *The psychoanalytic movement* (2nd ed.). London: Fontana.

Gershon, E. S., & Nurnberger, J. I. (1995). Bipolar illness. In J. M. Oldham, & M. B. Riba (Eds.), *Review of psychiatry, 14,* 405–424.

Gilmore, K. (1995). Gender identity disorder in a girl: Insights from adoption. *Journal of the American Psychoanalytic Association, 43,* 39–59.

Gleick, J. (1987). *Chaos.* New York: Viking.

Goldberg, D., & Huxley, P. (1992). *Common mental disorders: A bio-social model.* New York: Tavistock/Routledge.

Goodwin, D. W. (1985). Alchoholism and genetics: The sins of the fathers. *Archives of General Psychiatry, 42,* 171–174.

Gordon, T. (1970). *Parent effectiveness training.* New York: P. H. Wyden.

Gottesman, I. (1991). *Schizophrenia genesis.* New York: Freeman.

Gould, S. J. (1981). *The mismeasure of man.* New York: Norton.

Gould, S. J. (1989). *Wonderful life.* New York: Norton.

Gould, S. J. (1996). *Full house: The spread of excellence from Plato to Darwin.* New York: Harmony Books.

Green, B. L., Grace, M. C., Vary, M. G., Kramer, T. L., Gleser, G. C., & Leonard, A. C. (1994). Children of disaster in the second decade: A 17 year follow-up of Buffalo Creek survivors. *Journal of the American Academy of Child and Adolescent Psychiatry, 33,* 71–79.

Greenberg, J. R., & Mitchell, S. A. (1983). *Object relations in psychoanalytic theory.* Cambridge, MA: Harvard University Press.

Greenberg, M. T. (1999). Attachment and psychopathology in childhood. In J. Cassidy & P. R. Shaver (Eds.), *Handbook of attachment: Theory, research and clinical aspects* (pp. 469–496). New York: Guilford.

Gross, J. J. (1999). Emotion and emotion regulation. In L. A. Pervin & O. P. John (Eds.), *Handbook of personality: Theory and research* (2nd ed., pp. 525–552). New York: Guilford.

Grove, W. M., Eckert, E. D., Heston, L., & Bouchard, T. J. (1990). Heritability of substance abuse and antisocial behavior: A studies of monozygotic twins raised apart. *Biological Psychiatry, 27,* 1293–1304.

Groze, V., & Ileana, D. (1996). A follow-up study of adopted children from Romania. *Child & Adolescent Social Work Journal, 13,* 541–565.

Grunbaum, A. (1984). *The foundations of psychoanalysis: A philosophical critique.* Berkley, CA: University of California Press.

Gunderson, J. G. (1985). Conceptual risks of the Axis I-II division. In H. Klar & L. J. Siever (Eds.), *Biological response styles: Clinical implications* (pp. 81–95). Washington DC: American Psychiatric Press.

Gunderson, J. G., Frank, A. F., Ronningstam, E. F., Wahter, S., Lynch, V. J., & Wolf, P. J. (1989). Early discontinuance of borderline patients from psychotherapy. *Journal of Nervous and Mental Diseases, 177,* 38–42.

Gunderson, J. G., & Phillips, K. A. (1991). A current view of the interface between borderline personality disorder and depression. *American Journal of Psychiatry, 48,* 967–975.

Hale, R. (1995). *The rise and crisis of psychoanalysis in the United States.* New York: Oxford University Press.

Hamer, D. (1998). *Living with our genes.* New York: Doubleday.

Harlow, H. F. (1958). The nature of love. *American Psychologist, 13,* 673–670.

Harris, J. R. (1995). Where is the child's environment? A group socialization theory of development. *Psychology Review, 102,* 458–489.

Harris, J. R. (1998). *The nurture assumption.* New York: Free Press.

Hechtman, L. (1994). Genetic factors in attention deficit disorder. *Journal of Psychiatry and Neuroscience, 19,* 193–201.

Hechtman, L. (Ed.). (1996). *Do they grow out of it?* Washington DC: American Psychiatric Press.

Helzer, J. E., & Canino, G. J. (Eds.). (1992). *Alcoholism in North America, Europe, and Asia.* New York: Oxford University Press.

Helzer, J. E., Robins, L. B. N., & Wishe E. (1979). Depression in Vietnam veterans and civilian controls. *American Journal of Psychiatry, 136,* 526–529.

Herman, J. (1992). *Trauma and recovery.* New York: Basic Books.

Herman J. L., & Schatzow, E. (1987). Recovery and verification of memories of childhood sexual trauma. *Psychoanalytic Psychology, 4,* 11–14.

Hesse, E. (1999). The adult attachment interview: Historical and current perspectives. In J. Cassidy, & P. Shaver (Eds.), *Handbook of attachment: Theory, research, and clinical applications* (pp. 395–433). New York: Guilford.

Hetherington, E. M., Cox, M., & Cox, R. (1985). Long-term effects of divorce and remarriage on the adjustment of children. *Journal of the American Academy of Child Psychiatry, 24,* 518–530.

Hilgard, E. (1994). Neodissociation theory. In S. J. Lynn, & J. W. Rhue (Eds.), *Dissociation: Clinical and theoretical perspectives* (pp. 32–51). New York: Guilford.

Hobson, A. (1988). *The dreaming brain.* New York: Basic Books.

Hodges, J., & Tizard, B. (1989). Social and family relationships of ex-institutional adolescents. *Journal of Child Psychology and Psychiatry, 30,* 77–97.

Hogarty, G. E., Anderson, C., Reiss, D., & Kornblith, S. (1991). Family psychoeducation, social skills training and maintenance chemotherapy in the afteracre treatment of schizophrenia. *Archives of General Psychiatry, 48,* 340–347.

Holmes, D. (1990). The evidence for repression: An examination of sixty years of research. In J. Singer (Ed.), *Repression and dissociation: Implications for personality theory, psychopathology, and health* (pp. 85–102). Chicago: University of Chicago Press.

Holmes, J. (1998). Psychodynamics, narrative, and "intentional causality". *British Journal of Psychiatry, 173,* 279–280.

Holzman, P. S. (1996). On the trail of the genetics and pathophysiology of schizophrenia. *Psychiatry, 59,* 117–127.

Horowitz, M. (1993). Stress-response syndromes. In J. P. Wilson & B. Raphael (Eds.), *International handbook of traumatic stress syndromes* (pp. 49–60). New York: Plenum.

Horowitz, M., Marmar, C., Weiss, D., DeWitt, D., & Rosenbaum, R. (1984). Brief psychotherapy of bereavement reactions: The relationship of process to outcome. *Archives of General Psychiatry, 41,* 438–444.

Horwitz, L. (1974). *Clinical prediction in psychotherapy.* New York: Aronson.

Howard, K. I., Kopta, A. M., Krause, M. S., & Orlinsky, D. E. (1986). The dose-effect relationship to psychotherapy. *American Psychologist, 41,* 159-164.

Hubble, M. A., Duncan, B. L., & Miller, S. D. (Eds.). (1999). *The heart and soul of therapy.* Washington DC: American Psychological Association.

Hughes, R. (1993). *The culture of complaint.* New York: Oxford University Press.

Hull, C. (1951/1974). *Essentials of behavior.* New York: Greenwood.

Hwu, H. G., Yeh, E. K., Change, L.Y. (1989). Prevalence of psychiatric disorders in Taiwan defined by the Chinese Diagnostic Interview Schedule. *Acta Psychiatrica Scandinavica, 79,* 136–147.

Jamison, K. R. (1994). George Gordon, Lord Byron, 1788–1824. *American Journal of Psychiatry, 151,* 480–481.

Janet, P. (1907). *The major symptoms of hysteria.* New York: MacMillan.

Jang, K. L., Livesley, W. J., Vernon, P. A., & Jackson, D. N. (1996). Heritability of personality traits: A twin study. *Acta Psychiatrica Scandinavica, 94,* 438–444.

Jang, K., Paris, J., Zweig-Frank, H., & Livesley, J. (1998). A twin study of dissociative experience. *Journal of Nervous and Mental Diseases, 186,* 345–351.

Johnson, A. M. (1949). Sanctions for superego lacunae of adolescents. In K. R. Eissler (Ed.), *Searchlights on delinquency* (pp. 224–245). New York: International Universities Press.

Johnson, J. J., Cohen, P., Brown, J., Smailes, E. M., & Bernstein, D. P. (1999). Childhood maltreatment increases risk for personality disorders during early adulthood. *Archives of General Psychiatry, 56,* 600–606.

Kagan, J. (1989). *Unstable ideas: Temperament, cognition and self.* Cambridge, MA: Harvard University Press.

Kagan, J. (1994). *Galen's prophecy.* New York: Basic Books.

Kagan, J. (1997). Conceptualizing psychopathology: The importance of developmental profiles. *Development and Psychopathology, 9,* 321–334.

Kagan, J. (1998a). Biology and the child. In W. Damon (Editor-in-chief) & N. Eisenberg (Volume Editor), *Handbook of child psychology* (Vol. 3, 5th ed., pp. 177–236). New York: Wiley.

Kagan, J. (1998b). *Three seductive ideas.* Cambridge, MA: Harvard University Press.

Kagan, J., & Zentner, M. (1996). Early childhood predictors of adult psychopathology. *Harvard Review of Psychiatry, 3,* 341–350.

Kandel, E. R. (1998). A new intellectual framework for psychiatry. *American Journal of Psychiatry, 155,* 457–469.

Kandel, E. R. (1999). Biology and the future of psychoanalysis. *American Journal of Psychiatry, 156,* 505–524.

Kanner, L. (1943). Autistic disturbances of affective contact. *Nervous Child, 2,* 217–250.

Kasen, S., Cohen, P., Brook, J. S., & Hartmark, C. (1996). A multiple-risk interaction mode: Effects of temperament and divorce on psychiatric disorders in children. *Journal of Abnormal Child Psychology, 24,* 121–150.

Kaufman, C., Grunebaum, H., Cohler, B., & Gamer, E. (1979). Superkids: Competent children of schizophrenic mothers. *American Journal of Psychiatry, 136,* 1398–1402.

Kazdin, A. E. (1997). Parent management training: Evidence, outcomes, and issues. *Journal of the American Academy of Child & Adolescent Psychiatry, 36,* 1349–1356.

Kendler, K. S. (1995). Genetic epidemiology in psychiatry: Taking both genes and environment seriously. *Archives of General Psychiatry, 52,* 895–899

Kendler, K. S. (1996). Parenting: A genetic epidemiological perspective. *American Journal of Psychiatry, 153,* 11–20.

Kendler, K. S., & Eaves, L. J. (1986). Models for the joint effect of genotype and environment on liability to psychiatric illness. *American Journal of Psychiatry, 143,* 279–289.

Kendler, K. S., Heath, A., & Martin, N. G. (1987). Symptoms of anxiety and symptoms of depression: Same genes, different environment? *Archives of General Psychiatry, 44,* 451–457.

Kendler, K. S., Kessler, R. C., & Walters, E. E. (1995). Stressful life events, genetic liability, and onset of an episode of major depression in women. *American Journal of Psychiatry, 152,* 833–842.

Kendler, K. S., Neale, M. C., Kessler, R. C., Heath, A. C., & Eaves, L. J. (1992). Familial influences on the clinical characteristics of major depression: A twin study. *Acta Psychiatrica Scandinavica, 86,* 371–378.

Kendler, K. S., Neale, M. C., Kessler, R. C., Heath, A. C., & Eaves, L. J. (1993a). A test of the equal-environment assumption in twin studies of psychiatric illness. *Behavior Genetics, 23*, 21–27.

Kendler, K. S., Neale, M., Kessler, R., Heath, A., & Eavens, L. (1993b). A twin study of recent life events and difficulties. *Archives of General Psychology, 50*, 789–779.

Kernberg, O. F. (1984). *Severe personality disorders.* New Haven, CT: Yale University Press.

Kernberg, O. F., Coyne, L., Appelbaum, A., Horwitz, L., & Voth, H. (1972). Final report of the Menninger Psychotherapy Research Project. *Bulletin of the Menninger Clinic, 36*, 1–275.

Kessler, R. C., McGonagle, K. A., Nelson, C. B., Hughes, M., Eshelman, S., Wittchen, H. U., & Kendler, K. S. (1994). Lifetime and 12-month prevalence of DSM-III-R psychiatric disorders in the United States. *Archives of General Psychiatry, 51*, 8–19.

Kihlstrom, J. F. (1994). One hundred years of hysteria. In S. J. Lynn & J. W. Rhue (Eds.), *Dissociation: Clinical and theoretical perspectives* (pp. 365–394). New York: Guilford.

Kihlstrom, J. F. (1999). The psychological unconcious. In L. A. Pervin & O. P. John (Eds.), *Handbook of personality: Theory and research* (2nd ed., pp. 424–432). New York: Guilford.

Kirmayer, L. J. (1996). Landscapes of memory: Trauma, narrative and dissociation. In C. Pantze & M. Lambed (Eds.), *The subject of memory* (pp. 183–198). London: Routledge.

Kirmayer, & Laurence. (1986). Somatization and the social construction of illness experience. In S. McHugh, T. Vallis, & T. Michael (Eds.), *Illness behavior: A multidisciplinary model* (pp. 111–133). New York: Plenum Press.

Kirmayer, L. J., Robbins, J. M., & Paris, J. (1994). Somatoform disorders: Personality and the social matrix of somatic distress. *Journal of Abnormal Psychology, 103*, 125–136.

Kirsch, I., & Lynn, S. J. (1998). Dissociation theories of hypnosis. *Psychological Bulletin, 123*, 100–115.

Klaus, M. H., & Kennell, J. H. (1976). *Maternal-infant bonding.* St. Louis: Mosby.

Klein, M. (1946). *Envy and gratitude.* New York: International Universities Press.

Kochanska, G., Kuczynski, L., & Radke-Yarrow, M. (1989). Correspondence between mothers' self-reported and observed child-rearing practices. *Child Development, 60*, 56–63.

Kohut, H. (1970). *The analysis of the self.* New York: International Universities Press.

Kohut, H. (1977). *The restoration of the self.* New York: International Universities Press.

Kolvin, I., Miller, F. J. W., Fleeting, M., & Kolvin, P. A. (1988). Risk/protective factors for offending with particular reference to deprivation. In M. Rutter (Ed.), *Studies of psychosocial risk: The power of longitudinal data* (pp. 77–95). New York: Cambridge University Press.

Kopta, S. M., Howard, K. I., Lowry, J. L., & Beutler, L. E. (1994). Patterns of symptomatic recovery in psychotherapy. *Journal of Consulting and Clinical Psychology, 62*, 1009–1016.

Kroll, J. (1995, May). *Treatment of BPD with histories of abuse.* Paper presented to the American Psychiatric Association, Miami, FL.

Kroonenberg, P. M., van Dam, M., von IJzendoorn, M. H., & Mooijaart, A. (1997). Dynamics of behavior in the Strange Situation. *British Journal of Psychology, 88*, 311–332.

Kuhn, T. (1970). *The structure of scientific revolutions.* Chicago: University of Chicago Press.

Lambert, M. J., & Bergin, A. E. (1994). The effectiveness of psychotherapy. In A. E. Bergin & S. L. Garfield (Eds.), *Handbook of psychotherapy and behavior change* (pp. 143–189). New York: Wiley.

Langs, R. J. (1973). *The theory and practice of psychoanalytic psychotherapy.* New York: Aronson.

Larkin, P. (1988). *Collected poems.* London: Marvell Press.

Laurence, J. R., & Perry, C. (1983). Hypnotically created memory among highly hypnotizable subjects. *Science, 222*, 523–524.

Leach, P. (1984). *Child care encyclopedia.* New York: Knopf.

Leff, J. P. (1988). *Psychiatry around the globe.* London: Gaskell.

Leighton, D. C., Durding, J. S., & Macklin, D. B. (1963). *The character of danger.* New York: Basic.

Lesch, K. P., Bengel, D., Heils, A., Sabol, S. Z., Greenberg, B. D., Petri, S., Benjamin, J., Muller, C. R., Hamer, D. H., & Murphy, D. L. (1996). Association of anxiety-related traits with a polymorphism in the serotonin transporter gene regulatory region. *Science, 274*, 1527–1531.

Levy, D. (1943). *Overprotection.* New York: Columbia University Press.

Lewis, D. O. (1998). *Guilty by reason of insanity: A psychiatrist explores the minds of killers.* New York: Fawcett.

Lewis, M. (1997). *Altering fate.* New York: Guilford.

Lewis, M. (1999). On the development of personality. In L. A. Pervin & O. P. John (Eds.), *Handbook of personality: Theory and research* (2nd ed., pp. 327–346). New York: Guilford.

Lidz, T., & Fleck, S. (1985). *Schizophrenia and the family.* New York: International Universities Press.

Linehan, M. M. (1993). *Cognitive behavioral therapy of borderline personality disorder.* New York: Guilford.

Livesley, W. J. (1998). Suggestions for a framework for an empirically based classification of personality disorder. *Canadian Journal of Psychiatry, 43*, 137–147.

Livesley, W. J., Jang, K., Schroeder, M. L., & Jackson, D. N. (1993). Genetic and environmental factors in personality dimensions. *American Journal of Psychiatry, 150*, 1826–1831.

Livesley, W. J., Jang, K. L., & Vernon, P. A. (1998). Phenotypic and genetic structure of traits delineating personality disorder. *Archives of General Psychiatry, 55*, 941–948.

Livesley, W. J., Schroeder, M. L., Jackson, D. N., & Jang, K. (1994). Categorical distinctions in the study of personality disorder: Implications for classification. *Journal of Abnormal Psychology, 103*, 6–17.

Locke, J. (1693/1892). *Some thoughts concerning education.* Cambridge: Cambridge University Press.

Loftus, E. (1979). *Eyewitness testimony.* Cambridge, MA: Harvard University Press.

Loftus, E. F. (1993). The reality of repressed memories. *American Psychologist, 48*, 518–537.

Long, C. V. F., & Vaillant, G. E. (1984). Natural history of male psychological health XI: Escape from the underclass. *American Journal of Psychiatry, 141*, 341–346.

Lorenz, K. (1966). *On aggression.* London: Methuen.

Luborsky, L., & Crits-Christoph, P. (1990). *Understanding transference: The core conflict relationship theme method.* New York: Basic Books.

Luborsky, L., Crits-Christoph, P., & Alexander, K. J. (1990). Repressive style and relationship patterns. In J. Singer (Ed.), *Repression and dissociation: Implications for personality theory, psychopathology, and health* (pp. 275–298). Chicago: University of Chicago Press.

Luborsky, L., Singer, B., & Luborsky, L. (1975). Comparative studies of psychotherapy: Is it true that everyone has won and all shall have prizes? *Archives of General Psychiatry, 41*, 165–180.

Lykken, D. (1995). *The antisocial personalities.* Hillside, NJ: Erlbaum.

Lykken, D., & Tellegen, A. (1996). Happiness is a stochastic phenomenon. *Psychological Science, 7*, 186–189.

Lyons, M. J., Goldberg, J., Eisen, S. A., True, W., Tsuang, M. T., Meyer, J. M., & Henderson, W. G. (1993). Do genes influence exposure to trauma? A twin study of combat. *American Journal of Medical Genetics, 48*, 22–27.

Mack, J. (1995). *Abduction: Human encounters with aliens.* New York: Ballantine.

MacMillan, H. L., MacMillan, J. H., Offord, D. R., & Griffith, L. (1994a). Primary prevention of child sexual abuse: A critical review: *Journal of Child Psychology Psychiatry, 35*, 857–876.

MacMillan, H. L., MacMillan, J. H., Offord, D. R., & Griffith, L. (1994b). Primary prevention of child physical abuse and neglect: A critical review. *Journal of Child Psychology Psychiatry, 35*, 835–856.

Magai, S., & McFadden, S. H. (Eds.). (1996). *Handbook of emotion, adult development, and aging.* San Diego, CA: Academic Press.

Mahler, M., Pine, F., & Bergeman, A. (1975). *The psychological birth of the human infant.* New York: Basic Books.

Maier, T. (1998). *Dr. Spock: An American life.* New York: Harcourt Brace.

Main, M. (1995). Recent studies in attachment. In S. Goldberg, R. Muir, & J. Kerr (Eds.), *Attachment theory: Social, developmental and clinical issues* (pp. 407–474). New York: Analytic Press.

Main, M., & Solomon, J. (1986). Discovery of an insecure-disorganized-disoriented attachment pattern. In T. Brazelton, B. Berry, & M. W. Yogman (Eds.), *Affective development in infancy* (pp. 95–124). Norwood, NJ: Ablex.

Malan, D. (1979). *Individual psychotherapy and the science of psychodynamics.* Boston: Butterworth.

Malinovsky-Rummell, R., & Hansen, D. J. (1993). Long-term consequences of physical abuse. *Psychological Bulletin, 114,* 68–79.

Mann, J. J. (1998). The neurobiology of suicide. *Nature Medicine, 4,* 25–30.

Mannuzza, S., Klein, R. G., Bessler, A., Malloy, P., & LaPadula, M. (1998). Adult psychiatric status of hyperactive boys grown up. *American Journal of Psychiatry, 155,* 493–498.

Masson, J. (1984). *The assault on truth.* New York: Penguin.

Masten, A. S., & Coatsworth, J. D. (1995). Competence, resilience, and psychopathology. In D. Cicchetti & D. J. Cohen (Eds.), *Developmental psychopathology, Volume 2: Risk, disorder, and adaptation* (pp. 715–752). New York: Wiley.

Matheny, A. P. Jr. (1987). Developmental research of twin's temperament. *Acta Geneticae Medicae et Gemellogiae, 36,* 135–143.

Maughan, B., & Rutter, M. (1997). Retrospective reporting of childhood adversity. *Journal of Personality Disorders, 11,* 4–18.

Maziade, M., Caron, C., Coté, R., Boutin, P., & Thivierge, J. (1990). Extreme temperament and diagnosis: A study in a psychiatric sample of consecutive children. *Archives of General Psychiatry, 47,* 477–484.

Mazlish, B. (1963). *Psychoanalysis and history.* Englewood Cliffs, NJ: Prentice-Hall.

McCord, J. (1990). Long-term perspectives on parental absence. In L. Robins & M. Rutter (Eds.), *Straight and devious pathways from childhood to adulthood* (pp. 116–134). New York: Cambridge University Press.

McCrae, R. R., & Costa, P. T. (1990). *Personality in adulthood.* New York: Guilford.

McCrae, R. R., & Costa, P. T. (1997). Personality trait structure as a human universal. *American Psychologist, 52,* 509–516.

McCrae, R. R., & Costa, P. T. (1999). A five-factor theory of personality. In L. A. Pervin & O. P. John (Eds.), *Handbook of personality: Theory and research* (2nd ed., pp. 139–153). New York: Guilford.

McCullough, L., Winston, A., Farber, B. A., Porter, P., Pollack, J., Laitkin, M., Vingiano, W., & Trujillo, M. (1991). The relationship of patient-therapist interaction to outcome in brief psychotherapy. *Psychotherapy, 28,* 525–533.

McGue, M., & Lykken, D. T. (1992). Genetic influence on risk of divorce. *Psychological Science, 3,* 368–373.

McHugh, P. R. (1992). Psychiatric misadventures. *American Scholar, 61,* 498–510.

McLanahan, S., & Sandefur, G. (1994). *Growing up with a single parent: What hurts, what helps.* Cambridge, MA: Harvard University Press.

Mead, M. (1926/1971). *Coming of age in Samoa.* New York: Morrow.

Meehl, P. E. (1973). *Specific genetic etiology, psychodynamics, and therapeutic nihilism, in psychodiagnosis: Selected papers.* New York: Norton.

Meehl, P. E. (1990). Toward an integrated theory of schizotaxa, schizotypy, and schizophrenia. *Journal of Personality Disorders, 4,* 1–99

Merskey, H. (1992). The manufacture of personalities. *British Journal of Psychiatry, 160,* 327–340.

Merskey, H. (1995). *The analysis of hysteria* (2nd ed.). London: Gaskell.

Meyer-Williams, L. (1994). Recall of childhood trauma: A prospective study of women's memories of child sexual abuse. *Journal of Consulting and Clinical Psychology, 62,* 1167–1176.

Miller, A. (1984). *Thou shalt not be aware.* New York: Farrar, Strauss, and Giroux.

Millon, T. (1985). *Personality and its disorders: A biosocial learning approach.* New York: Wiley.

Mintz, J., Auerbach, A., Luborsky, L., & Johnson, M. (1973). Patient's, therapist's and observers' views of psychotherapy: A "Rashomon" experience or a reasonable consensus? *British Journal of Medical Psychology, 46,* 83–89.

Minuchin, S., Rosman, B. L., & Baker, L. (1978). *Psychosomatic families: Anorexia nervosa in context.* Cambridge, MA: Harvard University Press.

Monroe, S. M., & Simons, A. D. (1991). Diathesis-stress theories in the context of life stress research. *Psychological Bulletin, 110,* 406–425.

Morey, L. C., & Ochoa, E. S. (1989). An investigation of adherence to diagnostic criteria: Clinical diagnosis of the DSM-III personality disorders. *Journal of Personality Disorders, 3,* 180–192.

Morison, S. J., Ames, E, W., & Chisholm, K. (1995). The development of children adopted from Romanian orphanages. *Merrill-Palmer Quarterly, 41,* 411–430.

Motion, A. (1993). *A Writer's life: Phillip Larkin.* London: Faber & Faber.

Mulder, R. T., Beautrais, A., Joyce, P. R., & Fergusson, D. M. (1998). Relationship between dissociation, childhood sexual abuse, childhood physical abuse, and mental illness in a general population sample. *American Journal of Psychiatry, 155,* 806–811.

Myers, D. G., & Diener, E. (1995). Who is happy? *Psychological Science, 6,* 10–19.

Nandi, D. N., Banerjee, G., Nandi, S., & Nandi, P. (1992). Is hysteria on the wane? *British Journal of Psychiatry, 160,* 87–91.

Nash, M. R., Hulsely, T. L., Sexton, M. C., Harralson, T. L., & Lambert, W. (1993). Long-term effects of childhood sexual abuse: Perceived family environment, psychopathology, and dissociation. *Journal of Consulting and Clinical Psychology, 61,* 276–283.

Newman, D. L., Caspi, A., Moffit, T. E., & Silva, P. A. (1997). Antecedents of adult interpersonal functioning: Effects of individual differences in age 3 temperament. *Developmental Psychology, 33,* 206–217.

Norris, H. (1992). Epidemiology of trauma. *Journal of Consulting and Clinical Psychology, 60,* 409–418.

North, C. S., Ryall, J. M., Ricci, D. A., & Wetzel, R. D. (1993). *Multiple personalities, multiple disorders: Psychiatric classification and media influence.* New York: Oxford University Press.

North, C. S., Smith, E. M., & Spitznagel, E. L. (1997). One year follow-up of survivors of a mass shooting. *American Journal of Psychiatry, 154,* 1606–1702.

Ofshe, R., & Watters, E. (1994). *Making monsters: False memories, psychotherapy, and sexual hysteria.* New York: Scribner.

Orlinsky, D. E., Grawe, K., & Parks, B. K. (1994). Process and outcome in psychotherapy—noch einmal. In A. E. Bergin & S. L. Garfield (Eds.), *Handbook of psychotherapy and behavior change* (pp. 270–379). New York: Wiley.

Orne, M. T., Whitehouse, W. G., Dinges, D. F., & Orne, E. C. (1988). Reconstructing memory through hypnosis: Forensic and clinical implications. In H. M. Pettinati (Ed.), *Hypnosis and memory* (pp. 21–54). New York: Guilford.

Paris, J. (1976). The Oedipus complex: A critical re-examination. *Canadian Psychiatric Association Journal, 21,* 173–179.

Paris, J. (1994). *Borderline personality disorder: A multidimensional approach.* Washington DC: American Psychiatric Press.

Paris, J. (1996c). *Social factors in the personality disorders.* New York: Cambridge University Press.

Paris, J. (1997a). Antisocial and borderline personality: Two separate disorders or two aspects of the same psychopathology? *Comprehensive Psychiatry, 38,* 237–242.

Paris, J. (1998a). Anxious traits, anxious attachment, and anxious cluster personality disorders. *Harvard Review of Psychiatry, 6,* 142–148.

Paris, J. (1998b). *Working with traits: Psychotherapy in the personality disorders.* Northville, NJ: Jason Aronson.

Paris, J. (1999). *Nature and nurture in psychiatry.* Washington, DC: American Psychiatric Press.

Paris, J., Zelkowitz, P., Guzder, J., & Joseph, S. (1999). Neuropsychological factors associated with borderline pathology in children. *Journal of the American Academy of Child and Adolescent Psychiatry, 38,* 770–774.

Parker. G. (1983). *Parental overprotection: A risk factor in psychosocial development.* New York: Grune and Stratton.

Parker, G. (1992). Early environment. In E. S. Paykel (Ed.), *Handbook of affective disorders* (2nd ed., pp. 171–194). New York: Guilford.

Patience, D. A., McGuire, R. J., Scott, A. I. F., & Freeman, C. P. (1995). The Edinburgh Primary Care Depression Study: Personality disorder and outcome. *British Journal of Psychiatry, 167,* 324–330.

Pendergrast, M. (1995). *Victims of memory.* Hinesburg, VT: Upper Access.

Pepper, C. M., Klein, D. N., Anderson, R. L., Riso, L. P., Ouimette, P. C., & Lizardi, H. (1995). DSM-III-R Axis II comorbidity in dysthymia and major depression. *American Journal of Psychiatry, 152,* 239–247.

Pickering, A. D., & Gray, J. A. (1999). The neuroscience of personality. In L. A. Pervin & O. P. John (Eds.), *Handbook of personality: Theory and research* (2nd ed., pp. 277–299). New York: Guilford.

Pihl, R. O., & Peterson, J. (1990). Inherited predisposition to alcoholism. *Journal of Abnormal Psychology, 99,* 291–301.

Pike, A., & Plomin, R. (1996). Importance of nonshared environmental factors for childhood and adolescent psychopathology. *Journal of the American Academy of Child and Adolescent Psychiatry, 35,* 560–570.

Pinker, S. (1997). *How the mind works.* New York: Norton.

Piper, W. E., Azim, H. A., Joyce, A. S., & McCallum, M. (1991). Transference interpretations, therapeutic alliance, and outcome in short-term individual psychotherapy. *Archives of General Psychiatry, 48,* 946–953.

Piper, W. E., Joyce, A. S., McCallum, M., & Azim, H. A. (1998). Interpretive and supportive forms of psychotherapy and patient personality variables. *Journal of Consulting and Clinical Psychology, 66,* 558–567.

Plath, S. (1963). *The bell jar.* London: Heinemann.

Plomin, R., & Caspi, A. (1999). Behavioral genetics and personality. In L. A. Pervin & O. P. John (Eds.), *Handbook of personality: Theory and research* (2nd ed., pp. 251–276). New York: Guilford.

Plomin, R., DeFries, J. C., McClearn, G. E., & Rutter, M. (1997). *Behavioral genetics* (3rd ed.). New York: Freeman.

Plomin, R., Emde, R. N., Braungartm, J. M., & Campos, J. (1993). Genetic change and continuity from fourteen to twenty months. *Child Development, 64,* 1354–1376.

Plomin, R., & Rutter, M. M. (1998). Child development, molecular genetics, and what to do with genes once they are found. *Child Development, 69,* 1223–1242.

Pollak, R. (1997). *The creation of Dr. B.: A biography of Bruno Bettelheim.* New York: Touchstone.

Pope, H. G. (1997). *Psychology astray.* Boca Raton, FL: Upton.

Pope, H. G., & Hudson, J. I. (1995). Can memories of childhood sexual abuse be repressed? *Psychological Medicine, 25,* 121–126.

Popper, K. (1968). *Conjectures and refutations.* New York: Harper Torch.

Post, R. M. (1992). Transduction of psychosocial stress into the neurobiology of recurrent affective disorder. *American Journal of Psychiatry, 149,* 99–1010.

Propst, A., Paris, J., & Rosberger, Z. (1994). Do therapist experience, diagnosis, and functional level predict outcome in short-term psychotherapy? *Canadian Journal of Psychiatry, 39,* 178–183.

Rahe, R. H. (1995). Stress and psychiatry. In H. Kaplan, & B. Sadock (Eds.) *Comprehensive textbook of psychiatry* (5th ed., pp. 1545–1559).

Rank, O. (1926/1984). *Beyond psychology.* New York: Dover.

Rapaport-Bar-Sever, M., & Rapaport, J. (1994). The present state of people who survived the Holocaust as children. *Acta Psychiatrica Scandinavica, 89,* 242–245.

Rathbun, C., DiVirgilio, L., & Waldfogel, S. (1958). A restitutive process in childhood following radical separation from family and culture. *American Journal of Orthopsychiatry, 28,* 408–415.

Regier, D. A., & Burke, J. D. (1989). Epidemiology. In H. Kaplan & B. Sadock (Eds.), *Comprehensive textbook of psychiatry* (5th ed., pp. 308–326). Baltimore: Williams and Wilkins.

Reiss, D., Hetherington, E. M., Howe, G. W., Simmens, S. J., Henderson, S. H., O'Connor, T. J., Russell, D. A., Anderson, E. R., & Law, T. (1995). Genetic questions for environmental studies: Differential parenting and psychopathology in adolesence. *Archives of General Psychiatry, 52,* 925–936.

Reiss, D., Hetherington, E. M., & Plomin, R. (2000). *The relationship code.* Cambridge, MA: Harvard University Press.

Renaud, H., & Estes, F. (1961). Life history interviews with one hundred normal American males: Pathogenicity of childhood. *American Journal of Orthopsychiatry, 31,* 786–802.

Rende, R., & Plomin, R. (1995). Nature, nurture, and the development of psychopathology. In D. Cicchetti & D. J. Cohen (Eds.), *Developmental psychopathology* (Vol. 1: Theory and methods, pp. 291–314). New York: Wiley.

Rind, B., & Tromovitch, P. (1997). A meta-analytic review of findings from national samples on psychological correlates of child sexual abuse. *Journal of Sexuality Research, 34,* 237–255.

Rind, B., Tromovitch, P., & Bauserman, R. (1998). A meta-analytic examination of assumed properties of child sexual abuse using college samples. *Psychological Bulletin, 124,* 22–53.

Robins, L. N. (1966). *Deviant children grown up.* Baltimore: Williams and Wilkins.

Robins, L. N., & Regier, D. A. (Eds.). (1991). *Psychiatric disorders in America.* New York: Free Press.

Robins, L. N., Schoenberg, S. P., & Holmes, S. J. (1985). Early home environment and retrospective recall; A test for concordance between siblings with and without psychiatric disorders. *American Journal of Orthopsychiatry, 55,* 27–41.

Robinson, S., Rapaport-Bar-Sever, M., & Rapaport, J. (1994). The present state of people who survived the holocaust as children. *Acta Psychiatrica Scandinavica, 89,* 242–245.

Rodgers, B. (1990). Influences of early-life and recent factors on affective disorder in women. In L. Robins & M. Rutter (Eds.), *Straight and devious pathways from childhood to adulthood* (pp. 314–328). New York: Cambridge University Press.

Rosenbaum, R. (1998). *The search for Hitler.* New York: Random House.

Rosenzweig, S. (1936). Some implicit common factors in diverse methods of psychotherapy. *American Journal of Orthopsychiatry, 6,* 412–415.

Rothbart, M. K., & Ahad, S. A. (1994). Temperament and the development of personality. *Journal of Abnormal Psychology, 103,* 55–66.

Rothbart, M. K., & Bates, J. E. (1998). Temperament. In W. Damon (Editor-in-chief) & N.

Eisenberg (Volume Editor), *Handbook of child psychology* (Vol. 3, 5th ed., pp. 25–104). New York: John Wiley.

Rotter, J. B. (1966). Generalized expectancies for internal vs. external control of reinforcements. *Psychological Monographs: General and Applied, 80,* 1–28.

Rousseau, J. J. (1762/1978). *On the social contract.* London: St. Martin's Press.

Rowe, D. C. (1981). Environmental and genetic influences on dimensions of perceived parenting: A twin study. *Developmental Psychology, 17,* 203–208.

Rowe, D. C. (1994). *The limits of family influence: Genes, experience, and behavior.* New York: Guilford.

Russell, D. (1986). *The secret trauma: Incest in the lives of girls and women.* New York: Basic Books.

Rutter, M. (1971). Parent-child separation: Psychological effects on the children. *Jounal of Child Psychology and Psychiatry, 12,* 233–260.

Rutter, M. (1972). *Maternal deprivation reassessed.* New York: Penguin.

Rutter, M. (1985). Resilience in the face of adversity: Protective factors and resistance to psychiatric disorder. *British Journal of Psychiatry, 147,* 598–611.

Rutter, M. (1987a). Psychosocial resilience and protective mechanisms. *American Journal of Orthopsychiatry, 57,* 316–331.

Rutter, M. (l987b). Temperament, personality, and personality development. *British Journal of Psychiatry, 150,* 443–448.

Rutter, M. (1989). Pathways from childhood to adult life. *Journal of Child Psychology and Psychiatry, 30,* 23–51.

Rutter, M. (1991). Nature, nurture, and psychopathology: A new look at an old topic. *Development and Psychopathology, 3,* 125–136.

Rutter, M. (1995a). Clinical implications of attachment concepts: Retrospect and prospect. *Journal of Child Psychology and Psychiatry, 36,* 549–571.

Rutter, M. (1995b). Mental disorders in childhood and adulthood. *Acta Psychiatroca Scandinavica, 91,* 73–85.

Rutter, M. (1998). Some research considerations on intergenerational continuities. *Developmental Psychology, 34,* 1269–1273.

Rutter, M. (1999, April). *Follow-up of Romanian orphans in Britain.* Paper presented to the Society for Research in Child Development, Albuquerque, NM.

Rutter, M., Dunn, J., Plomin, R., Simonoff, E., Pickles, A., Maughan, B., Ormel, J., Meyer, J., & Eaves, L. (1997). Integrating nature and nurture: Implications of person-environment correlations and interactions for developmental psychopathology. *Development and Psychopathology, 9,* 335–364.

Rutter, M., Giller, A., & Hagele, A. (1999). *Antisocial behavior by young people.* Cambridge, England: Cambridge University Press.

Rutter, M., Quinton, D., & Hill, J. (1990). Adult outcome of institution-reared children: Males and females compared. In L. Robins & M. Rutter (Eds.), *Straight and devious pathways from childhood to adulthood* (pp. 135–157). New York: Cambridge University Press.

Rutter, M., & Rutter, M. (1993). *Developing minds: Challenge and continuity across the life span.* New York, Basic

Rutter, M., & Smith, D. J. (1995). *Psychosocial problems in young people.* Cambridge, England: Cambridge University Press.

Sapolsky, R. (1998). *Why zebras get ulcers* (2nd ed.). New York: Freeman.

Sarason, B. R., Sarason, I. G., & Pierce, G. R. (Eds.). (1990). *Social support: an interactional view.* New York: Wiley.

Scarr, S. (1992). Developmental theories for the 1990's: Development and individual differences. *Developmental Psychology, 63,* 1–19.

Scarr, S., & McCartney, K. (1983). How people make their own environments: A theory of genotype-environment effects. *Child Development, 54,* 424–435.

Schacter, D. L. (1996). *Searching for memory.* New York: Basic Books.

Seifer, R., Schiller, A. J., Sameroff, S., Resnick, S., & Riordan, K. (1996). Attachment, maternal sensitivity, and infant temperament during the first year of life. *Developmental Psychology, 32,* 12–25.

Seligman, M. E. (1975). *Helplessness.* New York: Freeman.

Seligman, M. E. P., & Hager, J. (Eds.). (1972). *The biological boundaries of learning.* New York: Appleton-Century-Crofts.

Shapiro, T., & Emde, R. (1994). *Research on psychoanalysis: Process, development, outcome.* New York: International Universities Press.

Shea, M. T., Pilkonis, P. A., & Beckahm, E. (1990). Personality disorders and treatment outcome in the NIMH Treatment of Depression Collaborative Research Program. *American Journal of Psychiatry, 147,* 711–718.

Shorter, E. (1994). *From mind to body.* New York: Free Press.

Shorter, E. (1997). *A history of psychiatry.* New York: Free Press.

Showalter, E. (1996). *Hystories: Hysterical epidemics and modern media.* New York: Columbia University Press.

Siever, L. J., & Davis, K. L. (1991). A psychobiological perspective on the personality disorders. *American Journal of Psychiatry, 148,* 1647–1658.

Sifneos, P. (1996). Alexithymia: Past and present. *American Journal of Psychiatry, 153,* 137–142.

Sigal, J. J. (1998). Long-term effects of the holocaust: Empirical evidence for resilience in the first, second, and third generations. *Psychoanalytic Review, 85,* 579–585.

Sigal, J. J., & Weinfeld, M. (1989). *Trauma and rebirth: Intergenerational effects of the holocaust.* New York: Praeger.

Simon, J. (1978). Observations of 67 patients who took Erhard Seminars Training. *American Journal of Psychiatry, 135,* 686–691.

Singer, J. (Ed.) (1990). *Repression and dissociation: Implications for personality theory, psychopathology, and health.* Chicago: University of Chicago Press.

Singer, J., & Sincoff, J. B. (1990). Beyond repression and the defenses. In J. Singer (Ed.), *Repression and dissociation: Implications for personality theory, psychopathology, and health* (pp. 471–496). Chicago: University of Chicago Press.

Singer, M. A., Gatz, M., Siri, M. L., & Pedersen, N. L. (1998). Childhood adoption: Long-term effects on adulthood. *Psychiatry, 61,* 191–205.

Sloane, R. B. (1975). *Psychotherapy vs. behavior therapy.* Cambridge, MA: Harvard University Press.

Smiley, J. (1990). *A thousand acres.* New York: Fawcett.

Smith, M. L., Glass, G. V., & Miller, T. I. (1980). *The benefits of psychotherapy.* Baltimore: Johns Hopkins Press.

Soloff, P. H. (1993). Psychopharmacological intervention in borderline personality disorder. In J. Paris (Ed.), *Borderline personality disorder: Etiology and treatment* (pp. 319–348). Washington, DC: American Psychiatric Press.

Spence, D. (1983). *Narrative truth and historical truth.* New York: Norton.

Spence, D. (1992). Interpretation: A critical perspective. In J. W. Barron, M. N. Eagle, & D. L. Wolitsky (Eds.), *Interface of psychoanalysis and psychology* (pp. 558–572). Washington, DC: American Psychological Association.

Spock, B. (1946). *Baby and child care.* New York: Pocket Books.

Srole, L. (1980). The Midtown Manhattan longitudinal study vs. "the mental paradise lost" doctrine. *Archives of General Psychiatry, 37,* 209–221.

Stannard, D. E. (1980). *Shrinking history: On Freud and the failure of psychohistory.* New York: Oxford University Press.

Steiger, H., Liquornik, K., Chapman, J., & Hussain, N. (1991). Personality and family disturbances in eating disorder patients. *International Journal of Eating Disorders, 10*, 501–512.

Steinberg, M. (1994). *Interviewer's guide to the structured clinical interview for DSM-IV dissociative disorders*. Washington, DC: American Psychiatric Press.

Stern, D. (1985). *The interpersonal world of the infant*. New York: Basic.

Strupp, H. H., Fox, R. E., & Lesser, K. (1969). *Patients view their psychotherapy*. Baltimore:
Johns Hopkins.

Strupp, H. H., & Hadley, S. W. (l979). Specific vs. non-specific factors in psychotherapy.
Archives of General Psychiatry, 36, 1125–1136.

Sulloway, F. (1996). *Born to rebel*. New York: Pantheon.

Sutherland, S. (1994). *Irrationality*. London: Penguin.

Tellegen, A., Lykken, D. T., Bouchard, T. J., Wilcox, K. J., Segal, N. L., & Rich, S. (1988).
Personality similarity in twins reared apart and together. *Journal of Personal and Social
Psychology, 54*, 1031–1039.

Tennant, C. (1988). Parental loss in childhood to adult life. *Archives of General Psychiatry, 45*,
1045–1050.

Terr, L. C. (1988). What happens to early memories of trauma? *Journal of the American
Academy of Child and Adolescent Psychiatry, 27*, 96–104.

Terr, L. C. (1991). Childhood traumas: An outline and an overview. *American Journal of
Psychiatry, 148*, 10–20.

Thapar, A., & McGuffin, P. (1996). Genetic influences on life events. *Psychological Medicine,
26*, 813–830.

Thompson, R. A. (1998). Early sociopersonality development. In W. Damon (Editor-in-
chief) & N. Eisenberg (Volume Editor), *Handbook of child psychology* (5th ed., Vol. 3, pp.
25–104). New York: Wiley.

Thompson, R. A., Connell, J. P., & Bridges, L. J. (1988). Temperament, emotion, and social
interactive behavior in the strange situation. *Child Development, 56*, 1106–1110.

Tillman, J. G., Nash, M. R., & Lerner, P. M. (1994). Does trauma cause disssociative pathology? In S. J. Lynn & J. W. Rhue (Eds.), *Dissociation: Clinical and theoretical perspectives*
(pp. 395–514). New York: Guilford.

Tinbergen, N. (1951). *The study of instinct*. New York: Oxford University Press.

Torgersen, S. (1995, June). *Correlates of personality disorder diagnoses*. Paper presentation to
the International Society for the Study of Personality Disorders, Dublin.

Torgersen, S. (1999, September). *Genetics and personality disorders*. Paper presentation to the
International Society for the Study of Personality Disorders, Geneva.

Torgersen, A. M., & Kringlen, E. (1978). Genetic aspects of temperamental differences in
infants. *Journal of the American Academy of Child and Adolescent Psychiatry, 17*, 433–444.

Treasure, J., & Holland, A. J. (1995). Genetics of eating disorders. In G. Szmukler, C. Dare,
& J. Treasure (Eds.), *Handbook of eating disorders: Theory, treatment and research* (pp. 65–
81). Chichester, UK: John Wiley.

True, W. R., Rice, J., Eisen, S. A., Heath, A. C., Goldberg, J., Lyons, M. J., & Nowak, J.
(1993). A twin study of genetic and environmental contributions to liability for post-
traumatic stress symptoms. *Archives of General Psychiatry, 50*, 257–264.

Vaillant, G. E. (1977). *Adaptation to life*. Cambridge, MA: Little Brown.

Vaillant, G. E. (1990). Repression in college men followed for half a century. In J. Singer
(Ed.), *Repression and dissociation: Implications for personality theory, psychopathology, and
health* (pp. 259–274). Chicago: University of Chicago Press.

Vaillant, G. E. (1993). *The wisdom of the ego*. Cambridge, MA: Harvard University Press.

Vaillant, G. E. (1994). *The natural history of alcoholism* (2nd ed.). Cambridge, MA: Harvard
University Press.

van der Kolk, B. A. (1994). The body keeps the score: Memory and the evolving psychobi-
ology of posttraumatic stress. *Harvard Review of Psychiatry, 1*, 253–265.

218   References

van IJzendoorn, M. H. (1992). Intergenerational transmission of parenting: A review of studies in nonclinical populations. *Developmental Review, 12,* 76–99.

van IJzendoorn, M. H., Schuengel, C., & Bakermans-Kranenbrug, M. J. (1999). Disorganized attachment in early childhood: Meta-analysis of precursors, concomitants, and sequelae. *Development & Psychopathology, 11,* 225–249.

van IJzendoorn, M. H., & Sagi, A. (1999). Cross-cultural patterns of attachment. In J. Cassidy & P. R. Shaver (Eds.), *Handbook of attachment: Theory, research and clinical aspects* (pp. 713–734). New York: Guilford.

Vaughan, B. E, & Bost, K.K. (1999). Attachment and temperament. In J. Cassidy & P. R. Shaver (Eds.), *Handbook of attachment: Theory, research and clinical aspects* (pp. 198–225). New York: Guilford.

Volkan, V., Itkovitz, N., & Dod, A. W. (1997). *Richard Nixon: A psychobiography.* New York: Columbia University Press.

Wachtel, P. L. (1994). Cyclical processes in personality and psychopathology. *Journal of Abnormal Psychology, 103,* 51–54.

Wadsworth, M. E. J. (1991). *The imprint of time: Childhood history and adult life.* Oxford, England: Oxford University Press.

Walker, A. (1982). *The color purple.* New York: Harbrace.

Wallerstein, J. (1989). *Second chances: Men, women, and children a decade after divorce.* New York: Ticknor and Fields.

Wallerstein, R. (1986). *Forty-two lives in treatment.* New York: Guilford.

Wampold, B. E., Mondin, G. W., Moody, M., Stich, F., & Benson, K. (1997). A meta-analysis of outcome studies comparing bona fide psychotherapies: Empirically, "all must have prizes". *Psychological Bulletin, 122,* 203–215.

Watson, J. (1924/1970). *Behaviorism.* New York: Norton.

Webster, S. (1995). *Why Freud was wrong.* New York: Basic Books.

Weinberger, D. R. (1987). Implications of normal brain development for the pathogenesis of schizophrenia. *Archives of General Psychiatry, 44,* 660–669.

Weiner, B. (1999). Attribution in personality psychology. In L. A. Pervin, & O. P. John (Eds.), *Handbook of personality: Theory and research* (2nd ed., pp. 605–628). New York: Guilford.

Weiner, J. (1998). Orphanages: An idea whose time has come? *American Journal of Psychiatry, 155,* 1307–1308.

Weiss, G., & Hechtman, L. (1992). *Hyperactive children grown up* (2nd ed.). New York: Guilford.

Weissman, M. M., Bland, R. C., Canino, G. J., & Faravelli, C. (1996). Cross-national epidemiology of major depressive and bipolar disorder. *Journal of the American Medical Association, 276,* 298–299.

Werner, E. E. (1984). *Child care: Kith, kin, and hired hands.* Baltimore: University Park Press.

Werner, E. E., & Smith, R. S. (1992). *Overcoming the odds: High risk children from birth to adulthood.* New York: Cornell University Press.

Westen, D. (1998). The scientific legacy of Sigmund Freud: Towards a psychodynamically informed psychological science. *Psycholoigical Bulletin, 124,* 333–371.

Westen, D., & Gabbard, G. O. (1999). Psychoanalytic approaches to personality. In L. A. Pervin & O. P. John (Eds.), *Handbook of personality: Theory and research* (2nd ed., pp. 57–101). New York: Guilford.

Widiger, T. A., Verheul, R., & van den Brink, W. (1999). Personality and psychopathology. In L. A. Pervin & O. P. John (Eds.), *Handbook of personality: Theory and research* (2nd ed., pp. 347–366). New York: Guilford.

Widom, C. S. (1989). The cycle of violence. *Science, 244,* 16–166.

Widom, C. S. (1999). Posttraumatic stress disorder in abused and neglected children grown up. *American Journal of Psychiatry, 156,* 1223–1229.

Wilson, E. O. (1998). *Consilience: The unity of knowledge.* New York: Knopf.

Winick, M., Meyer, K. K., & Harris, R. C. (1975). Malnutrition and environmental enrichment by early adoption. *Science, 190,* 1173–1175.

Winnicott, D. W. (1958). *Collected papers.* London: Tavistock.

Yalom, I. D., & Lieberman, M. A. (1973). *Encounter groups: First facts.* New York: Basic Books.

Yarrow, M. R., Campbell, J. D., & Burton, R. V. (1970). Recollections of childhood: A study of the retrospective method. *Monograph of the Society for Research in Child Development 138.* Chicago: University of Chicago Press.

Yochelson, S., & Samenow, S. (1976). *The criminal personality.* New York: Jason Aronson.

Zanarini, M. C. (1993). Borderline personality as an impulse spectrum disorder. In J. Paris (Ed.), *Borderline personality disorder: Etiology and treatment* (pp. 67–86). Washington DC: American Psychiatric Press.

Zeitlin, D. (1986). *The natural history of psychiatric disorders in children.* Oxford, England: Oxford University Press.

Zoccolillo, M., Pickles, A., Quinton, D., & Rutter, M. (1992). The outcome of childhood conduct disorder: Implications for defining adult personality disorder and conduct disorder. *Psychological Medicine, 22,* 971–986.

Zweig-Frank, H., Paris, J., & Guzder, J. (1994). Psychological risk factors for dissociation in female patients with borderline and non-borderline personality disorders. *Journal of Personality Disorders, 8,* 203–209.

INDEX